HARLEY QUINN
AND THE BIRDS OF PREY

cover by JOËLLE JONES and LAURA ALLRED

HARLEY QUINN created by Paul Dini and Bruce Timm

PETER J. TOMASI, FRANK PITTARESE, SCOTT PETERSON,
MATT IDELSON, DARREN VINCENZO Editors – Original Series
JOSEPH ILLIDGE, NACHIE CASTRO Associate Editors – Original Series
ELISABETH V. GEHRLEIN, CHRIS DUFFY Assistant Editors – Original Series
JEB WOODARD Group Editor – Collected Editions
ALEX GALER Editor – Collected Edition
STEVE COOK Design Director – Books
MONIQUE NARBONETA Publication Design
DANIELLE DIGRADO Publication Production

BOB HARRAS Senior VP – Editor-in-Chief, DC Comics
PAT McCALLUM Executive Editor, DC Comics

DAN DiDIO Publisher
JIM LEE Publisher & Chief Creative Officer
BOBBIE CHASE VP – New Publishing Initiatives & Talent Development
DON FALLETTI VP – Manufacturing Operations & Workflow Management
LAWRENCE GANEM VP – Talent Services
ALISON GILL Senior VP – Manufacturing & Operations
HANK KANALZ Senior VP – Publishing Strategy & Support Services
DAN MIRON VP – Publishing Operations
NICK J. NAPOLITANO VP – Manufacturing Administration & Design
NANCY SPEARS VP – Sales
MICHELE R. WELLS VP & Executive Editor, Young Reader

DC Comics, 2900 West Alameda Ave., Burbank, CA 91505
Printed by LSC Communications, Kendallville, IN, USA. 10/4/19. First Printing.
ISBN: 978-1-4012-9483-0

Library of Congress Cataloging-in-Publication Data is available.

PEFC Certified

This product is from sustainably managed forests and controlled sources

PEFC
PEFC/29-31-337

www.pefc.org

TABLE OF CONTENTS

Ooooh Fun!

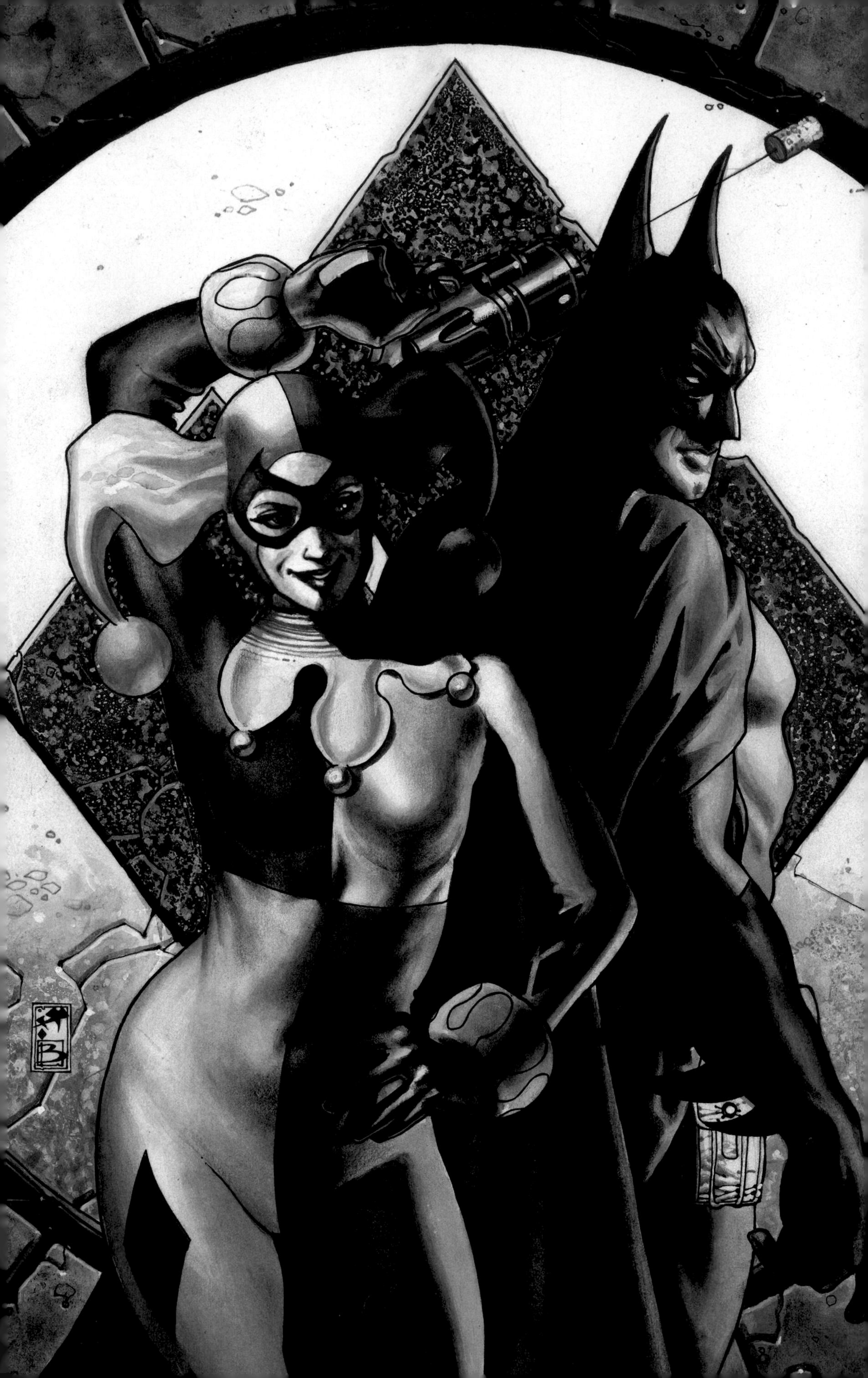

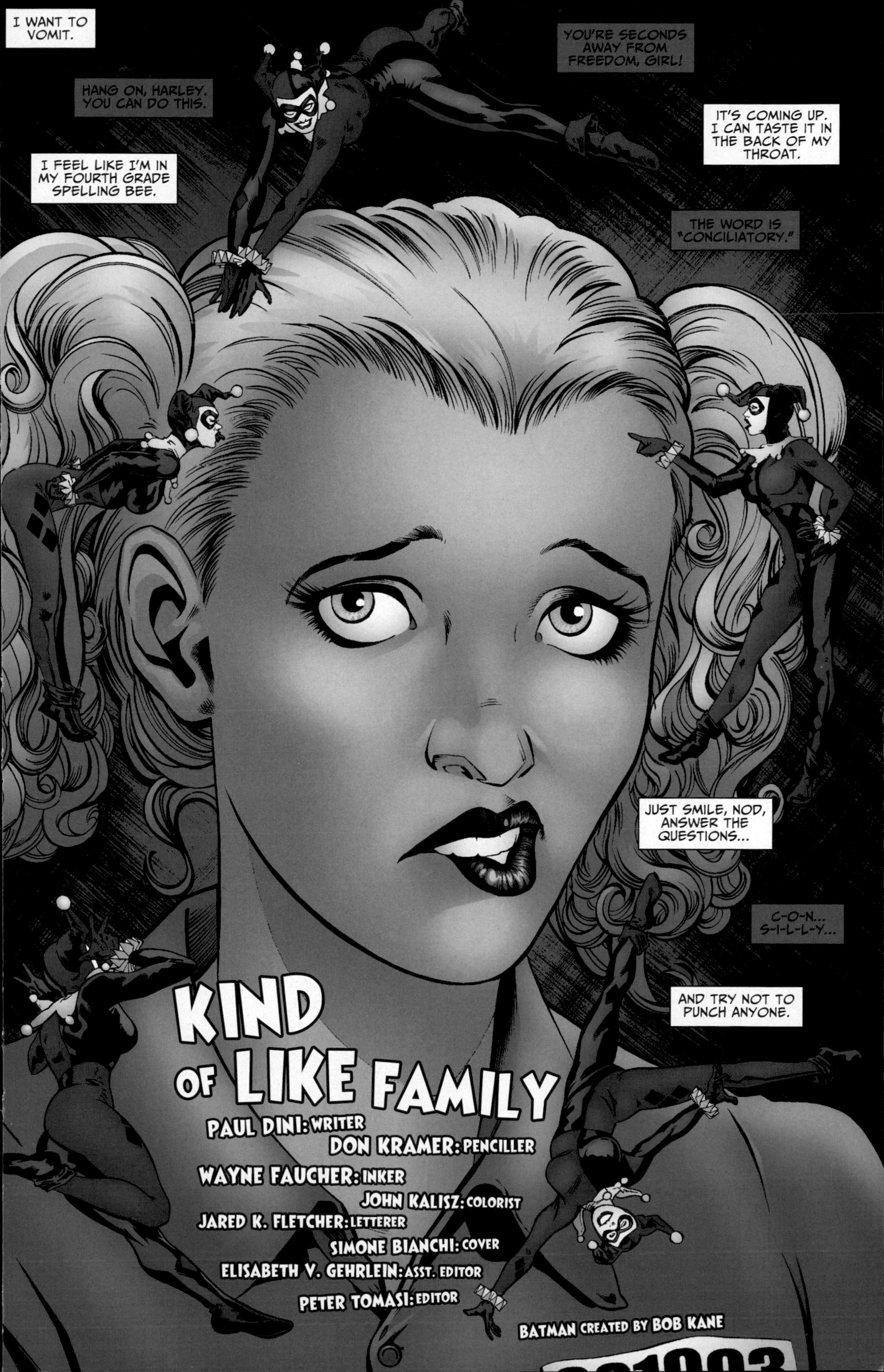
I WANT TO VOMIT.
HANG ON, HARLEY. YOU CAN DO THIS.
I FEEL LIKE I'M IN MY FOURTH GRADE SPELLING BEE.
YOU'RE SECONDS AWAY FROM FREEDOM, GIRL!
IT'S COMING UP. I CAN TASTE IT IN THE BACK OF MY THROAT.
THE WORD IS "CONCILIATORY."
JUST SMILE, NOD, ANSWER THE QUESTIONS...
C-O-N... S-I-L-L-Y...
AND TRY NOT TO PUNCH ANYONE.
KIND OF LIKE FAMILY
PAUL DINI: WRITER
DON KRAMER: PENCILLER
WAYNE FAUCHER: INKER
JOHN KALISZ: COLORIST
JARED K. FLETCHER: LETTERER
SIMONE BIANCHI: COVER
ELISABETH V. GEHRLEIN: ASST. EDITOR
PETER TOMASI: EDITOR
BATMAN CREATED BY BOB KANE

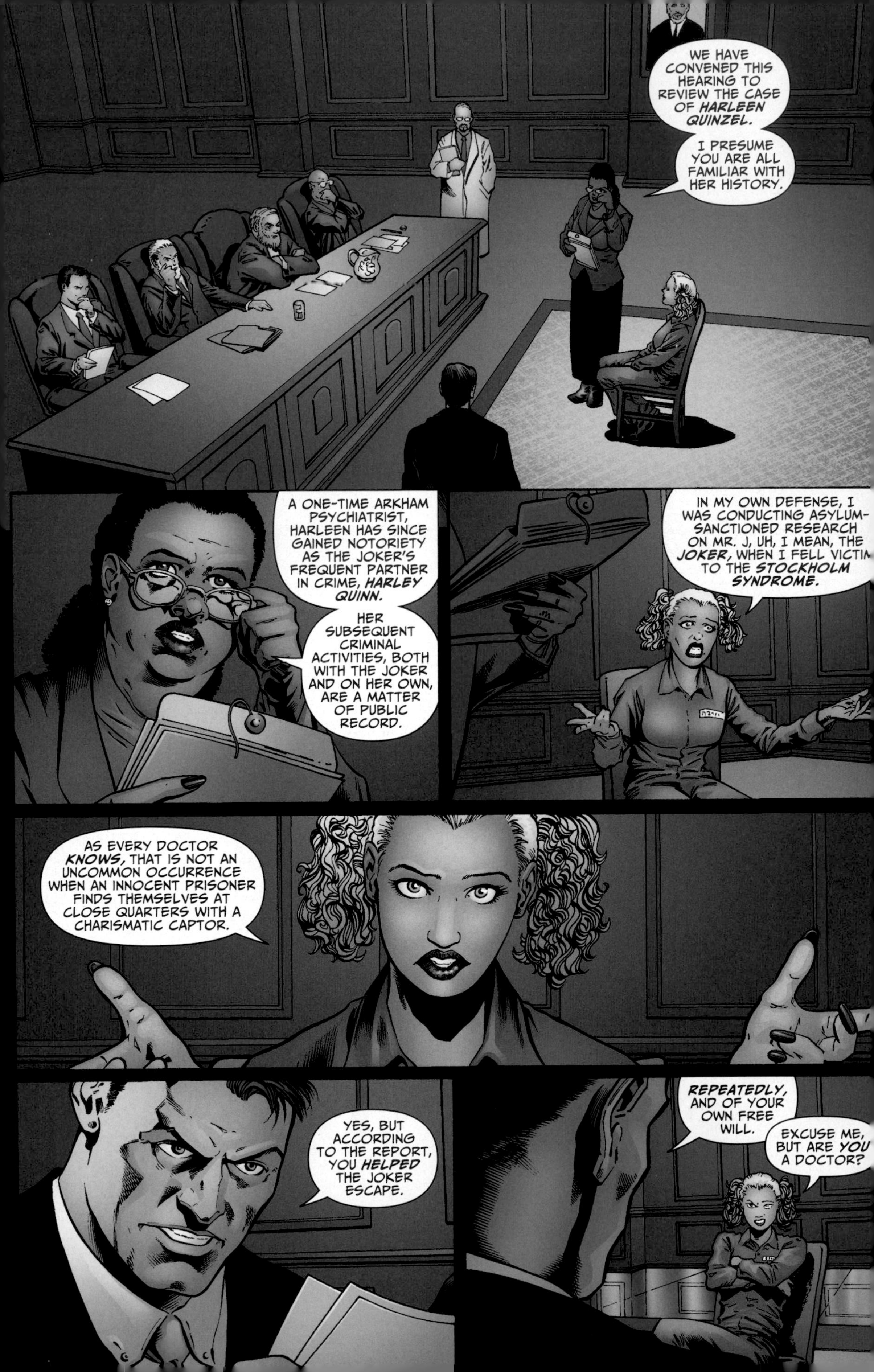
WE HAVE CONVENED THIS HEARING TO REVIEW THE CASE OF HARLEEN QUINZEL.
I PRESUME YOU ARE ALL FAMILIAR WITH HER HISTORY.
A ONE-TIME ARKHAM PSYCHIATRIST, HARLEEN HAS SINCE GAINED NOTORIETY AS THE JOKER'S FREQUENT PARTNER IN CRIME, HARLEY QUINN.
HER SUBSEQUENT CRIMINAL ACTIVITIES, BOTH WITH THE JOKER AND ON HER OWN, ARE A MATTER OF PUBLIC RECORD.
IN MY OWN DEFENSE, I WAS CONDUCTING ASYLUM-SANCTIONED RESEARCH ON MR. J, UH, I MEAN, THE JOKER, WHEN I FELL VICTIM TO THE STOCKHOLM SYNDROME.
AS EVERY DOCTOR KNOWS, THAT IS NOT AN UNCOMMON OCCURRENCE WHEN AN INNOCENT PRISONER FINDS THEMSELVES AT CLOSE QUARTERS WITH A CHARISMATIC CAPTOR.
YES, BUT ACCORDING TO THE REPORT, YOU HELPED THE JOKER ESCAPE.
REPEATEDLY, AND OF YOUR OWN FREE WILL.
EXCUSE ME, BUT ARE YOU A DOCTOR?

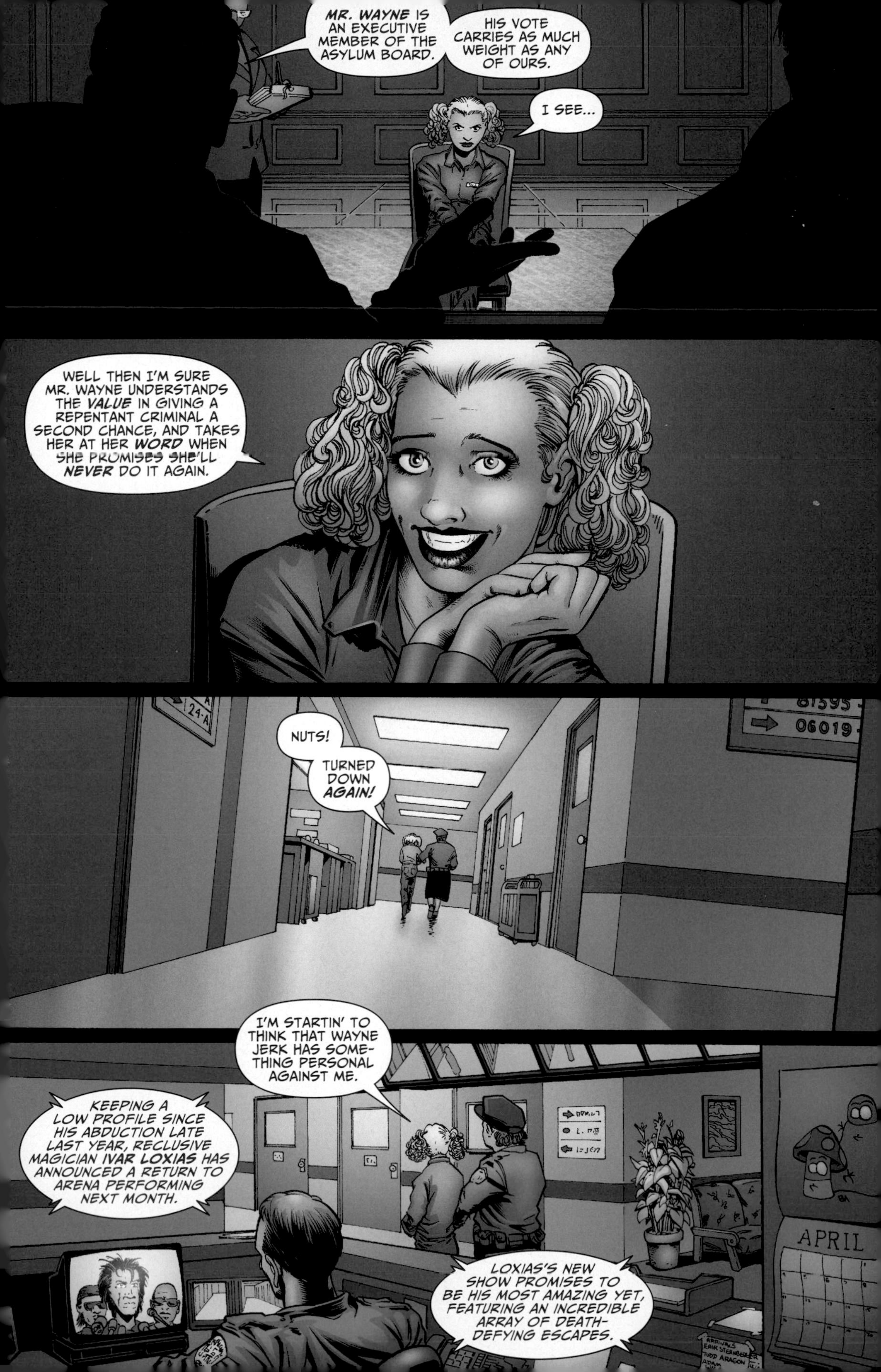

MR. WAYNE IS AN EXECUTIVE MEMBER OF THE ASYLUM BOARD.
HIS VOTE CARRIES AS MUCH WEIGHT AS ANY OF OURS.
I SEE...
WELL THEN I'M SURE MR. WAYNE UNDERSTANDS THE VALUE IN GIVING A REPENTANT CRIMINAL A SECOND CHANCE, AND TAKES HER AT HER WORD WHEN SHE PROMISES SHE'LL NEVER DO IT AGAIN.
06019
NUTS!
TURNED DOWN AGAIN!
I'M STARTIN' TO THINK THAT WAYNE JERK HAS SOME-THING PERSONAL AGAINST ME.
KEEPING A LOW PROFILE SINCE HIS ABDUCTION LATE LAST YEAR, RECLUSIVE MAGICIAN IVAR LOXIAS HAS ANNOUNCED A RETURN TO ARENA PERFORMING NEXT MONTH.
LOXIAS'S NEW SHOW PROMISES TO BE HIS MOST AMAZING YET, FEATURING AN INCREDIBLE ARRAY OF DEATH-DEFYING ESCAPES.
APRIL

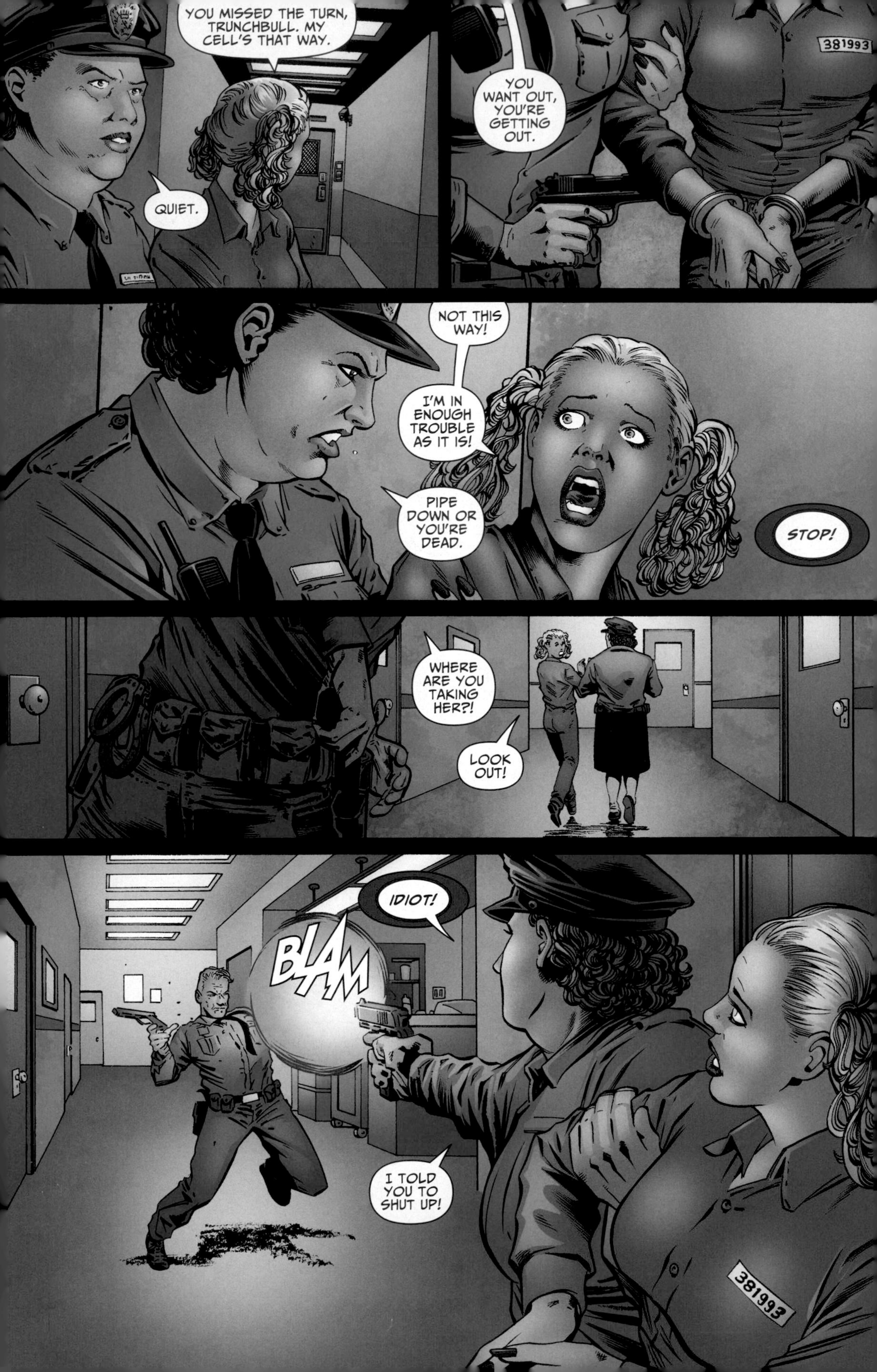
381993
YOU MISSED THE TURN, TRUNCHBULL. MY CELL'S THAT WAY.
QUIET.
YOU WANT OUT, YOU'RE GETTING OUT.
NOT THIS WAY!
I'M IN ENOUGH TROUBLE AS IT IS!
PIPE DOWN OR YOU'RE DEAD.
STOP!
WHERE ARE YOU TAKING HER?!
LOOK OUT!
IDIOT!
BLAM
I TOLD YOU TO SHUT UP!
381993

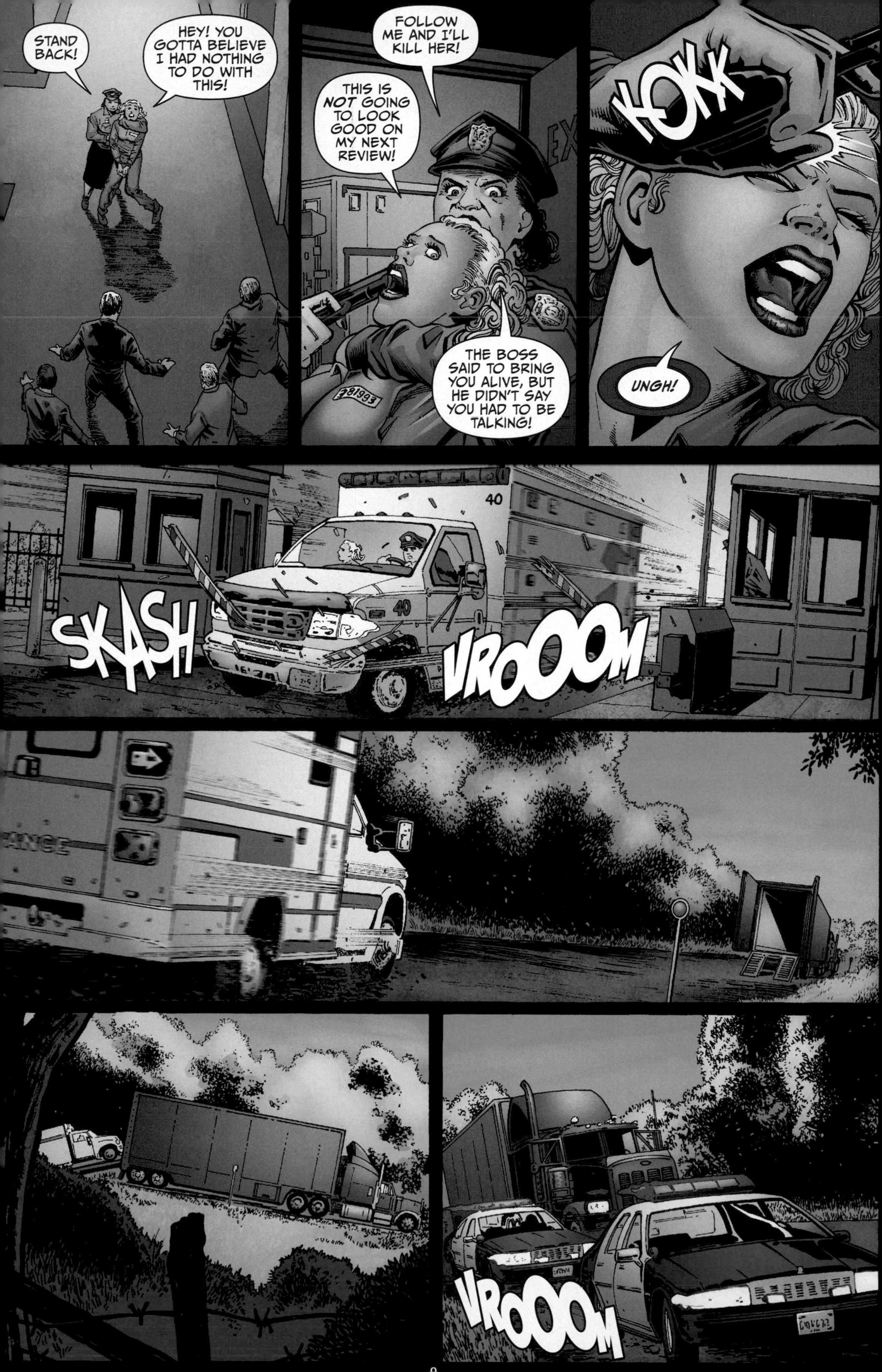
STAND BACK!
HEY! YOU GOTTA BELIEVE I HAD NOTHING TO DO WITH THIS!
FOLLOW ME AND I'LL KILL HER!
THIS IS NOT GOING TO LOOK GOOD ON MY NEXT REVIEW!
THE BOSS SAID TO BRING YOU ALIVE, BUT HE DIDN'T SAY YOU HAD TO BE TALKING!
KOKK
UNGH!
SKASH
VROOOM
VROOOM

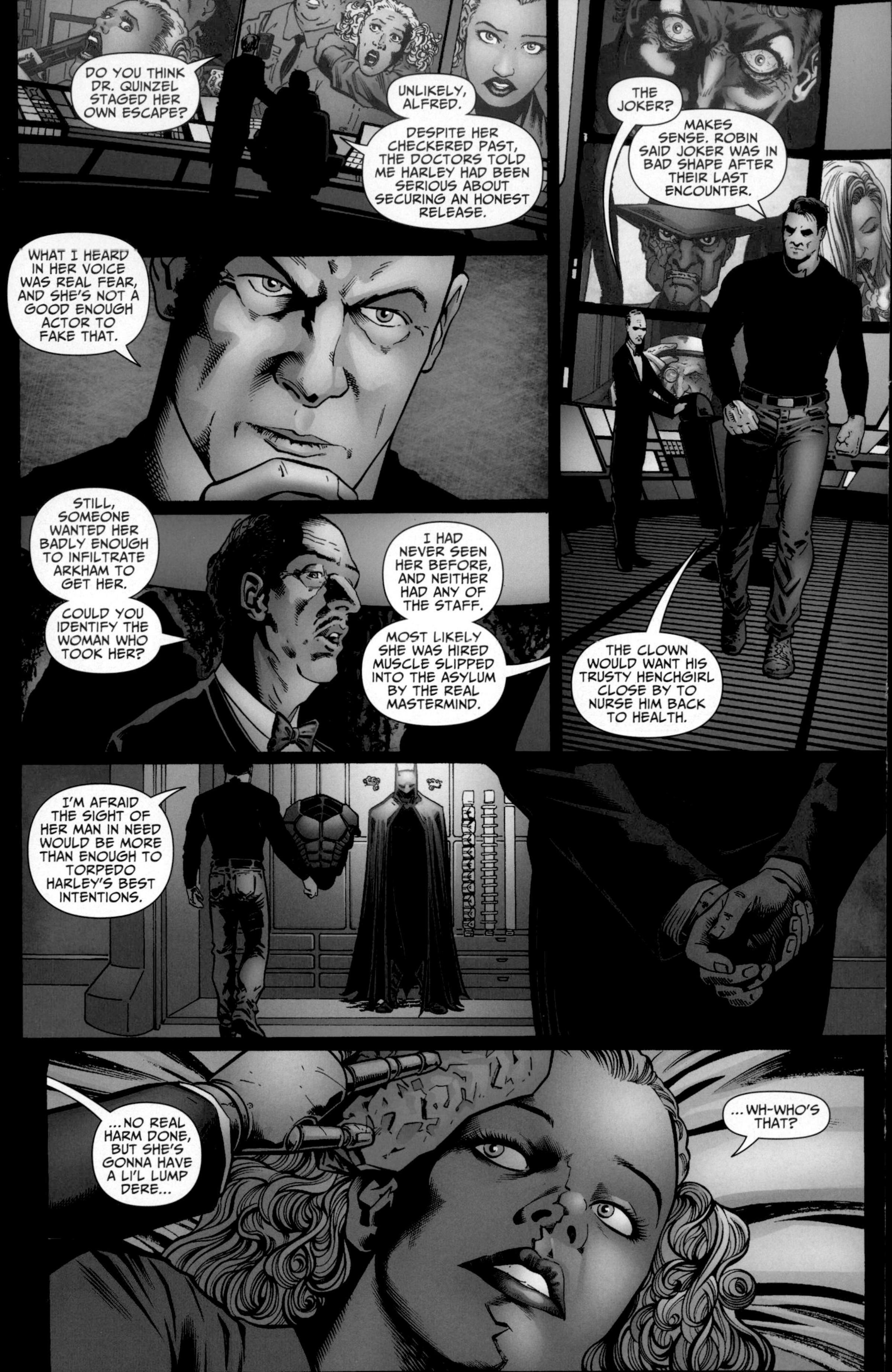
DO YOU THINK DR. QUINZEL STAGED HER OWN ESCAPE?
UNLIKELY, ALFRED.
DESPITE HER CHECKERED PAST, THE DOCTORS TOLD ME HARLEY HAD BEEN SERIOUS ABOUT SECURING AN HONEST RELEASE.
WHAT I HEARD IN HER VOICE WAS REAL FEAR, AND SHE'S NOT A GOOD ENOUGH ACTOR TO FAKE THAT.
STILL, SOMEONE WANTED HER BADLY ENOUGH TO INFILTRATE ARKHAM TO GET HER.
COULD YOU IDENTIFY THE WOMAN WHO TOOK HER?
I HAD NEVER SEEN HER BEFORE, AND NEITHER HAD ANY OF THE STAFF.
MOST LIKELY SHE WAS HIRED MUSCLE SLIPPED INTO THE ASYLUM BY THE REAL MASTERMIND.
THE JOKER?
MAKES SENSE. ROBIN SAID JOKER WAS IN BAD SHAPE AFTER THEIR LAST ENCOUNTER.
THE CLOWN WOULD WANT HIS TRUSTY HENCHGIRL CLOSE BY TO NURSE HIM BACK TO HEALTH.
I'M AFRAID THE SIGHT OF HER MAN IN NEED WOULD BE MORE THAN ENOUGH TO TORPEDO HARLEY'S BEST INTENTIONS.
...NO REAL HARM DONE, BUT SHE'S GONNA HAVE A LI'L LUMP DERE...
...WH-WHO'S THAT?

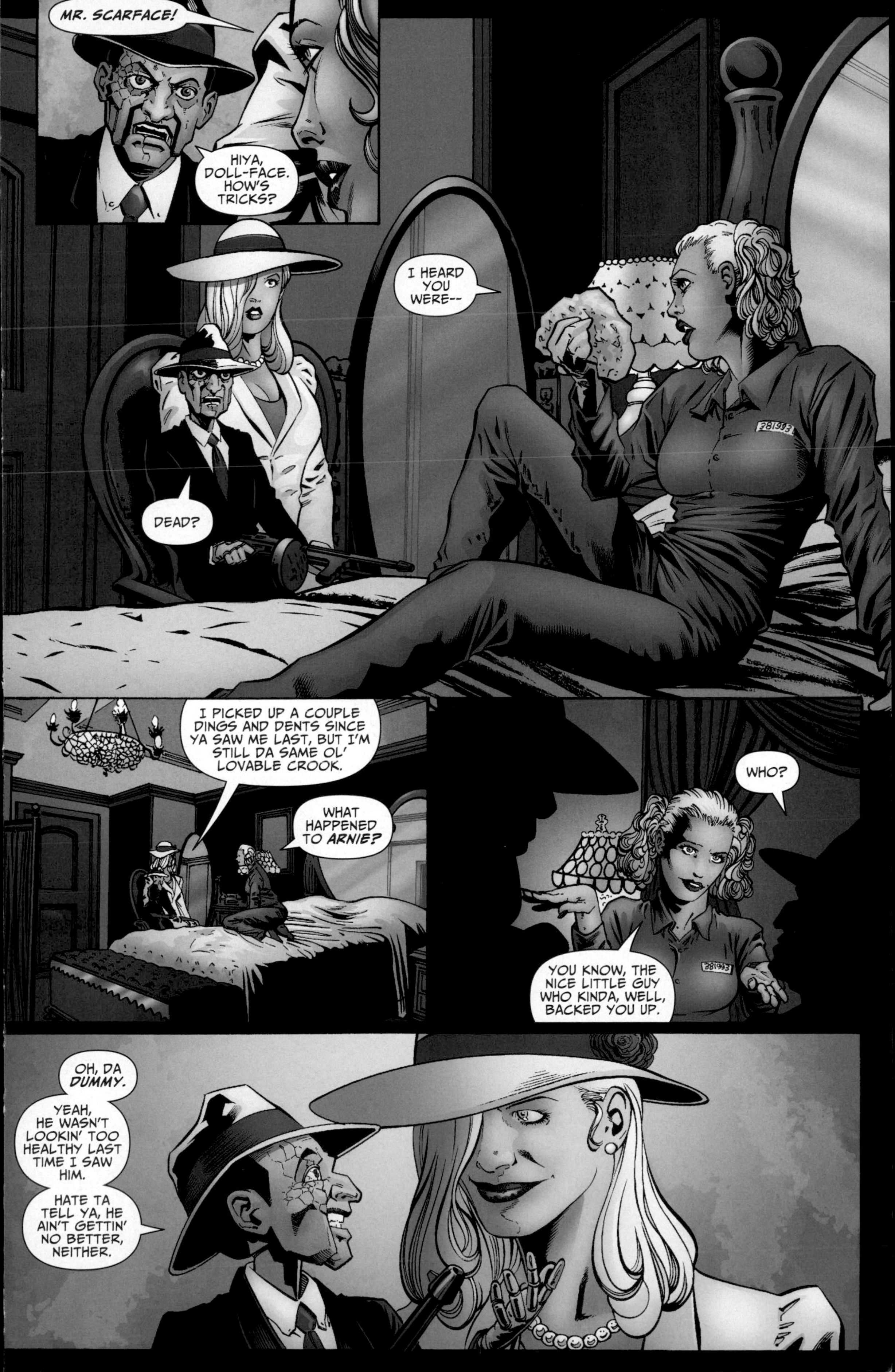
MR. SCARFACE!
HIYA, DOLL-FACE. HOW'S TRICKS?
I HEARD YOU WERE--
DEAD?
I PICKED UP A COUPLE DINGS AND DENTS SINCE YA SAW ME LAST, BUT I'M STILL DA SAME OL' LOVABLE CROOK.
WHAT HAPPENED TO ARNIE?
WHO?
YOU KNOW, THE NICE LITTLE GUY WHO KINDA, WELL, BACKED YOU UP.
OH, DA DUMMY.
YEAH, HE WASN'T LOOKIN' TOO HEALTHY LAST TIME I SAW HIM.
HATE TA TELL YA, HE AIN'T GETTIN' NO BETTER, NEITHER.

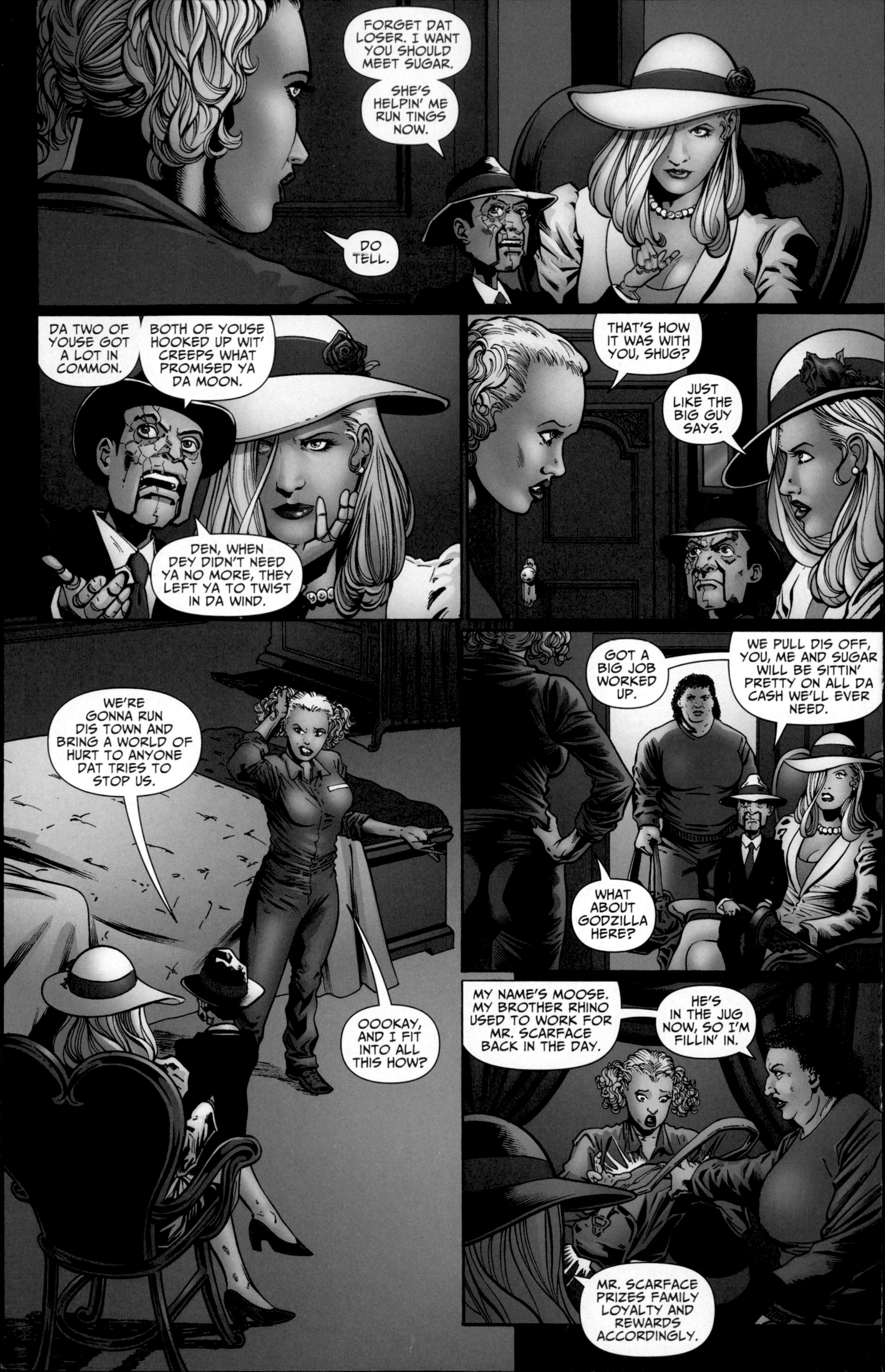
FORGET DAT LOSER. I WANT YOU SHOULD MEET SUGAR.
SHE'S HELPIN' ME RUN TINGS NOW.
DO TELL.
DA TWO OF YOUSE GOT A LOT IN COMMON.
BOTH OF YOUSE HOOKED UP WIT' CREEPS WHAT PROMISED YA DA MOON.
DEN, WHEN DEY DIDN'T NEED YA NO MORE, THEY LEFT YA TO TWIST IN DA WIND.
THAT'S HOW IT WAS WITH YOU, SHUG?
JUST LIKE THE BIG GUY SAYS.
WE'RE GONNA RUN DIS TOWN AND BRING A WORLD OF HURT TO ANYONE DAT TRIES TO STOP US.
OOOKAY, AND I FIT INTO ALL THIS HOW?
GOT A BIG JOB WORKED UP.
WE PULL DIS OFF, YOU, ME AND SUGAR WILL BE SITTIN' PRETTY ON ALL DA CASH WE'LL EVER NEED.
WHAT ABOUT GODZILLA HERE?
MY NAME'S MOOSE. MY BROTHER RHINO USED TO WORK FOR MR. SCARFACE BACK IN THE DAY.
HE'S IN THE JUG NOW, SO I'M FILLIN' IN.
MR. SCARFACE PRIZES FAMILY LOYALTY AND REWARDS ACCORDINGLY.

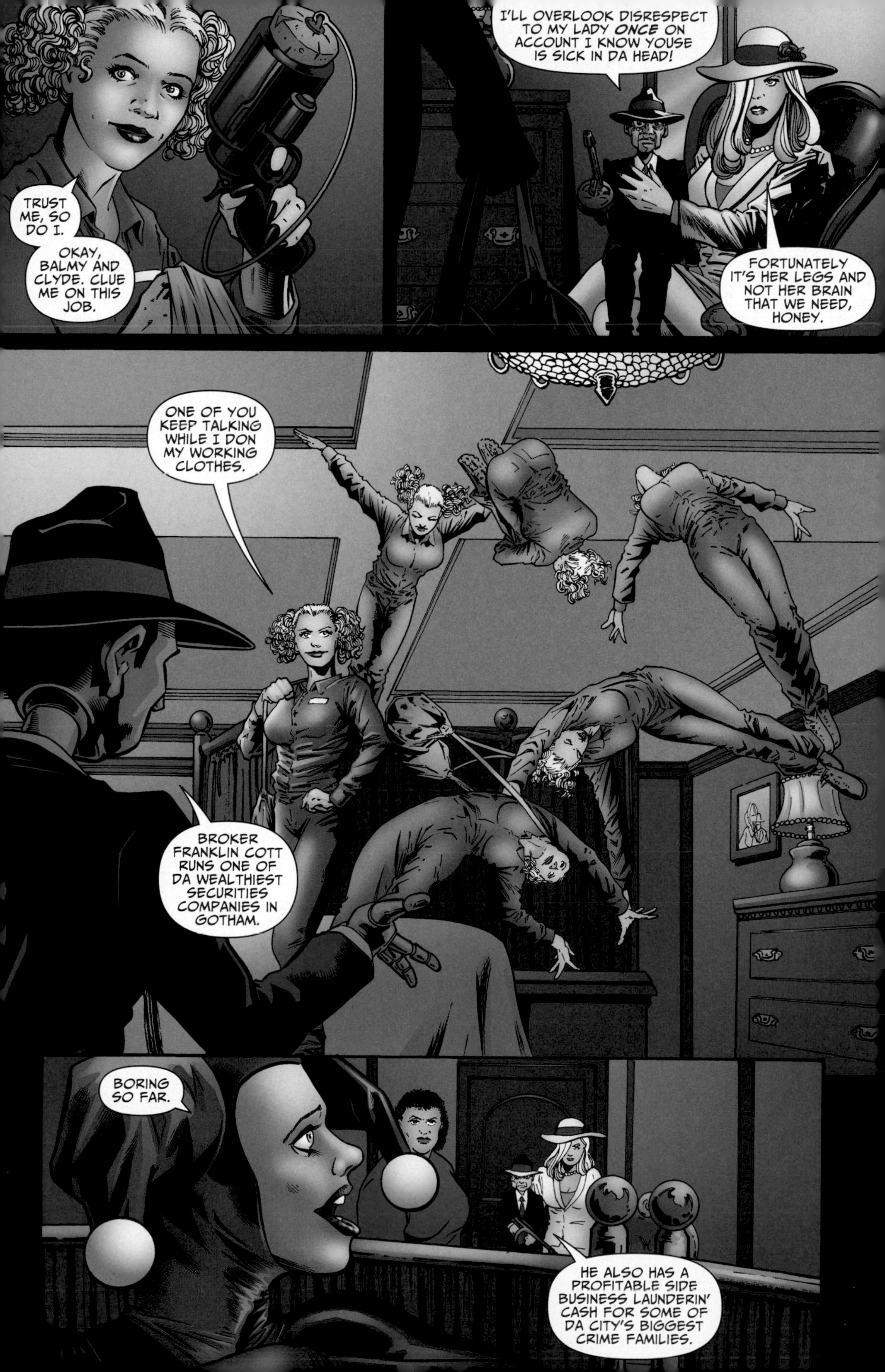
TRUST ME, SO DO I.
OKAY, BALMY AND CLYDE. CLUE ME ON THIS JOB.
I'LL OVERLOOK DISRESPECT TO MY LADY ONCE ON ACCOUNT I KNOW YOUSE IS SICK IN DA HEAD!
FORTUNATELY IT'S HER LEGS AND NOT HER BRAIN THAT WE NEED, HONEY.
ONE OF YOU KEEP TALKING WHILE I DON MY WORKING CLOTHES.
BROKER FRANKLIN COTT RUNS ONE OF DA WEALTHIEST SECURITIES COMPANIES IN GOTHAM.
BORING SO FAR.
HE ALSO HAS A PROFITABLE SIDE BUSINESS LAUNDERIN' CASH FOR SOME OF DA CITY'S BIGGEST CRIME FAMILIES.

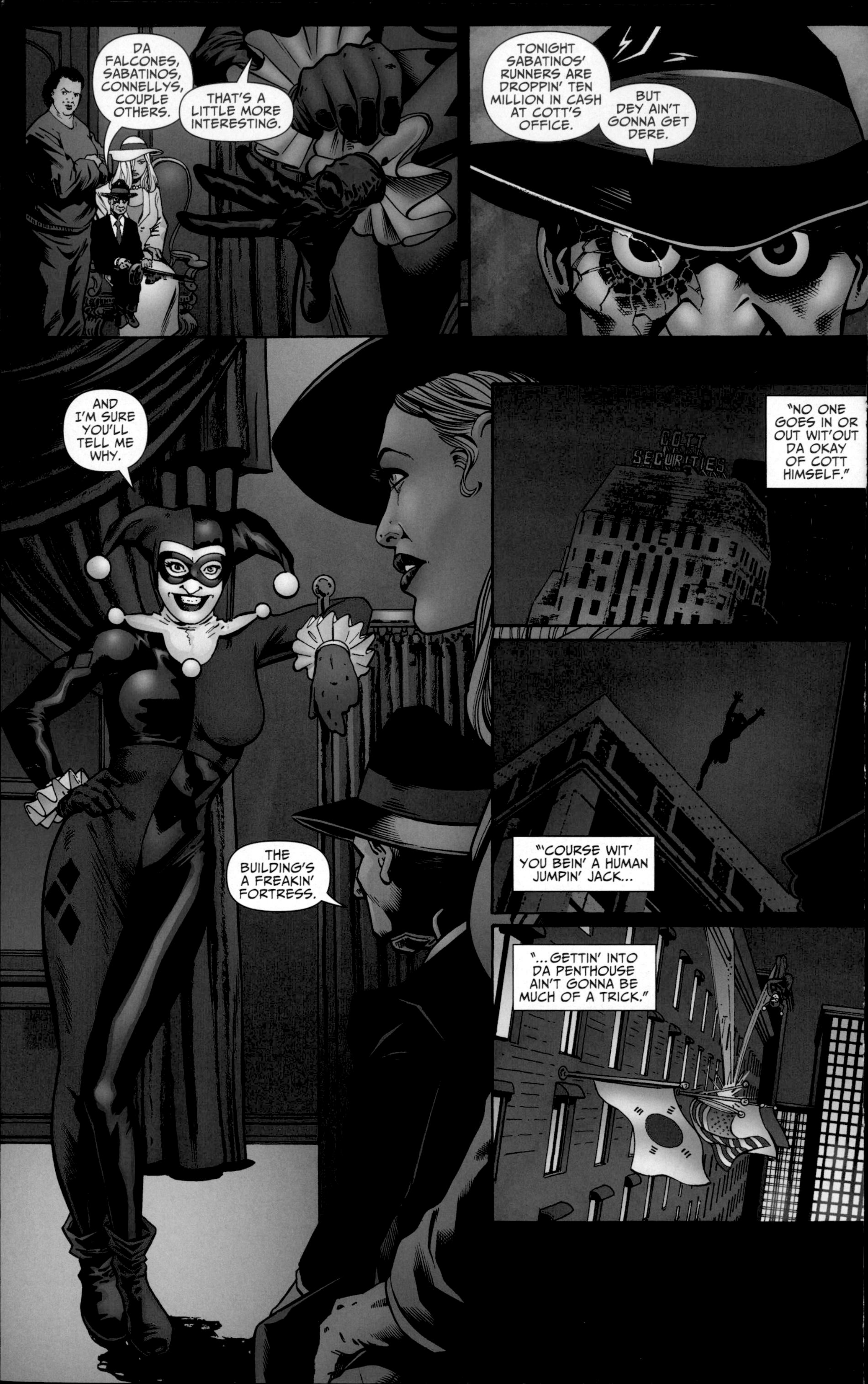
DA FALCONES, SABATINOS, CONNELLYS, COUPLE OTHERS.
THAT'S A LITTLE MORE INTERESTING.
TONIGHT SABATINOS' RUNNERS ARE DROPPIN' TEN MILLION IN CASH AT COTT'S OFFICE.
BUT DEY AIN'T GONNA GET DERE.
AND I'M SURE YOU'LL TELL ME WHY.
THE BUILDING'S A FREAKIN' FORTRESS.
COTT SECURITIES
"NO ONE GOES IN OR OUT WIT'OUT DA OKAY OF COTT HIMSELF."
"COURSE WIT' YOU BEIN' A HUMAN JUMPIN' JACK...
"...GETTIN' INTO DA PENTHOUSE AIN'T GONNA BE MUCH OF A TRICK."

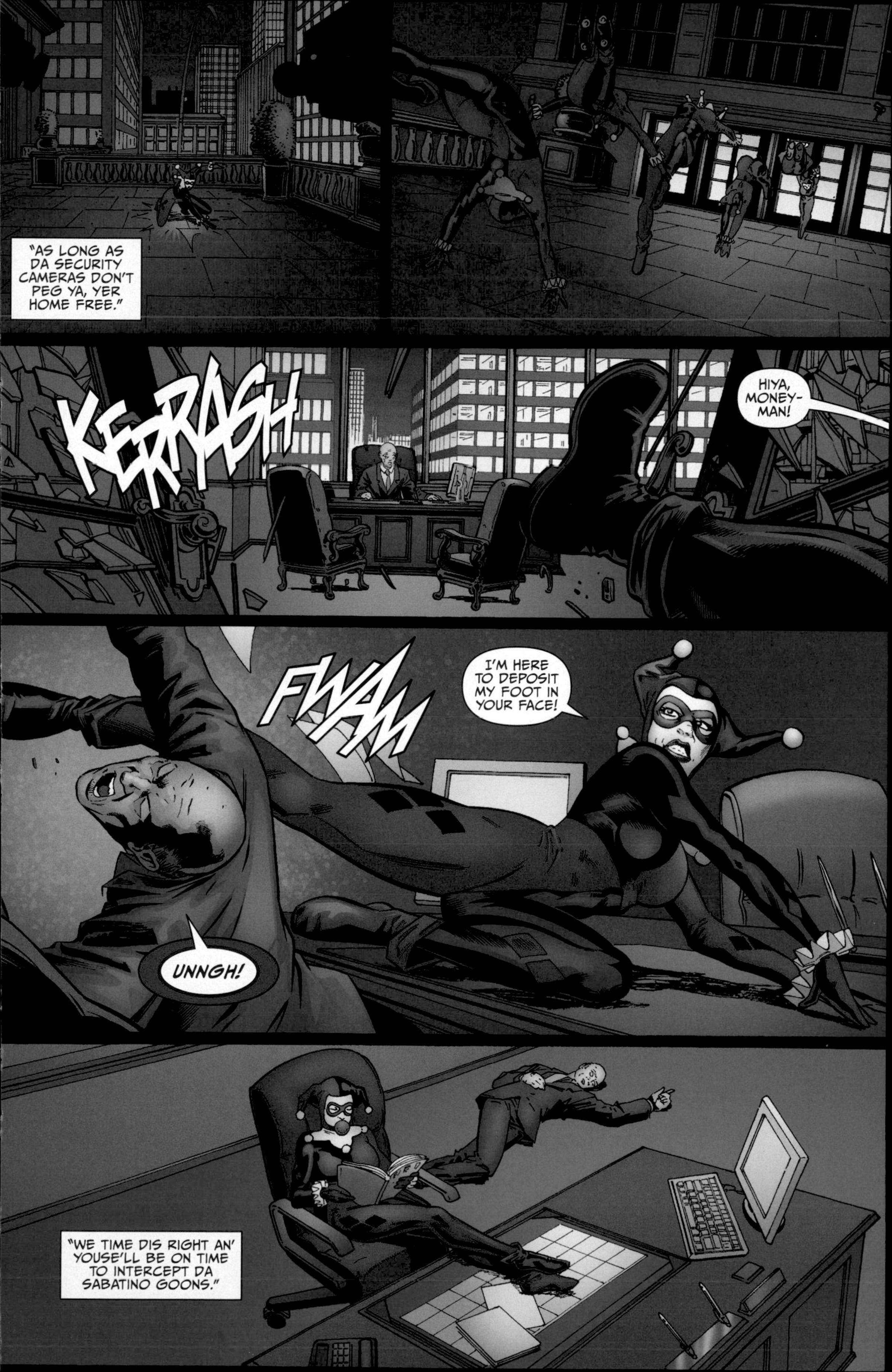
"AS LONG AS DA SECURITY CAMERAS DON'T PEG YA, YER HOME FREE."
KERRASH
HIYA, MONEY-MAN!
FWAM
I'M HERE TO DEPOSIT MY FOOT IN YOUR FACE!
UNNGH!
"WE TIME DIS RIGHT AN' YOUSE'LL BE ON TIME TO INTERCEPT DA SABATINO GOONS."

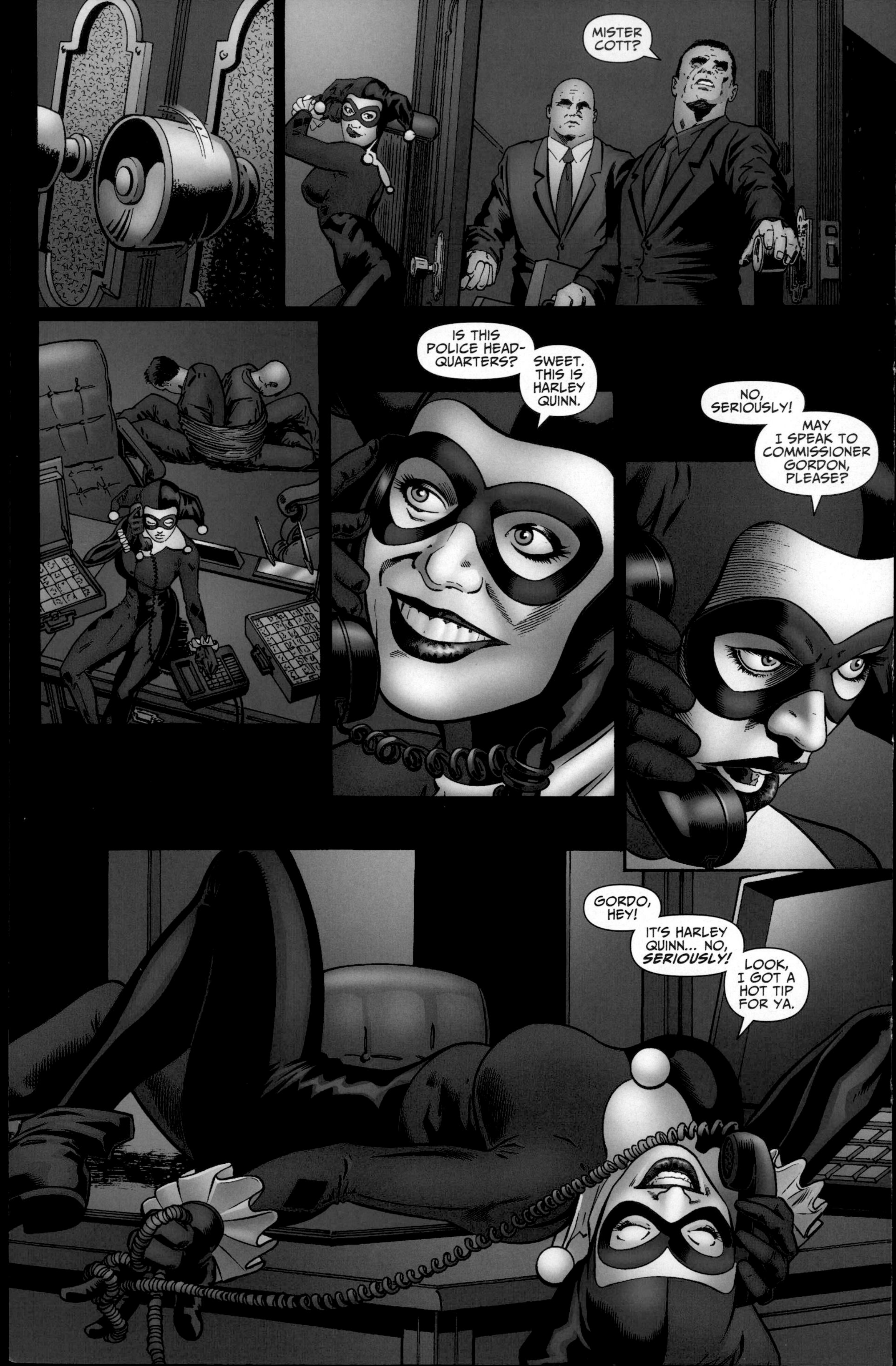
MISTER COTT?
IS THIS POLICE HEAD-QUARTERS?
SWEET. THIS IS HARLEY QUINN.
NO, SERIOUSLY!
MAY I SPEAK TO COMMISSIONER GORDON, PLEASE?
GORDO, HEY!
IT'S HARLEY QUINN... NO, *SERIOUSLY!*
LOOK, I GOT A HOT TIP FOR YA.

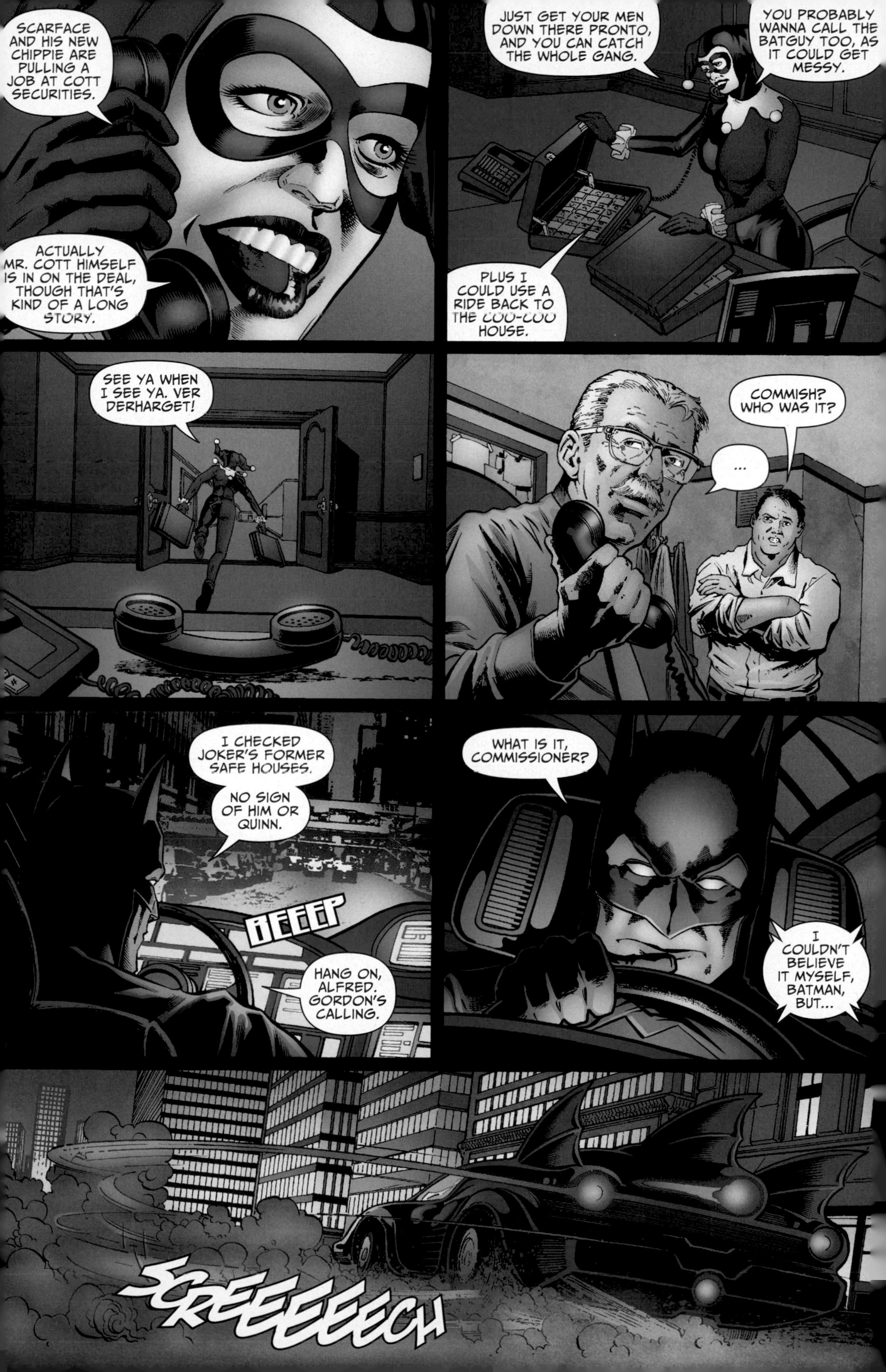
SCARFACE AND HIS NEW CHIPPIE ARE PULLING A JOB AT COTT SECURITIES.
ACTUALLY MR. COTT HIMSELF IS IN ON THE DEAL, THOUGH THAT'S KIND OF A LONG STORY.
JUST GET YOUR MEN DOWN THERE PRONTO, AND YOU CAN CATCH THE WHOLE GANG.
YOU PROBABLY WANNA CALL THE BATGUY TOO, AS IT COULD GET MESSY.
PLUS I COULD USE A RIDE BACK TO THE COO-COO HOUSE.
SEE YA WHEN I SEE YA. VER DERHARGET!
COMMISH? WHO WAS IT?
...
I CHECKED JOKER'S FORMER SAFE HOUSES.
NO SIGN OF HIM OR QUINN.
BEEEP
HANG ON, ALFRED. GORDON'S CALLING.
WHAT IS IT, COMMISSIONER?
I COULDN'T BELIEVE IT MYSELF, BATMAN, BUT...
SCREEEEEECH

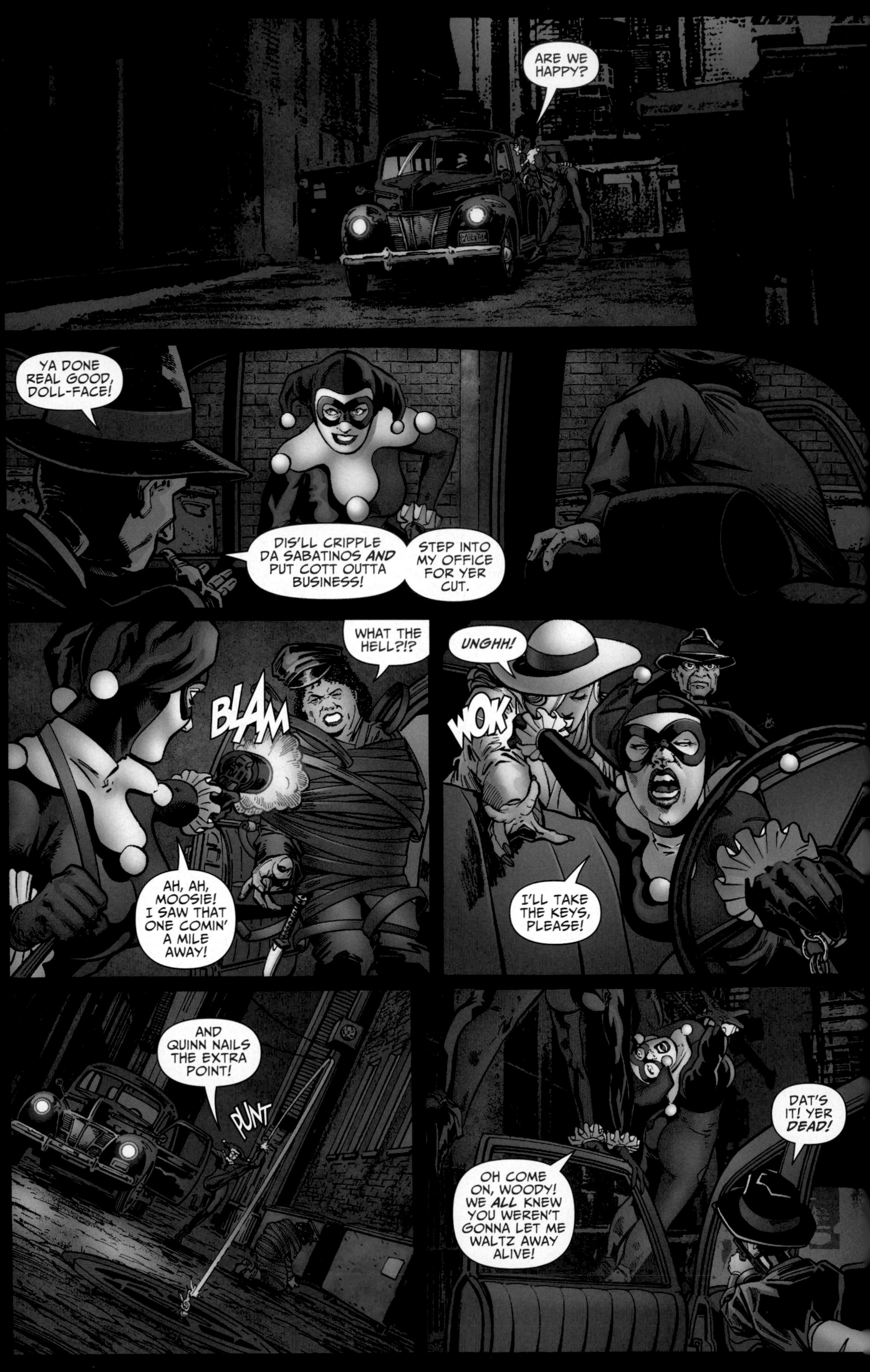
ARE WE HAPPY?
YA DONE REAL GOOD, DOLL-FACE!
DIS'LL CRIPPLE DA SABATINOS **AND** PUT COTT OUTTA BUSINESS!
STEP INTO MY OFFICE FOR YER CUT.
WHAT THE HELL?!?
BLAM
AH, AH, MOOSIE! I SAW THAT ONE COMIN' A MILE AWAY!
UNGHH!
WOK
I'LL TAKE THE KEYS, PLEASE!
AND QUINN NAILS THE EXTRA POINT!
PUNT
DAT'S IT! YER **DEAD!**
OH COME ON, WOODY! WE **ALL** KNEW YOU WEREN'T GONNA LET ME WALTZ AWAY ALIVE!

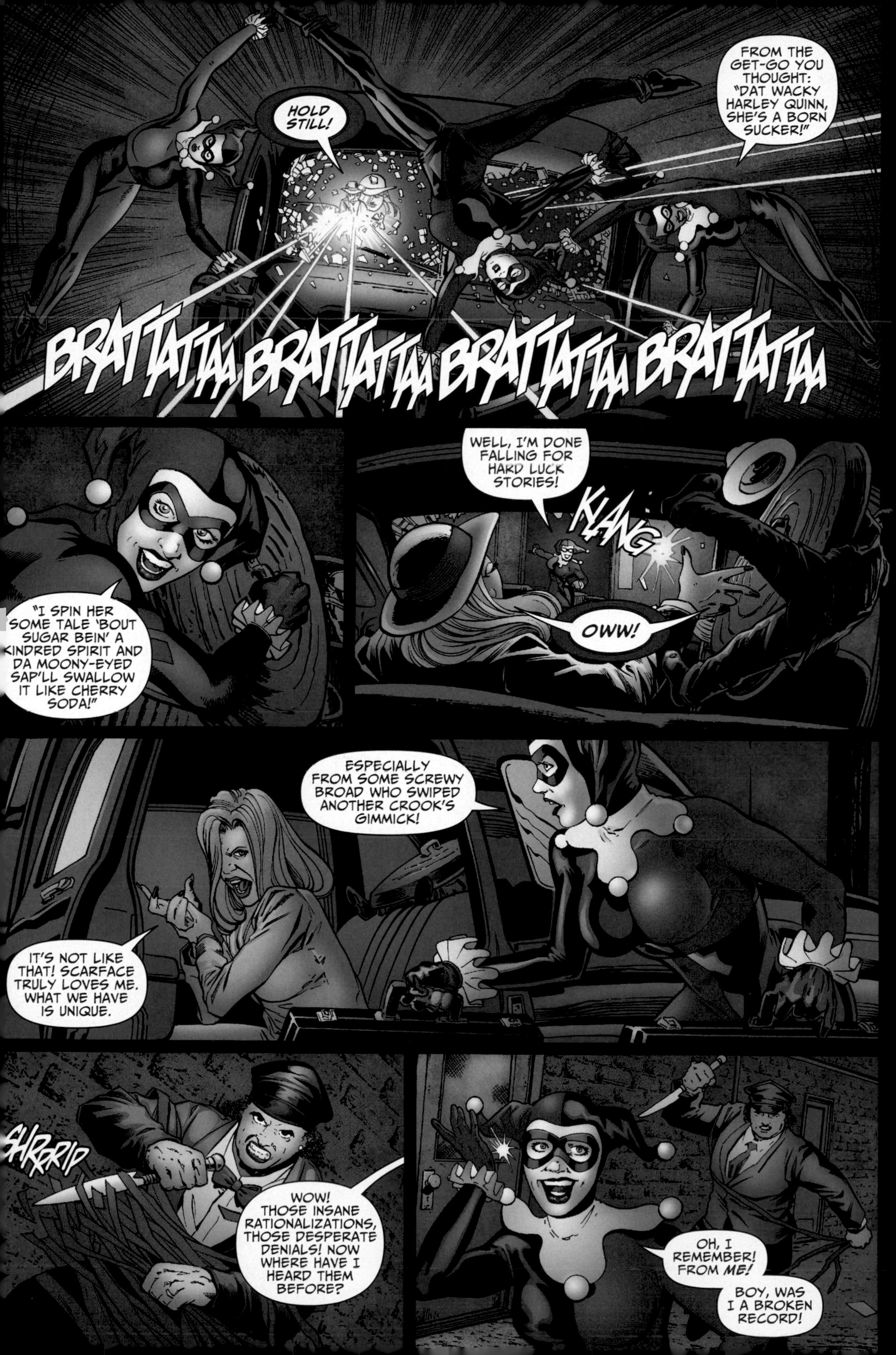
HOLD STILL!
FROM THE GET-GO YOU THOUGHT: "DAT WACKY HARLEY QUINN, SHE'S A BORN SUCKER!"
BRATTATTAA BRATTATTAA BRATTATTAA BRATTATTAA
"I SPIN HER SOME TALE 'BOUT SUGAR BEIN' A KINDRED SPIRIT AND DA MOONY-EYED SAP'LL SWALLOW IT LIKE CHERRY SODA!"
WELL, I'M DONE FALLING FOR HARD LUCK STORIES!
KLANG
OWW!
ESPECIALLY FROM SOME SCREWY BROAD WHO SWIPED ANOTHER CROOK'S GIMMICK!
IT'S NOT LIKE THAT! SCARFACE TRULY LOVES ME. WHAT WE HAVE IS UNIQUE.
SHRRRIP
WOW! THOSE INSANE RATIONALIZATIONS, THOSE DESPERATE DENIALS! NOW WHERE HAVE I HEARD THEM BEFORE?
OH, I REMEMBER! FROM ME!
BOY, WAS I A BROKEN RECORD!

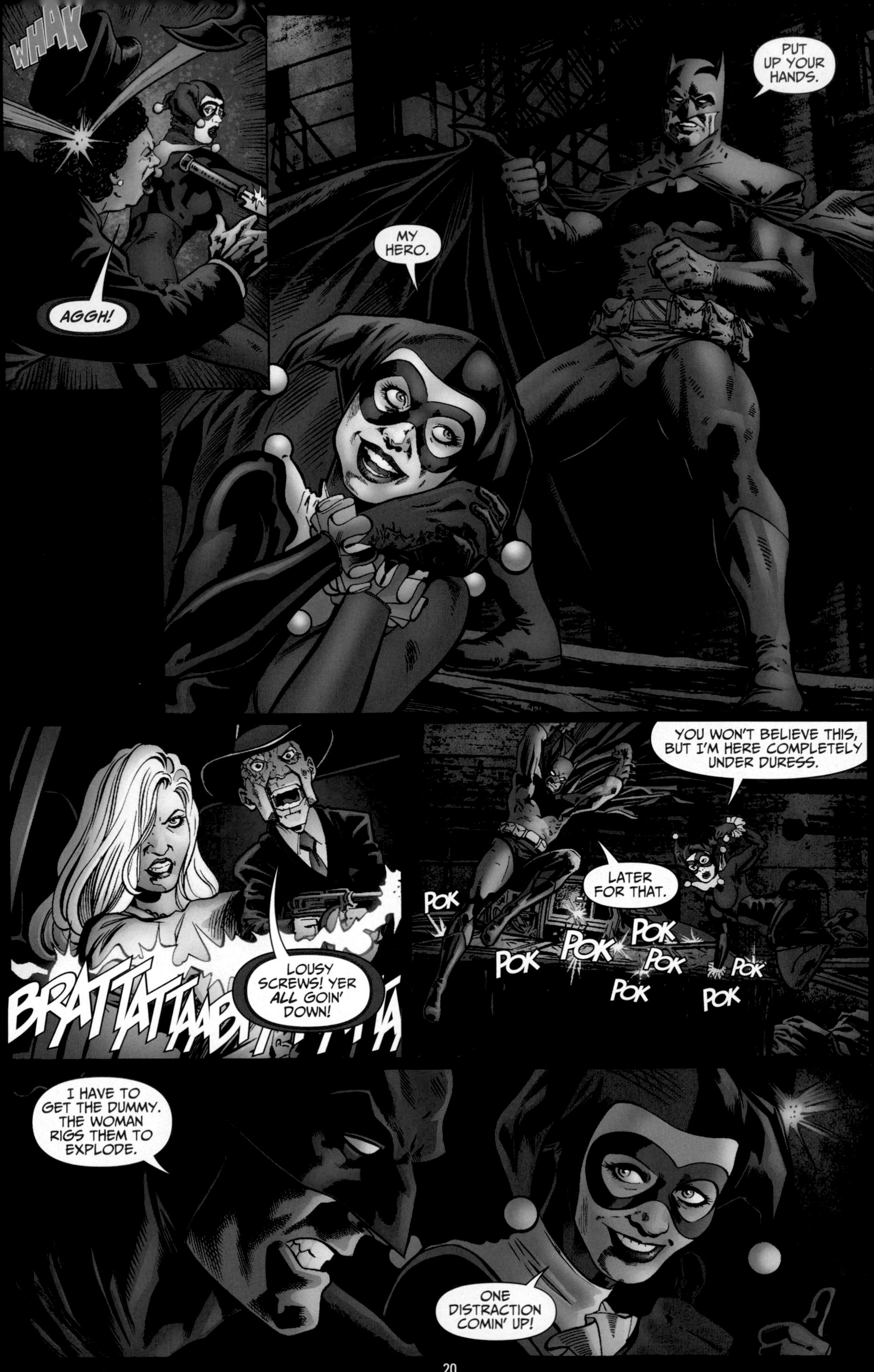
WHAK
AGGH!
PUT UP YOUR HANDS.
MY HERO.
BRATTATTAAB
LOUSY SCREWS! YER ALL GOIN' DOWN!
YOU WON'T BELIEVE THIS, BUT I'M HERE COMPLETELY UNDER DURESS.
LATER FOR THAT.
POK
POK
POK
POK
POK
POK
POK
POK
I HAVE TO GET THE DUMMY. THE WOMAN RIGS THEM TO EXPLODE.
ONE DISTRACTION COMIN' UP!

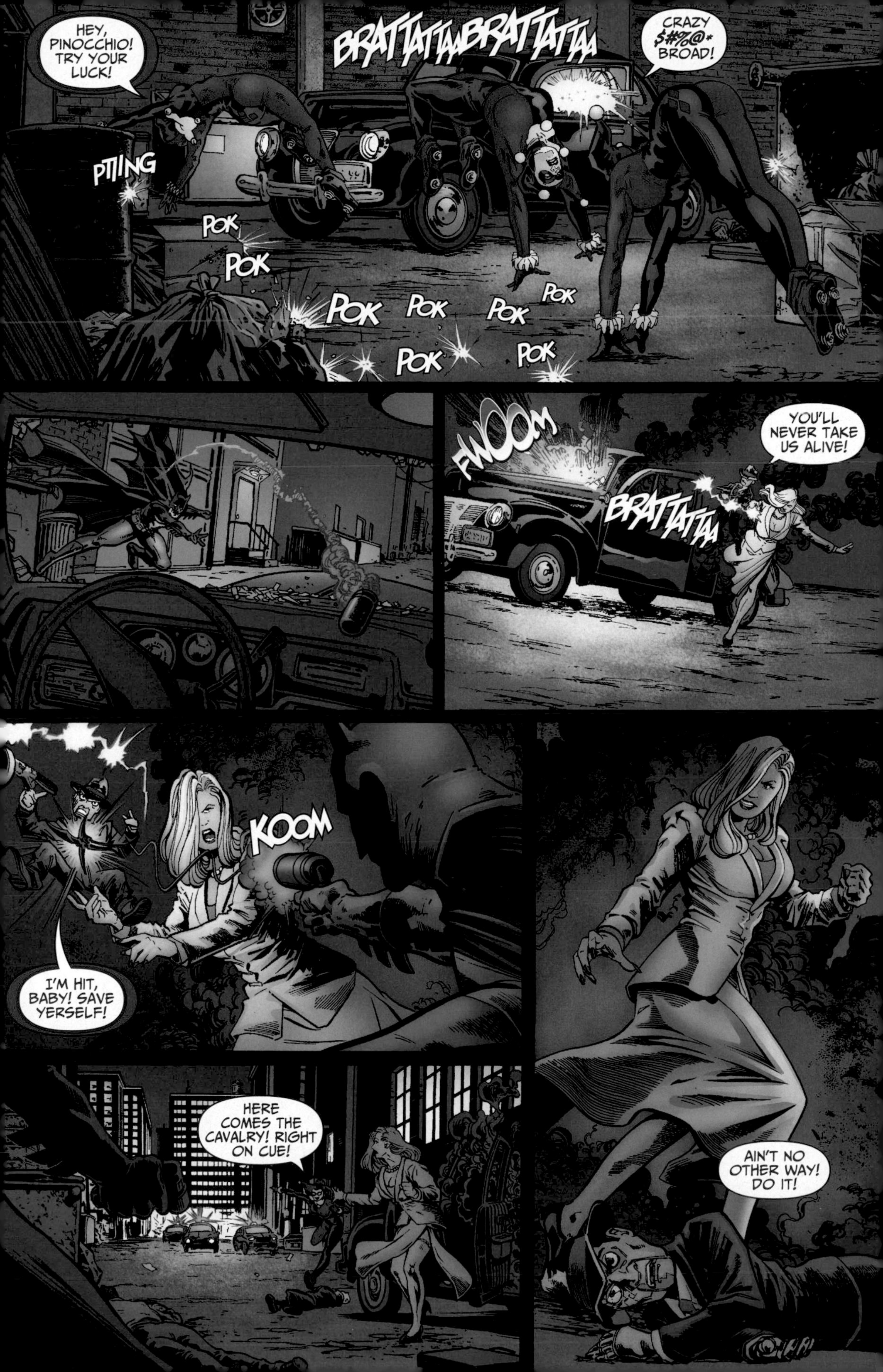

HEY, PINOCCHIO! TRY YOUR LUCK!
BRATTATTAABRATTATTAA
CRAZY $#%@* BROAD!
PTIING
POK
POK
POK
POK
POK
POK
POK
POK
FWOOM
YOU'LL NEVER TAKE US ALIVE!
BRATTATTAA
KOOM
I'M HIT, BABY! SAVE YERSELF!
HERE COMES THE CAVALRY! RIGHT ON CUE!
AIN'T NO OTHER WAY! DO IT!

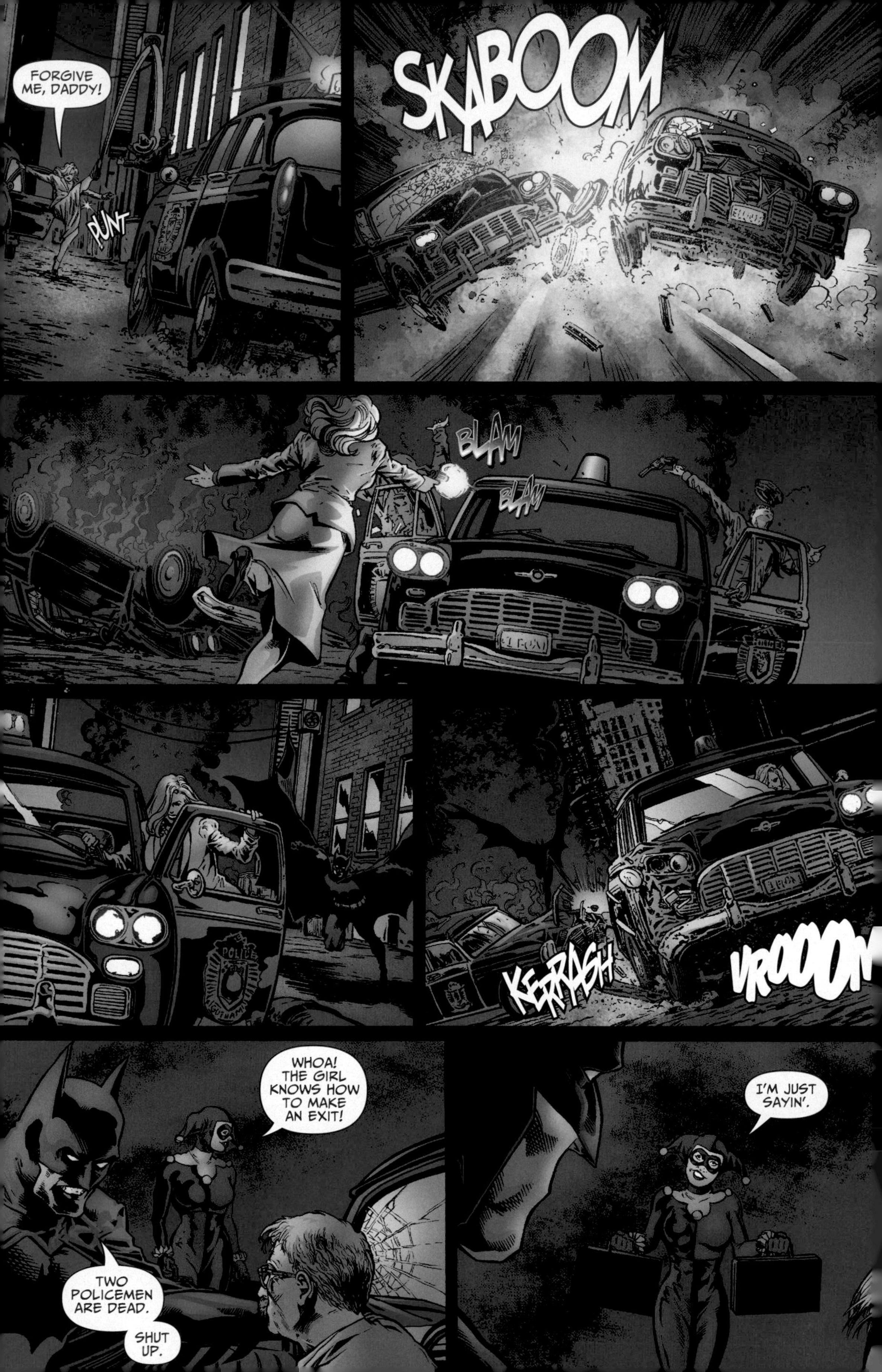
FORGIVE ME, DADDY!
PUNT
SKABOOM
BLAM
BLAM
KERRASH
VROOOOM
WHOA! THE GIRL KNOWS HOW TO MAKE AN EXIT!
TWO POLICEMEN ARE DEAD.
SHUT UP.
I'M JUST SAYIN'.

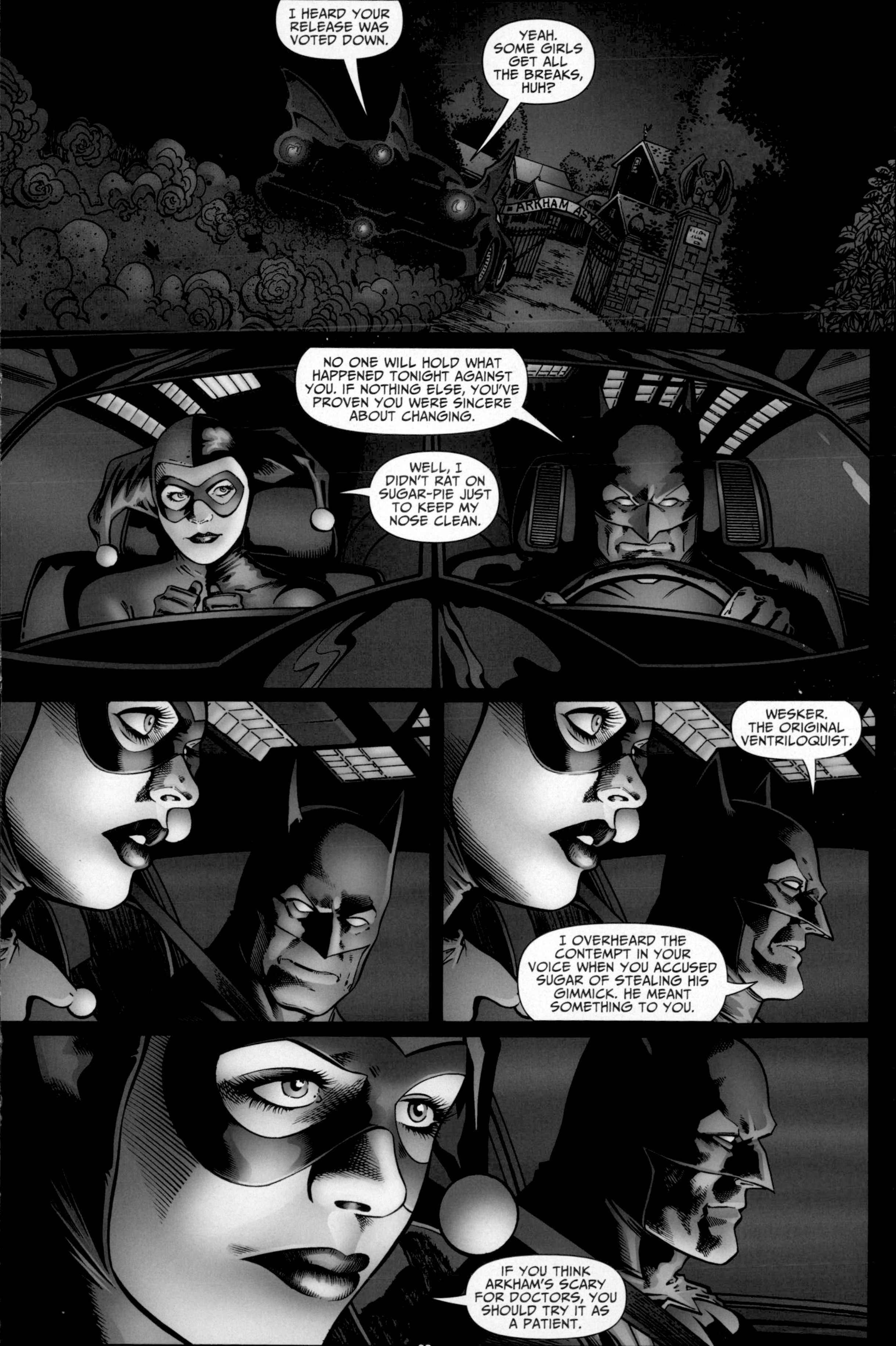
I HEARD YOUR RELEASE WAS VOTED DOWN.
YEAH. SOME GIRLS GET ALL THE BREAKS, HUH?
ARKHAM ASYLUM
NO ONE WILL HOLD WHAT HAPPENED TONIGHT AGAINST YOU. IF NOTHING ELSE, YOU'VE PROVEN YOU WERE SINCERE ABOUT CHANGING.
WELL, I DIDN'T RAT ON SUGAR-PIE JUST TO KEEP MY NOSE CLEAN.
WESKER. THE ORIGINAL VENTRILOQUIST.
I OVERHEARD THE CONTEMPT IN YOUR VOICE WHEN YOU ACCUSED SUGAR OF STEALING HIS GIMMICK. HE MEANT SOMETHING TO YOU.
IF YOU THINK ARKHAM'S SCARY FOR DOCTORS, YOU SHOULD TRY IT AS A PATIENT.

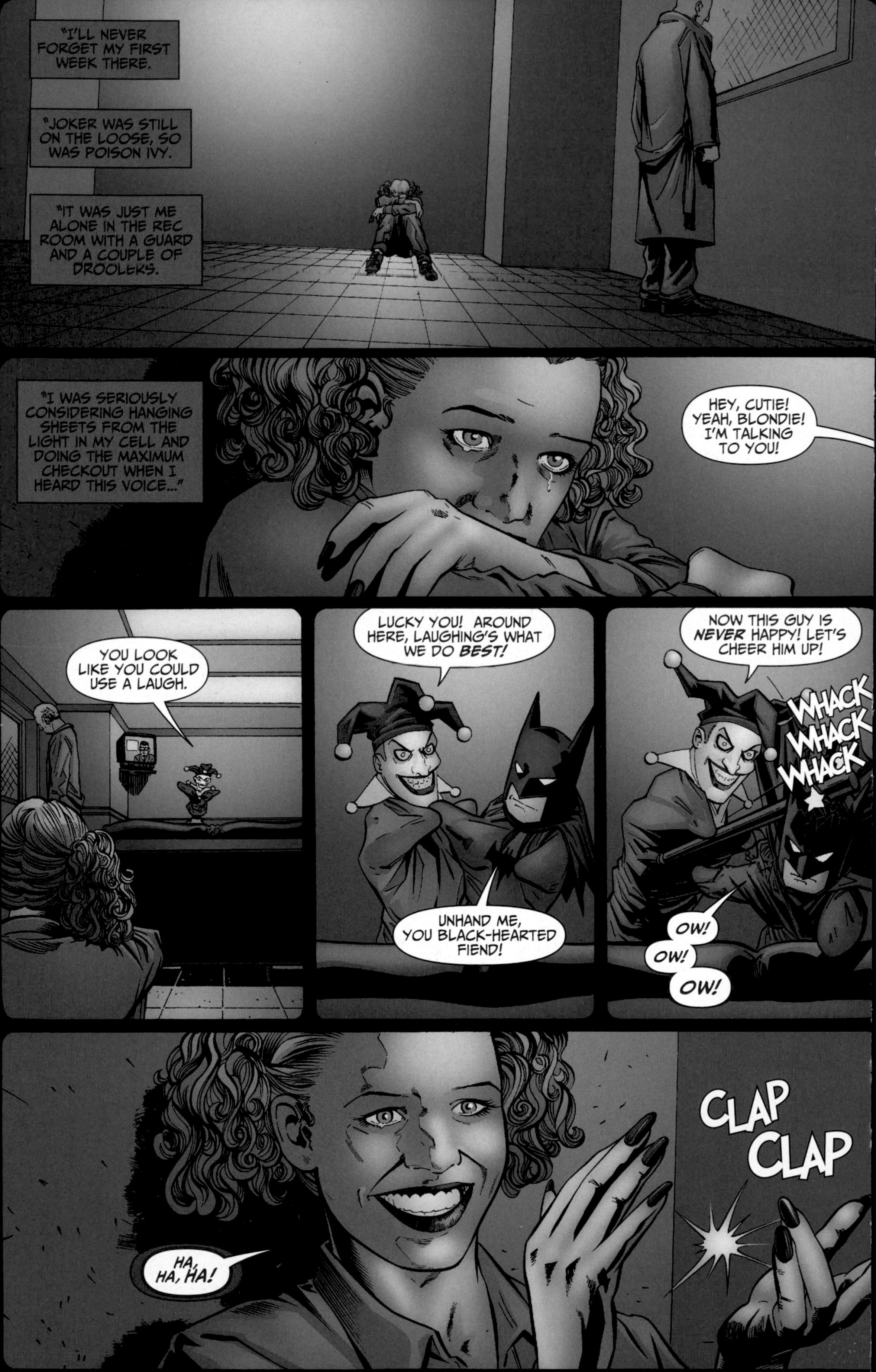
"I'LL NEVER FORGET MY FIRST WEEK THERE.
"JOKER WAS STILL ON THE LOOSE, SO WAS POISON IVY.
"IT WAS JUST ME ALONE IN THE REC ROOM WITH A GUARD AND A COUPLE OF DROOLERS.
"I WAS SERIOUSLY CONSIDERING HANGING SHEETS FROM THE LIGHT IN MY CELL AND DOING THE MAXIMUM CHECKOUT WHEN I HEARD THIS VOICE..."
HEY, CUTIE! YEAH, BLONDIE! I'M TALKING TO YOU!
YOU LOOK LIKE YOU COULD USE A LAUGH.
LUCKY YOU! AROUND HERE, LAUGHING'S WHAT WE DO *BEST!*
UNHAND ME, YOU BLACK-HEARTED FIEND!
NOW THIS GUY IS *NEVER* HAPPY! LET'S CHEER HIM UP!
WHACK
WHACK
WHACK
OW!
OW!
OW!
CLAP
CLAP
HA, HA, HA!

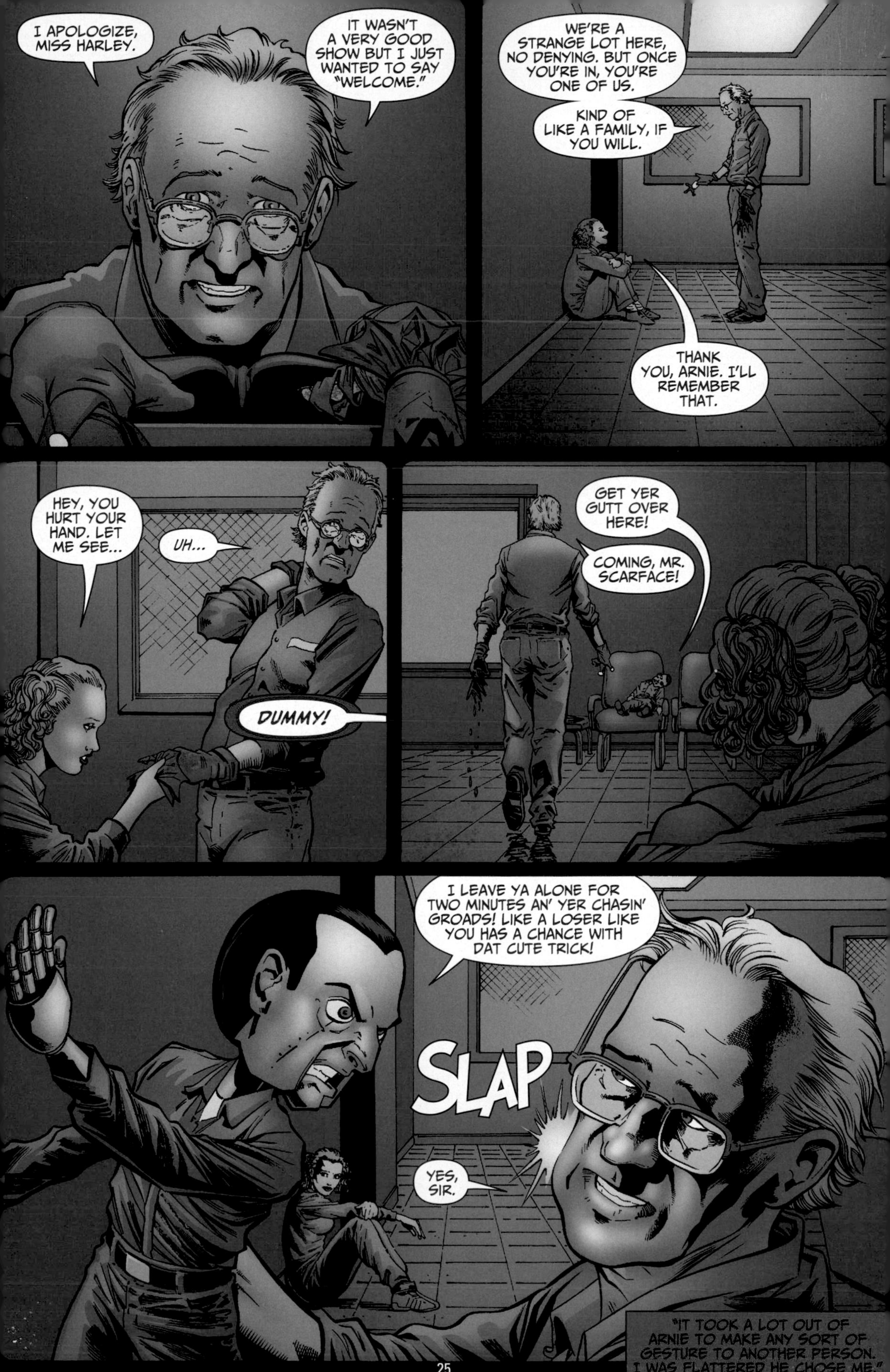
I APOLOGIZE, MISS HARLEY.
IT WASN'T A VERY GOOD SHOW BUT I JUST WANTED TO SAY "WELCOME."
WE'RE A STRANGE LOT HERE, NO DENYING. BUT ONCE YOU'RE IN, YOU'RE ONE OF US.
KIND OF LIKE A FAMILY, IF YOU WILL.
THANK YOU, ARNIE. I'LL REMEMBER THAT.
HEY, YOU HURT YOUR HAND. LET ME SEE...
UH...
DUMMY!
GET YER GUTT OVER HERE!
COMING, MR. SCARFACE!
I LEAVE YA ALONE FOR TWO MINUTES AN' YER CHASIN' GROADS! LIKE A LOSER LIKE YOU HAS A CHANCE WITH DAT CUTE TRICK!
SLAP
YES, SIR.
"IT TOOK A LOT OUT OF ARNIE TO MAKE ANY SORT OF GESTURE TO ANOTHER PERSON. I WAS FLATTERED HE CHOSE ME."

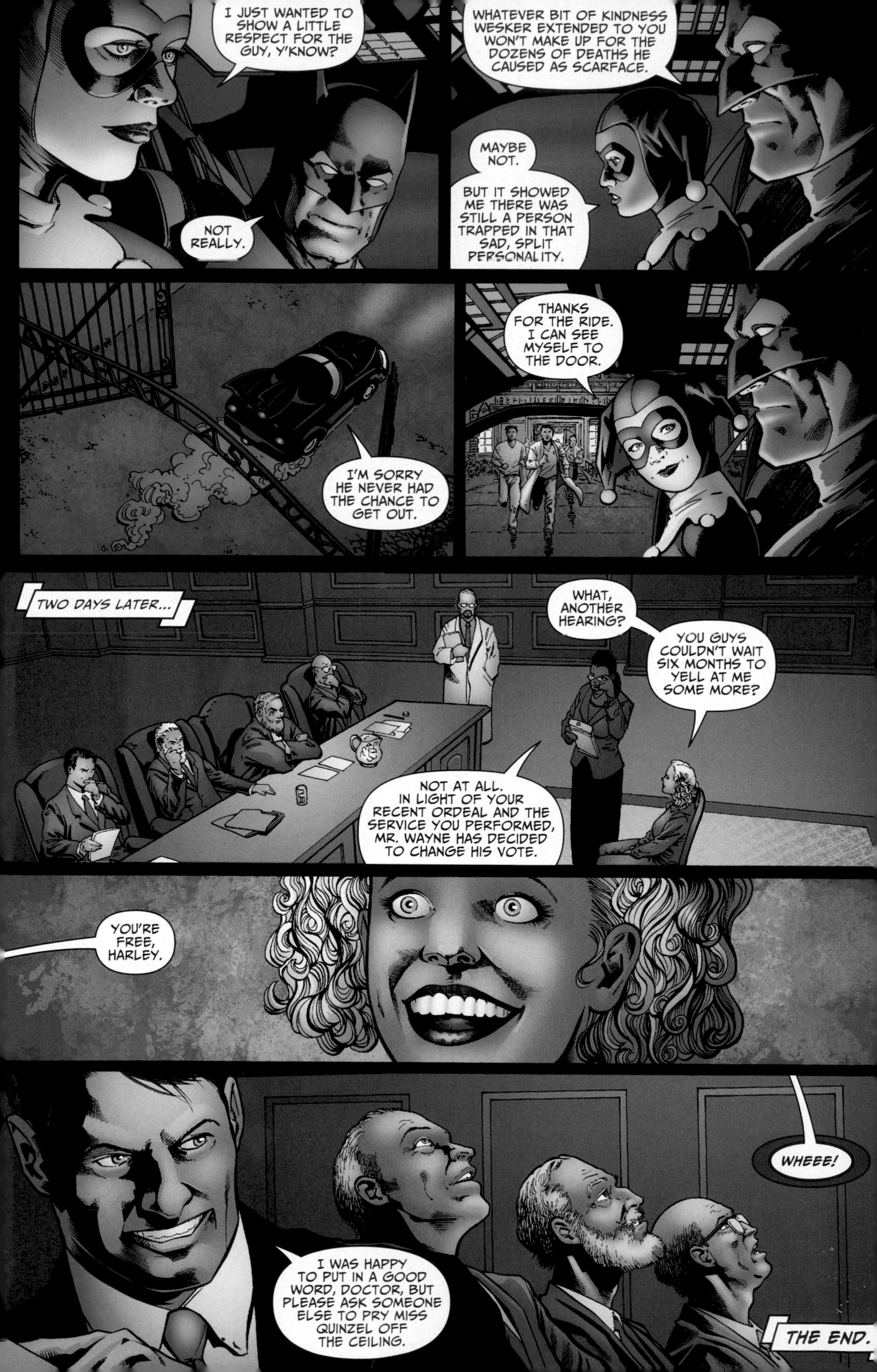

I JUST WANTED TO SHOW A LITTLE RESPECT FOR THE GUY, Y'KNOW?
NOT REALLY.
WHATEVER BIT OF KINDNESS WESKER EXTENDED TO YOU WON'T MAKE UP FOR THE DOZENS OF DEATHS HE CAUSED AS SCARFACE.
MAYBE NOT.
BUT IT SHOWED ME THERE WAS STILL A PERSON TRAPPED IN THAT SAD, SPLIT PERSONALITY.
I'M SORRY HE NEVER HAD THE CHANCE TO GET OUT.
THANKS FOR THE RIDE. I CAN SEE MYSELF TO THE DOOR.
TWO DAYS LATER...
WHAT, ANOTHER HEARING?
YOU GUYS COULDN'T WAIT SIX MONTHS TO YELL AT ME SOME MORE?
NOT AT ALL. IN LIGHT OF YOUR RECENT ORDEAL AND THE SERVICE YOU PERFORMED, MR. WAYNE HAS DECIDED TO CHANGE HIS VOTE.
YOU'RE FREE, HARLEY.
WHEEE!
I WAS HAPPY TO PUT IN A GOOD WORD, DOCTOR, BUT PLEASE ASK SOMEONE ELSE TO PRY MISS QUINZEL OFF THE CEILING.
THE END.

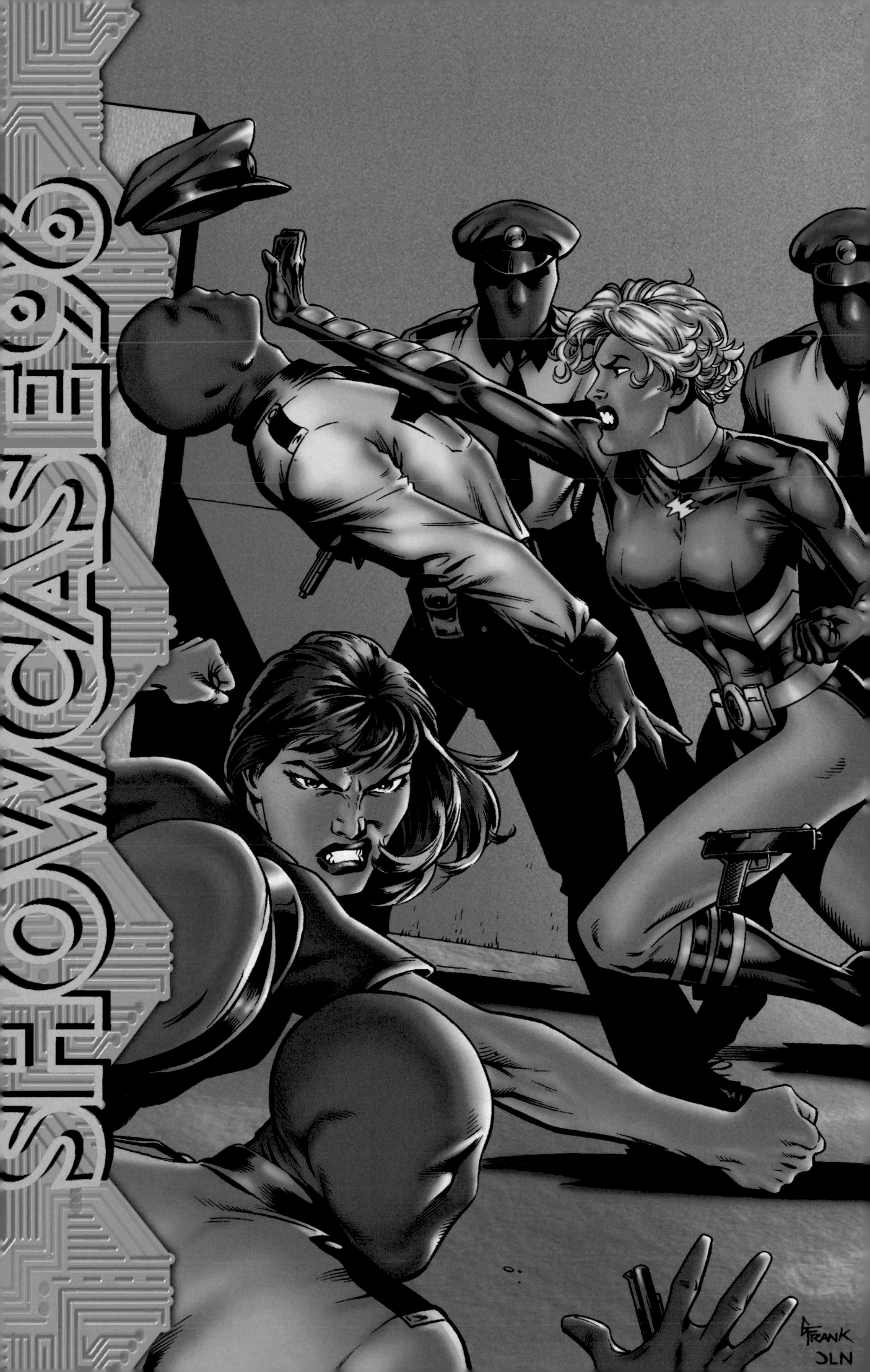
SHOWCASE 96
G FRANK
JLN

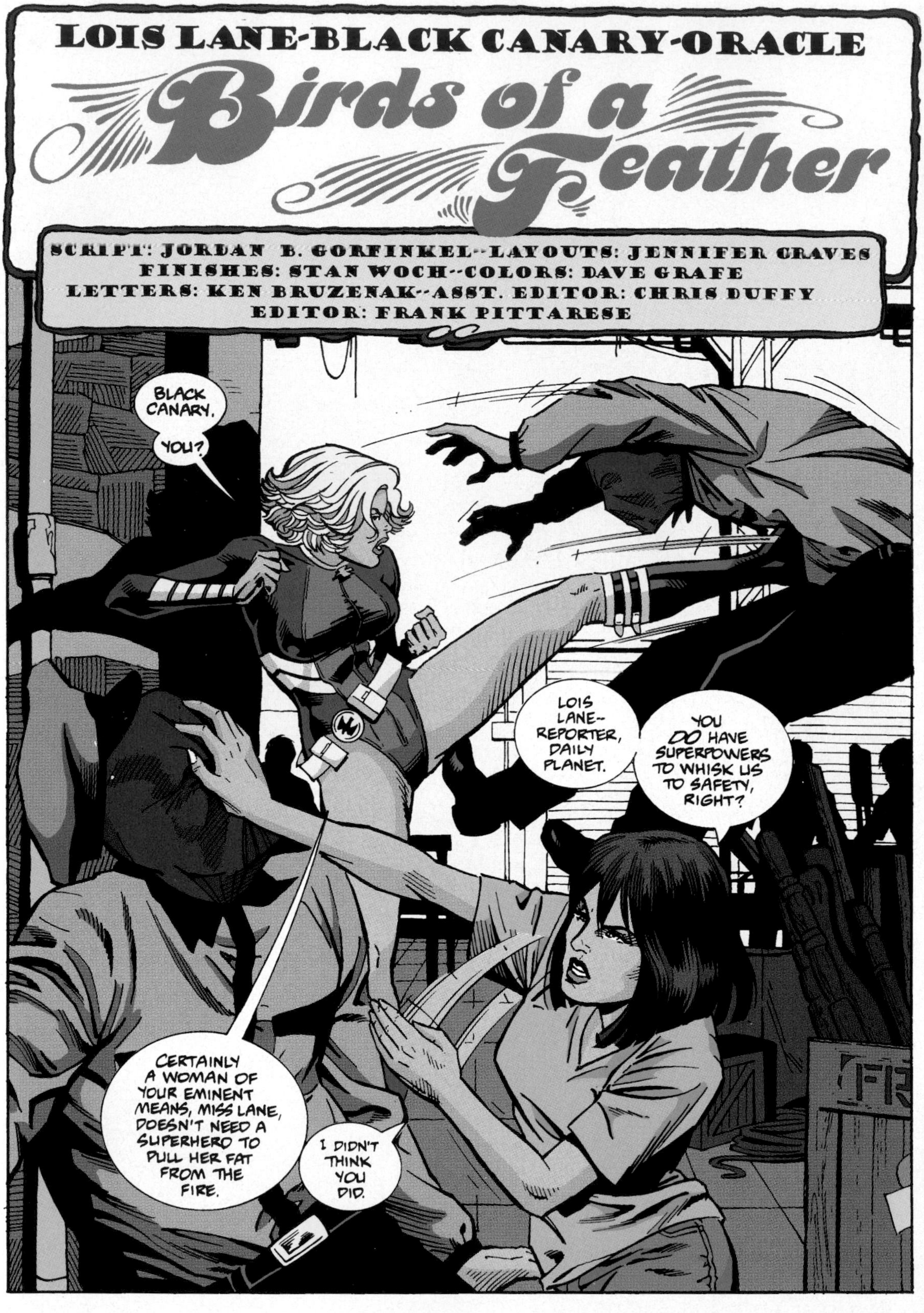
LOIS LANE-BLACK CANARY-ORACLE
Birds of a Feather
SCRIPT: JORDAN B. GORFINKEL--LAYOUTS: JENNIFER GRAVES
FINISHES: STAN WOCH--COLORS: DAVE GRAFE
LETTERS: KEN BRUZENAK--ASST. EDITOR: CHRIS DUFFY
EDITOR: FRANK PITTARESE
BLACK CANARY.
YOU?
LOIS LANE-- REPORTER, DAILY PLANET.
YOU DO HAVE SUPERPOWERS TO WHISK US TO SAFETY, RIGHT?
CERTAINLY A WOMAN OF YOUR EMINENT MEANS, MISS LANE, DOESN'T NEED A SUPERHERO TO PULL HER FAT FROM THE FIRE.
I DIDN'T THINK YOU DID.

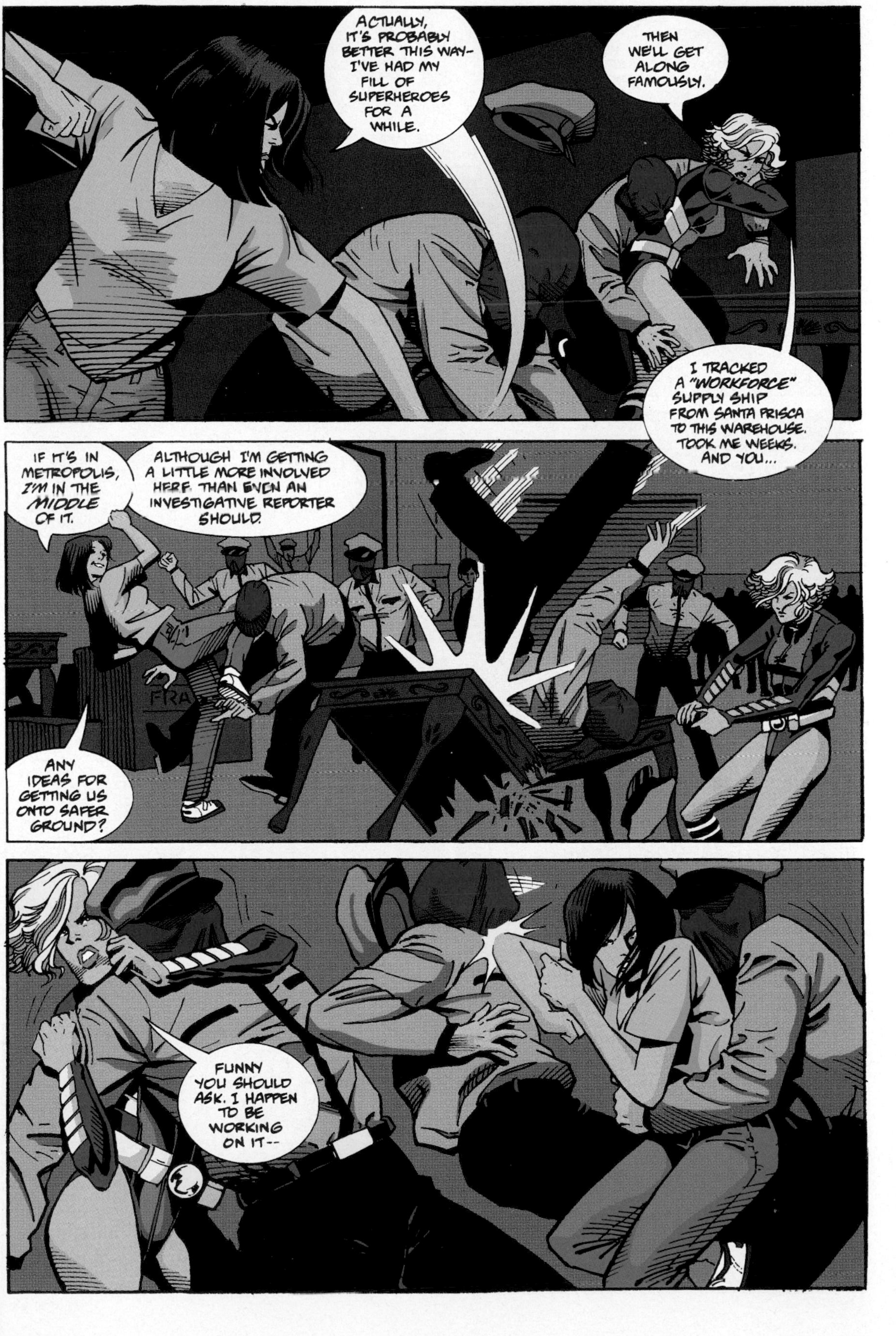
ACTUALLY, IT'S PROBABLY BETTER THIS WAY- I'VE HAD MY FILL OF SUPERHEROES FOR A WHILE.
THEN WE'LL GET ALONG FAMOUSLY.
I TRACKED A "WORKFORCE" SUPPLY SHIP FROM SANTA PRISCA TO THIS WAREHOUSE. TOOK ME WEEKS. AND YOU...
IF IT'S IN METROPOLIS, I'M IN THE MIDDLE OF IT.
ALTHOUGH I'M GETTING A LITTLE MORE INVOLVED HERE THAN EVEN AN INVESTIGATIVE REPORTER SHOULD.
ANY IDEAS FOR GETTING US ONTO SAFER GROUND?
FUNNY YOU SHOULD ASK. I HAPPEN TO BE WORKING ON IT--

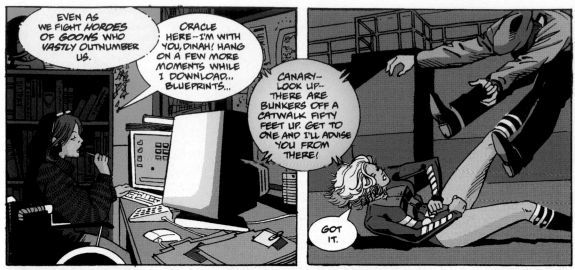

EVEN AS WE FIGHT *HORDES* OF *GOONS* WHO *VASTLY* OUTNUMBER US.

ORACLE HERE--I'M WITH YOU, DINAH! HANG ON A FEW MORE MOMENTS WHILE I DOWNLOAD... BLUEPRINTS...

CANARY-- LOOK UP-- THERE ARE BUNKERS OFF A CATWALK FIFTY FEET UP. GET TO ONE AND I'LL ADVISE YOU FROM THERE!

GOT IT.

YOU LIKE BASEBALL, MISS LANE?

LOIS!-- PLAYING, NOT WATCHING.

GOOD-- BATTER UP!

WUUUMF!

NICE BUNT.

LITTLE LEAGUE--MY SECRET TO MAINTAINING A FIVE HUNDRED BATTING AVERAGE.

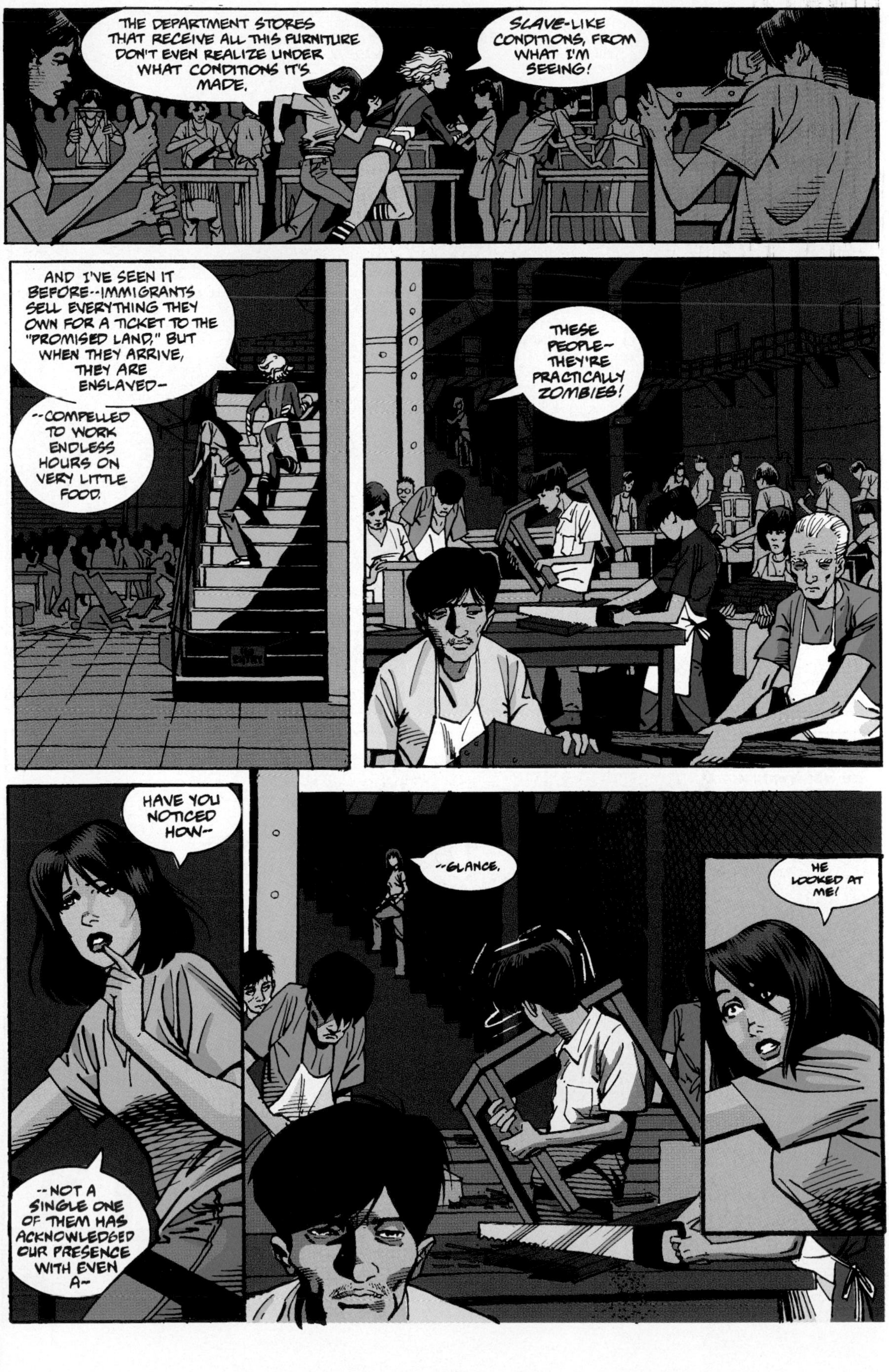
THE DEPARTMENT STORES THAT RECEIVE ALL THIS FURNITURE DON'T EVEN REALIZE UNDER WHAT CONDITIONS IT'S MADE.
SLAVE-LIKE CONDITIONS, FROM WHAT I'M SEEING!
AND I'VE SEEN IT BEFORE--IMMIGRANTS SELL EVERYTHING THEY OWN FOR A TICKET TO THE "PROMISED LAND," BUT WHEN THEY ARRIVE, THEY ARE ENSLAVED--
--COMPELLED TO WORK ENDLESS HOURS ON VERY LITTLE FOOD.
THESE PEOPLE-- THEY'RE PRACTICALLY ZOMBIES!
HAVE YOU NOTICED HOW--
--NOT A SINGLE ONE OF THEM HAS ACKNOWLEDGED OUR PRESENCE WITH EVEN A--
--GLANCE.
HE LOOKED AT ME!

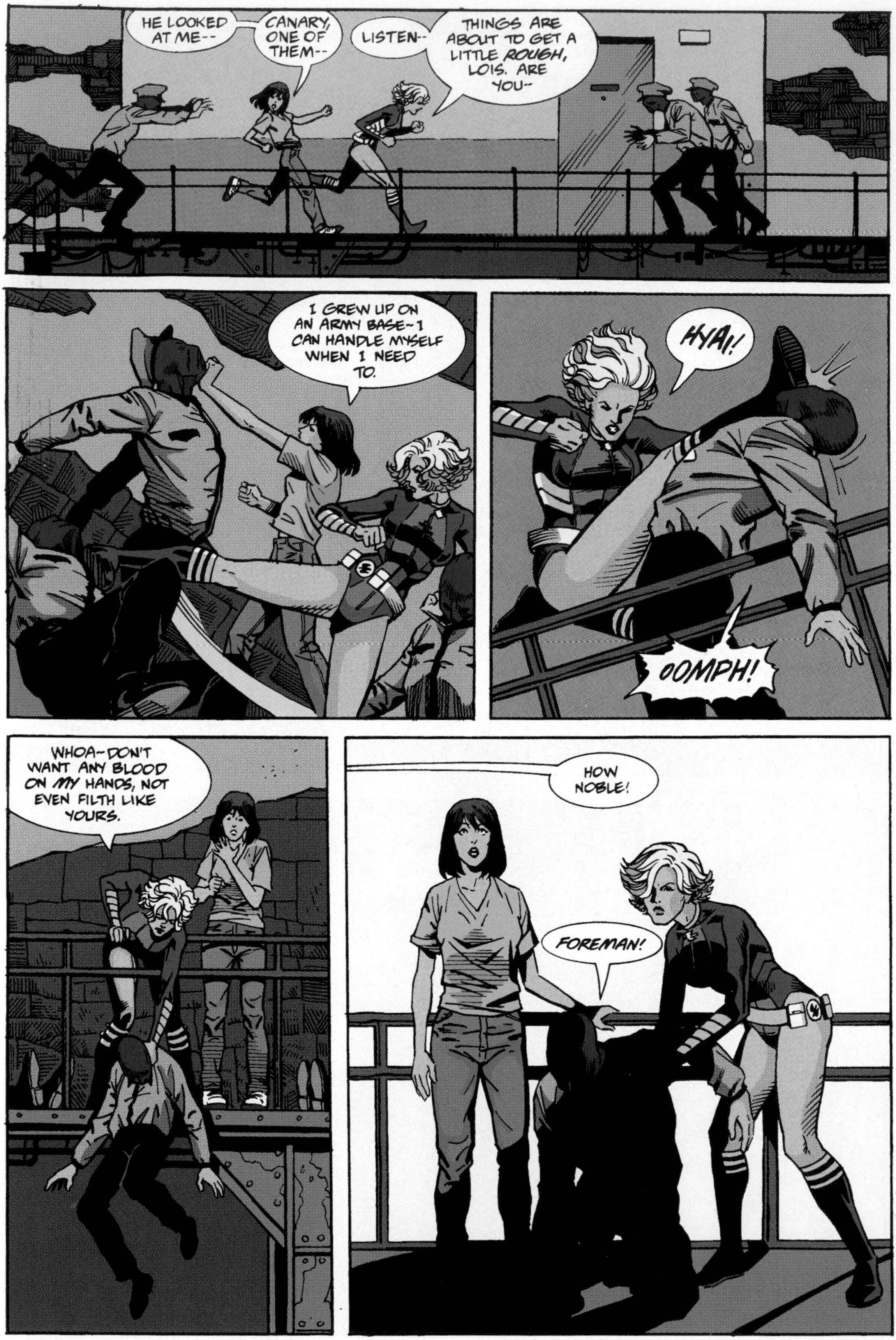
HE LOOKED AT ME--
CANARY, ONE OF THEM--
LISTEN--
THINGS ARE ABOUT TO GET A LITTLE ROUGH, LOIS. ARE YOU--
I GREW UP ON AN ARMY BASE--I CAN HANDLE MYSELF WHEN I NEED TO.
KYAI!
OOMPH!
WHOA--DON'T WANT ANY BLOOD ON MY HANDS, NOT EVEN FILTH LIKE YOURS.
HOW NOBLE!
FOREMAN!

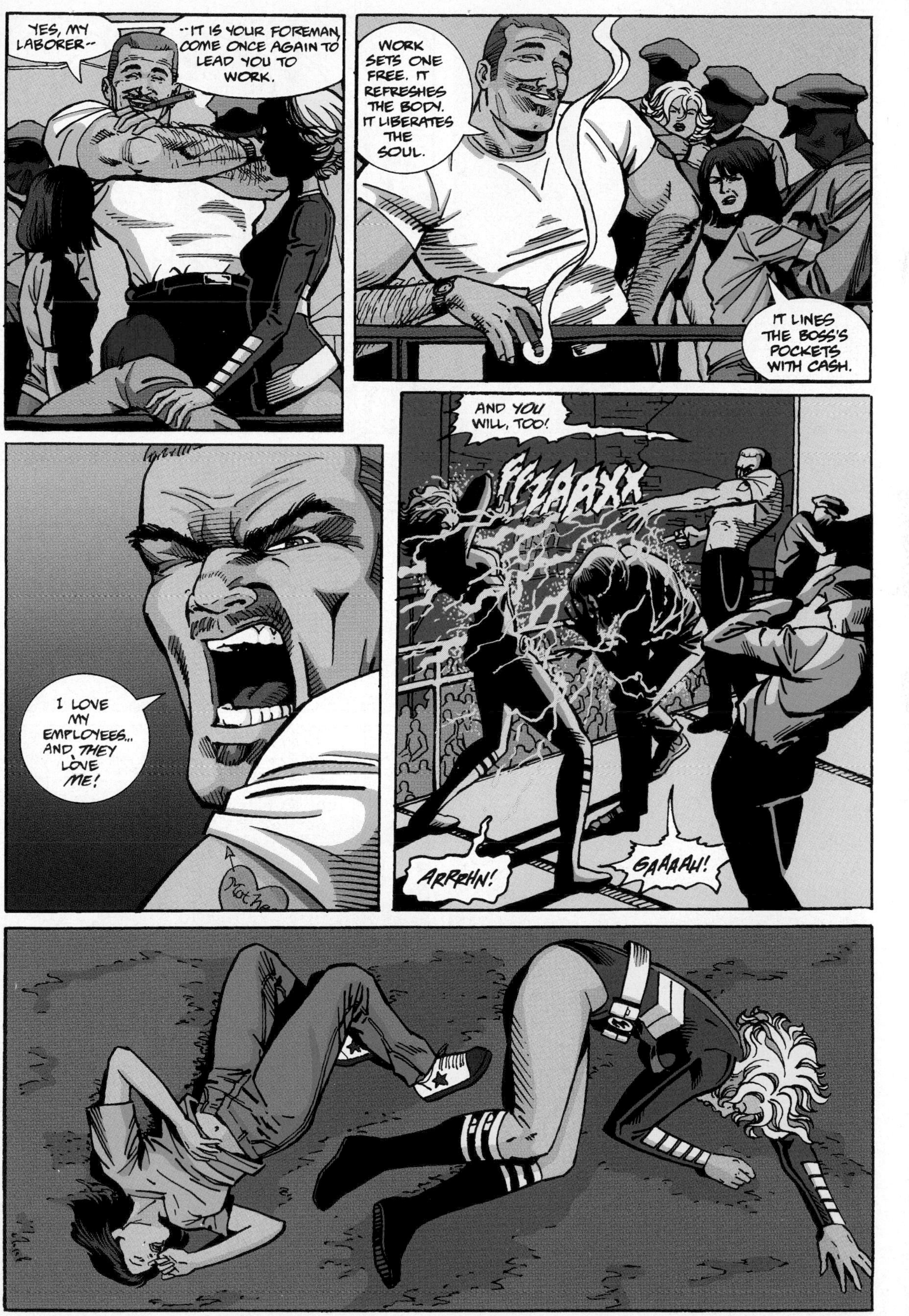
YES, MY LABORER--
--IT IS YOUR FOREMAN, COME ONCE AGAIN TO LEAD YOU TO WORK.
WORK SETS ONE FREE. IT REFRESHES THE BODY. IT LIBERATES THE SOUL.
IT LINES THE BOSS'S POCKETS WITH CASH.
I LOVE MY EMPLOYEES... AND THEY LOVE ME!
AND YOU WILL, TOO!
FFZAAXX
ARRRHN!
GAAAAH!

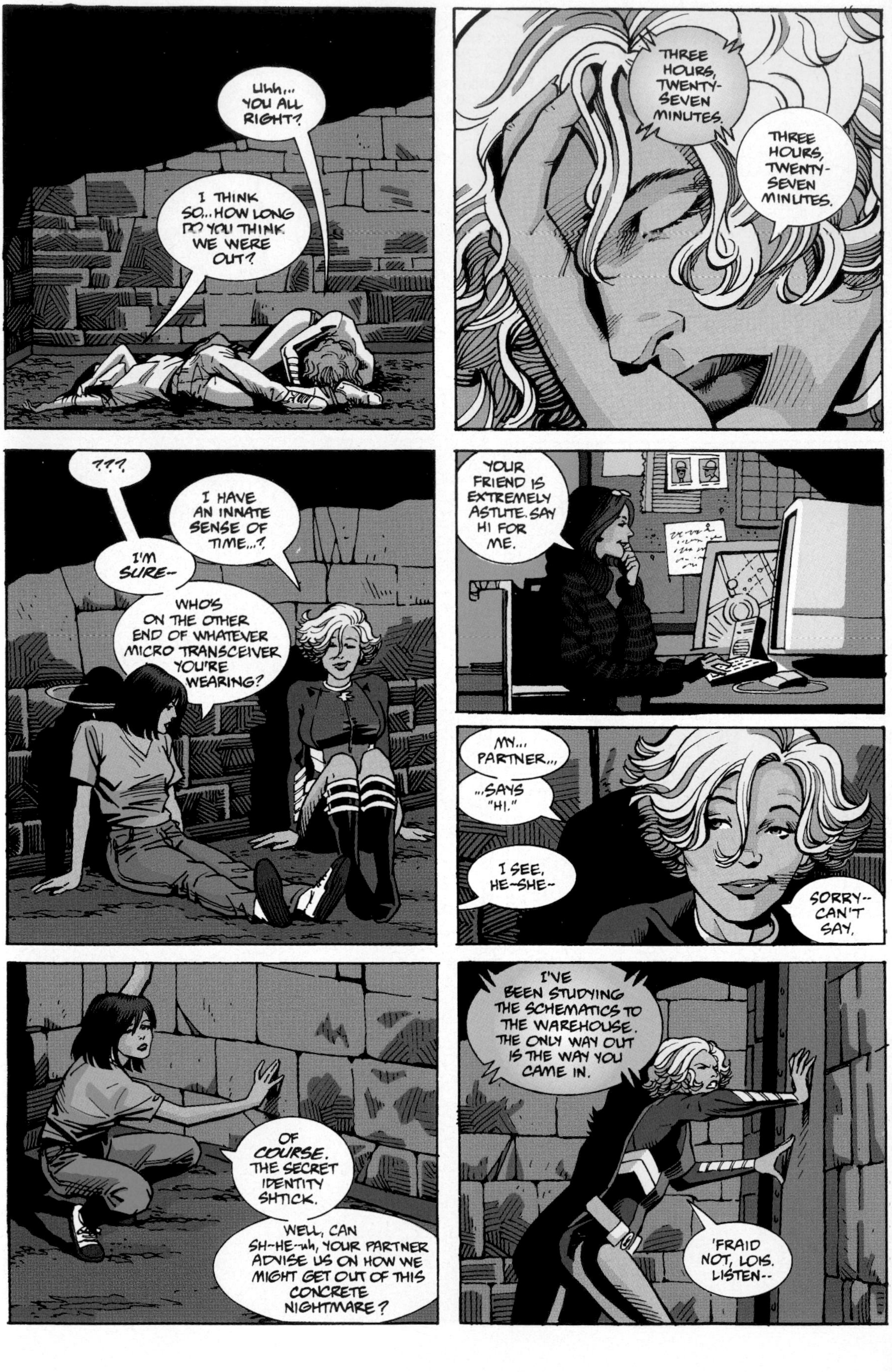
Uhh,... YOU ALL RIGHT?
I THINK SO... HOW LONG DO YOU THINK WE WERE OUT?
THREE HOURS, TWENTY-SEVEN MINUTES.
THREE HOURS, TWENTY-SEVEN MINUTES.
???
I HAVE AN INNATE SENSE OF TIME...?
I'M SURE--
WHO'S ON THE OTHER END OF WHATEVER MICRO TRANSCEIVER YOU'RE WEARING?
YOUR FRIEND IS EXTREMELY ASTUTE. SAY HI FOR ME.
MY... PARTNER...,
...SAYS "HI."
I SEE, HE-SHE-
SORRY-- CAN'T SAY.
OF COURSE. THE SECRET IDENTITY SHTICK.
WELL, CAN SH-HE-uh, YOUR PARTNER ADVISE US ON HOW WE MIGHT GET OUT OF THIS CONCRETE NIGHTMARE?
I'VE BEEN STUDYING THE SCHEMATICS TO THE WAREHOUSE. THE ONLY WAY OUT IS THE WAY YOU CAME IN.
'FRAID NOT, LOIS. LISTEN--

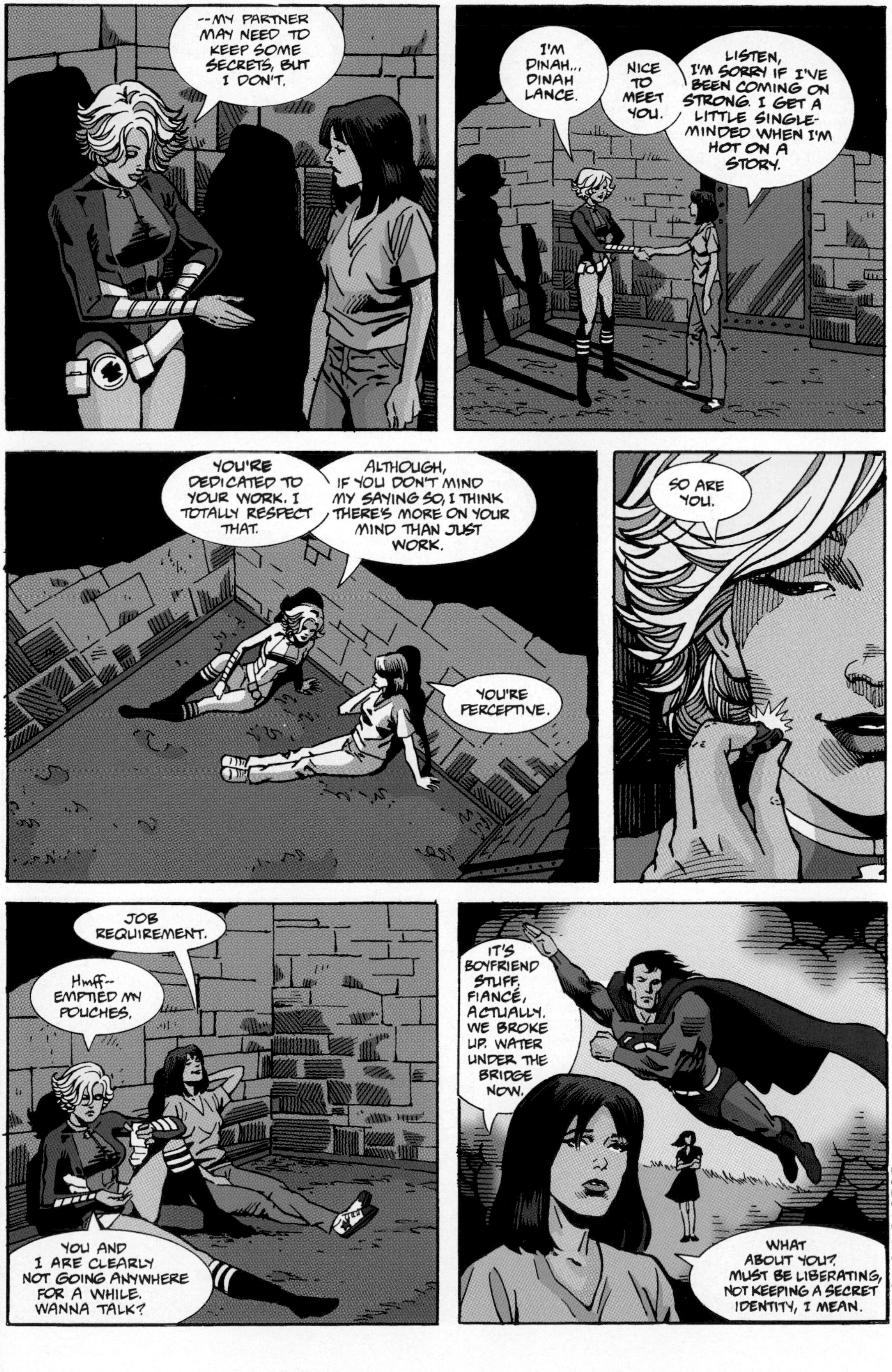
--MY PARTNER MAY NEED TO KEEP SOME SECRETS, BUT I DON'T.
I'M DINAH... DINAH LANCE.
NICE TO MEET YOU.
LISTEN, I'M SORRY IF I'VE BEEN COMING ON STRONG. I GET A LITTLE SINGLE-MINDED WHEN I'M HOT ON A STORY.
YOU'RE DEDICATED TO YOUR WORK. I TOTALLY RESPECT THAT.
ALTHOUGH, IF YOU DON'T MIND MY SAYING SO, I THINK THERE'S MORE ON YOUR MIND THAN JUST WORK.
YOU'RE PERCEPTIVE.
SO ARE YOU.
JOB REQUIREMENT.
Hmff-- EMPTIED MY POUCHES.
YOU AND I ARE CLEARLY NOT GOING ANYWHERE FOR A WHILE. WANNA TALK?
IT'S BOYFRIEND STUFF. FIANCÉ, ACTUALLY. WE BROKE UP. WATER UNDER THE BRIDGE NOW.
WHAT ABOUT YOU? MUST BE LIBERATING, NOT KEEPING A SECRET IDENTITY, I MEAN.

CONSEQUENCE OF NOT HAVING A REAL LIFE TO PROTECT.

THE LAST PERSON ALIVE WHO ONCE MEANT SOMETHING TO ME DIED--IRONICALLY, IN A PLANE OVER THIS VERY CITY.

GREEN ARROW!

YOU HEARD ABOUT IT.

I'VE COVERED A LOT OF SUPERMAN STORIES--THAT WAS ONE OF THEM. I'M SO SORRY.

S'OKAY. JERK DESERVED IT.

THAT WAS OFF THE RECORD.

MAYBE WE OUGHT TO TALK SHOP.

YEAH.

EL-ZAP-O--YOU KNOW, ALL BUFFED-UP-AND-NO-PLACE-TO-GO...

HIS GUARDS CALLED HIM FOREMAN.

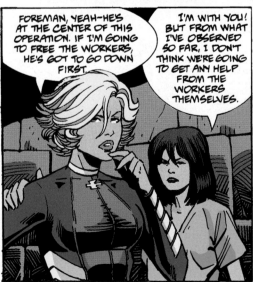

FOREMAN, YEAH--HE'S AT THE CENTER OF THIS OPERATION. IF I'M GOING TO FREE THE WORKERS, HE'S GOT TO GO DOWN FIRST.

I'M WITH YOU! BUT FROM WHAT I'VE OBSERVED SO FAR, I DON'T THINK WE'RE GOING TO GET ANY HELP FROM THE WORKERS THEMSELVES.

NOT TO MENTION, YOU'RE NO GOOD TO ANYONE LOCKED UP IN HE--

KKKRR... KKKRR... KKKRR...

YOU HEAR THAT? COMING FROM BEHIND THE WALL...

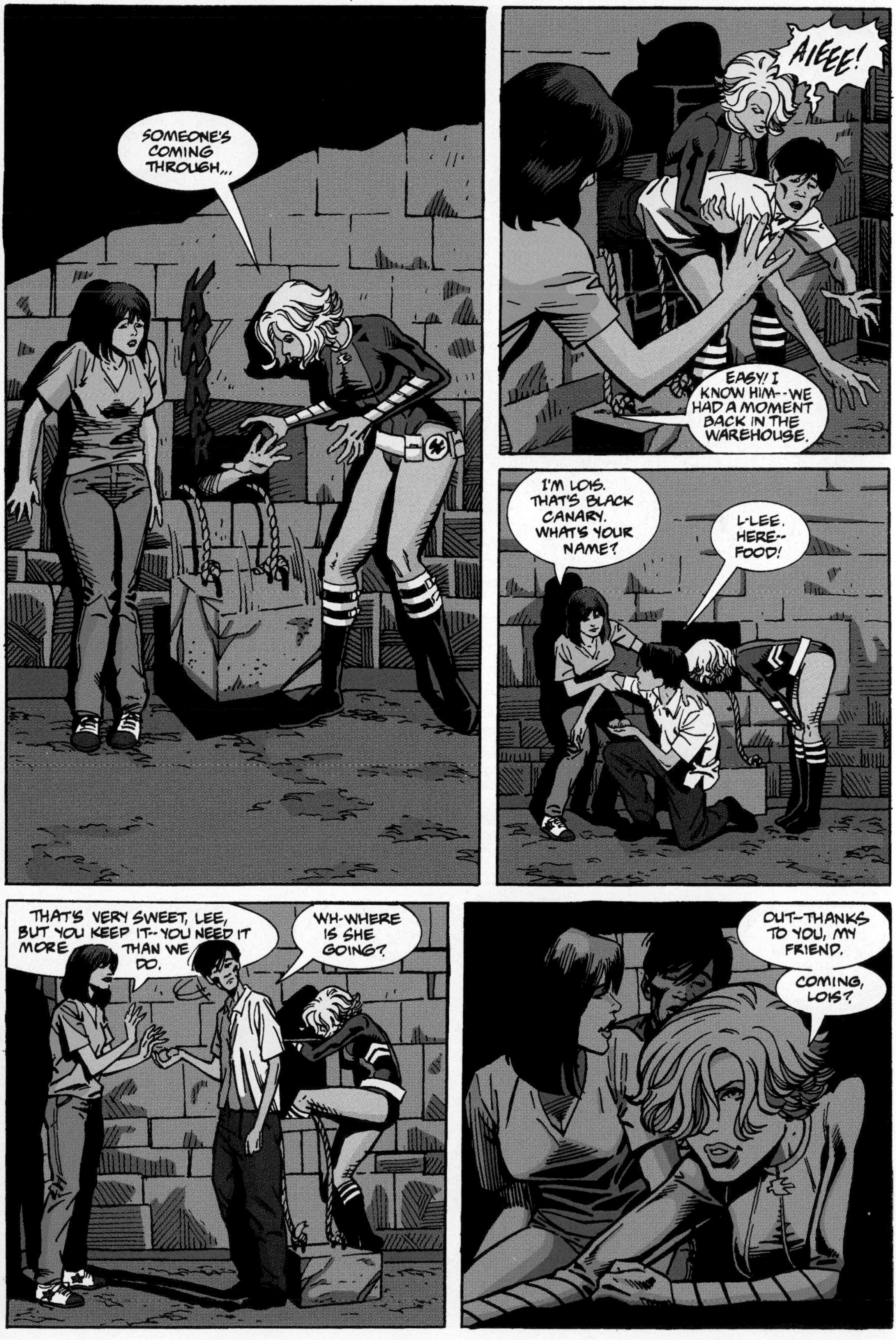
SOMEONE'S COMING THROUGH...
AIEEE!
EASY! I KNOW HIM--WE HAD A MOMENT BACK IN THE WAREHOUSE.
I'M LOIS. THAT'S BLACK CANARY. WHAT'S YOUR NAME?
L-LEE. HERE-- FOOD!
THAT'S VERY SWEET, LEE, BUT YOU KEEP IT--YOU NEED IT MORE THAN WE DO.
WH-WHERE IS SHE GOING?
OUT--THANKS TO YOU, MY FRIEND.
COMING, LOIS?

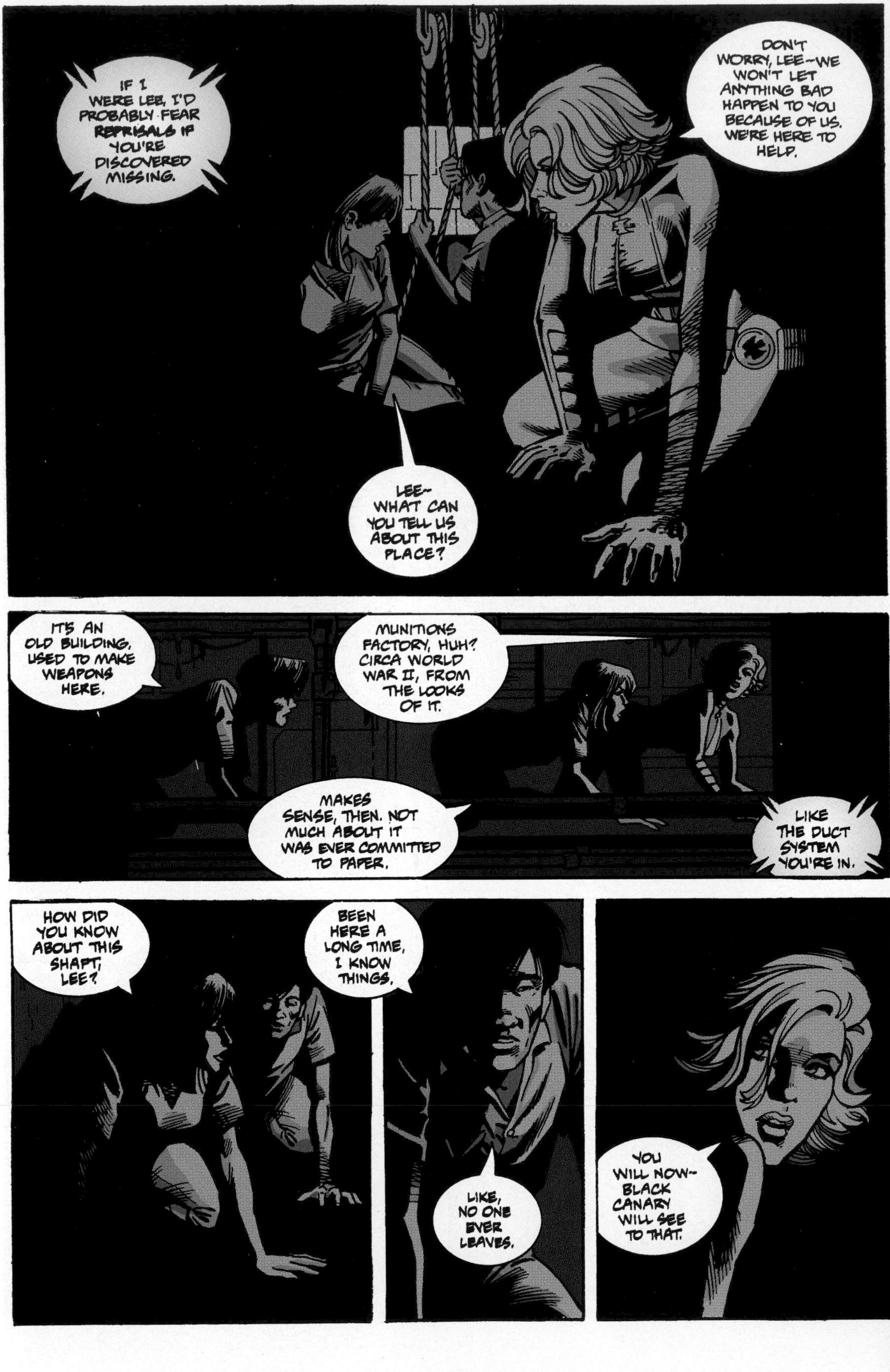
IF I WERE LEE, I'D PROBABLY FEAR REPRISALS IF YOU'RE DISCOVERED MISSING.
DON'T WORRY, LEE--WE WON'T LET ANYTHING BAD HAPPEN TO YOU BECAUSE OF US. WE'RE HERE TO HELP.
LEE-- WHAT CAN YOU TELL US ABOUT THIS PLACE?
IT'S AN OLD BUILDING. USED TO MAKE WEAPONS HERE.
MUNITIONS FACTORY, HUH? CIRCA WORLD WAR II, FROM THE LOOKS OF IT.
MAKES SENSE, THEN. NOT MUCH ABOUT IT WAS EVER COMMITTED TO PAPER.
LIKE THE DUCT SYSTEM YOU'RE IN.
HOW DID YOU KNOW ABOUT THIS SHAFT, LEE?
BEEN HERE A LONG TIME. I KNOW THINGS.
LIKE, NO ONE EVER LEAVES.
YOU WILL NOW-- BLACK CANARY WILL SEE TO THAT.

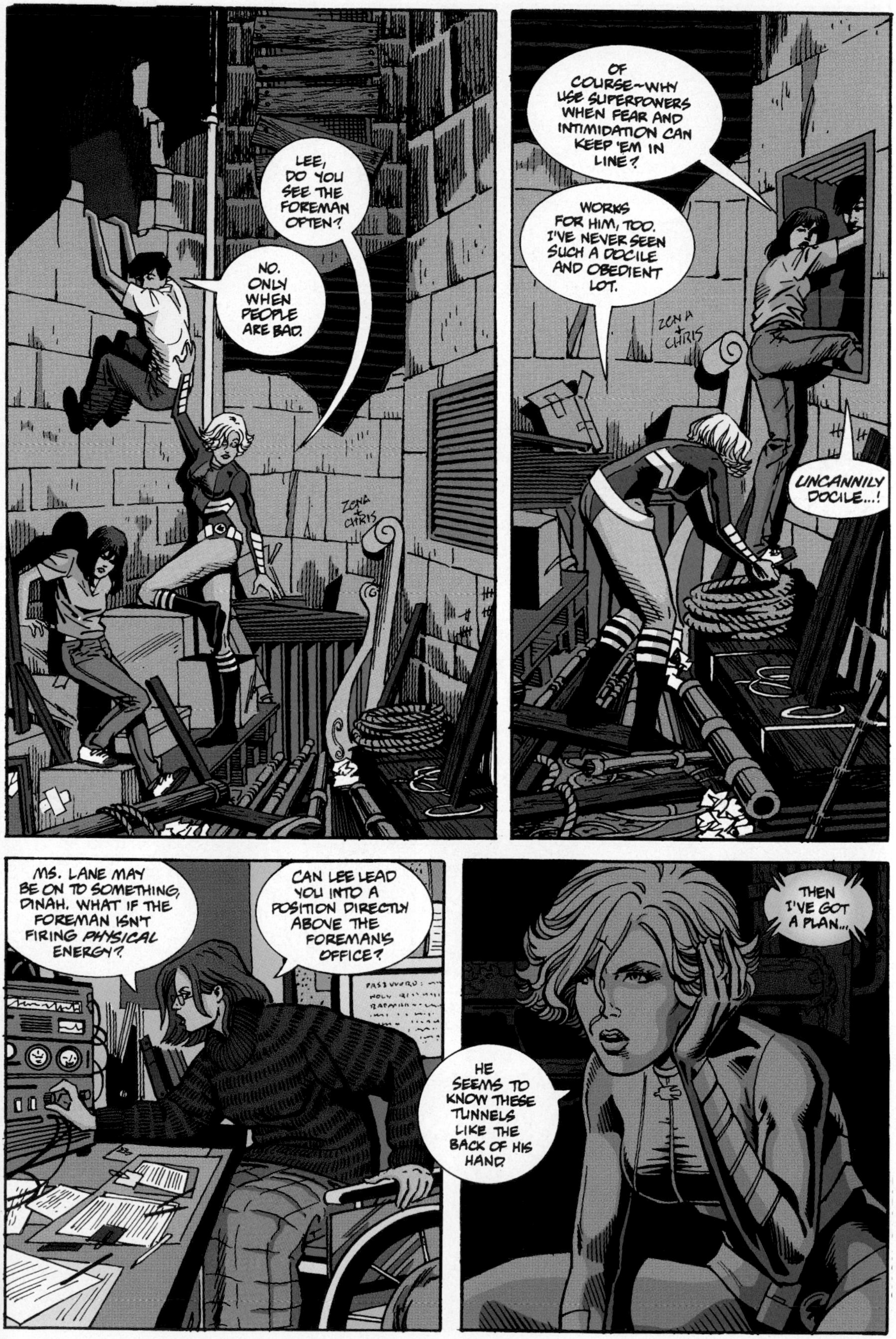
LEE, DO YOU SEE THE FOREMAN OFTEN?
NO. ONLY WHEN PEOPLE ARE BAD.
ZONA + CHRIS
OF COURSE-- WHY USE SUPERPOWERS WHEN FEAR AND INTIMIDATION CAN KEEP 'EM IN LINE?
WORKS FOR HIM, TOO. I'VE NEVER SEEN SUCH A DOCILE AND OBEDIENT LOT.
ZONA + CHRIS
UNCANNILY DOCILE...!
MS. LANE MAY BE ON TO SOMETHING, DINAH. WHAT IF THE FOREMAN ISN'T FIRING *PHYSICAL* ENERGY?
CAN LEE LEAD YOU INTO A POSITION DIRECTLY ABOVE THE FOREMAN'S OFFICE?
HE SEEMS TO KNOW THESE TUNNELS LIKE THE BACK OF HIS HAND.
THEN I'VE GOT A PLAN...

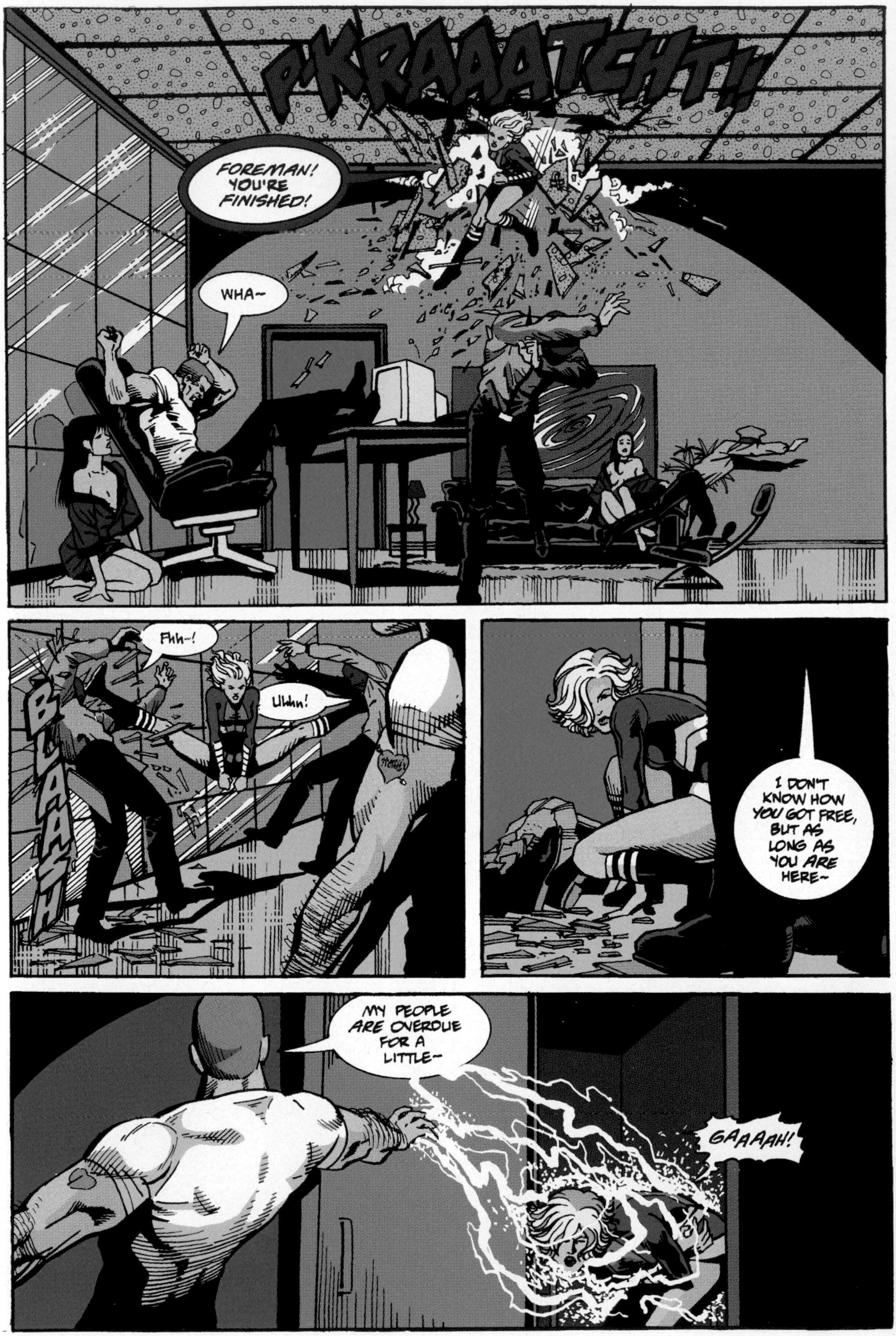
P-KRAAAATCHT!!
FOREMAN! YOU'RE FINISHED!
WHA--
Fhh--!
Uhhn!
BLAAASH
I DON'T KNOW HOW YOU GOT FREE, BUT AS LONG AS YOU ARE HERE--
MY PEOPLE ARE OVERDUE FOR A LITTLE--
GAAAAH!

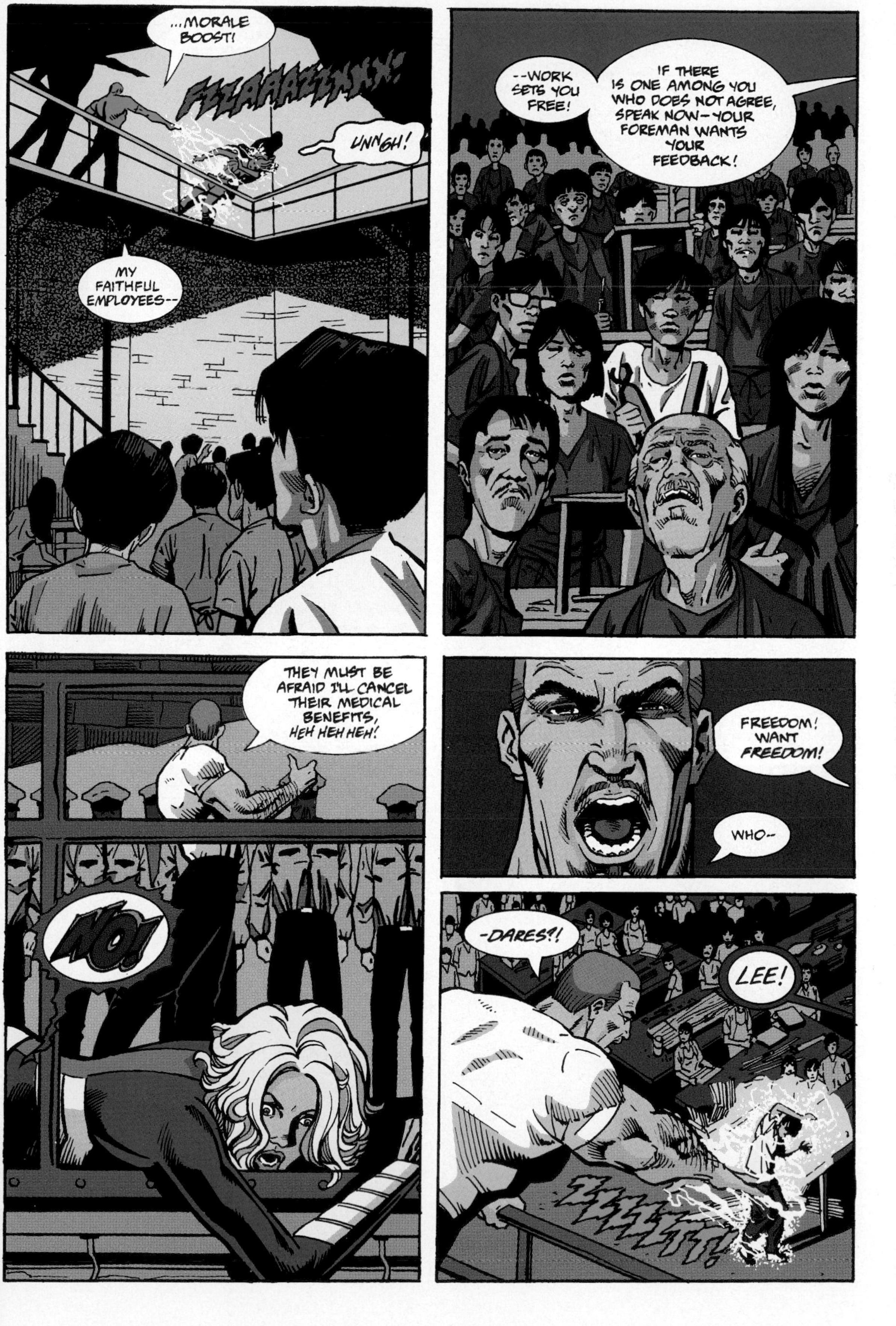
...MORALE BOOST!
FZZAAAAZZXXX!
UNNGH!
MY FAITHFUL EMPLOYEES--
--WORK SETS YOU FREE!
IF THERE IS ONE AMONG YOU WHO DOES NOT AGREE, SPEAK NOW—YOUR FOREMAN WANTS YOUR FEEDBACK!
THEY MUST BE AFRAID I'LL CANCEL THEIR MEDICAL BENEFITS, HEH HEH HEH!
FREEDOM! WANT FREEDOM!
WHO-
-DARES?!
NO!
LEE!

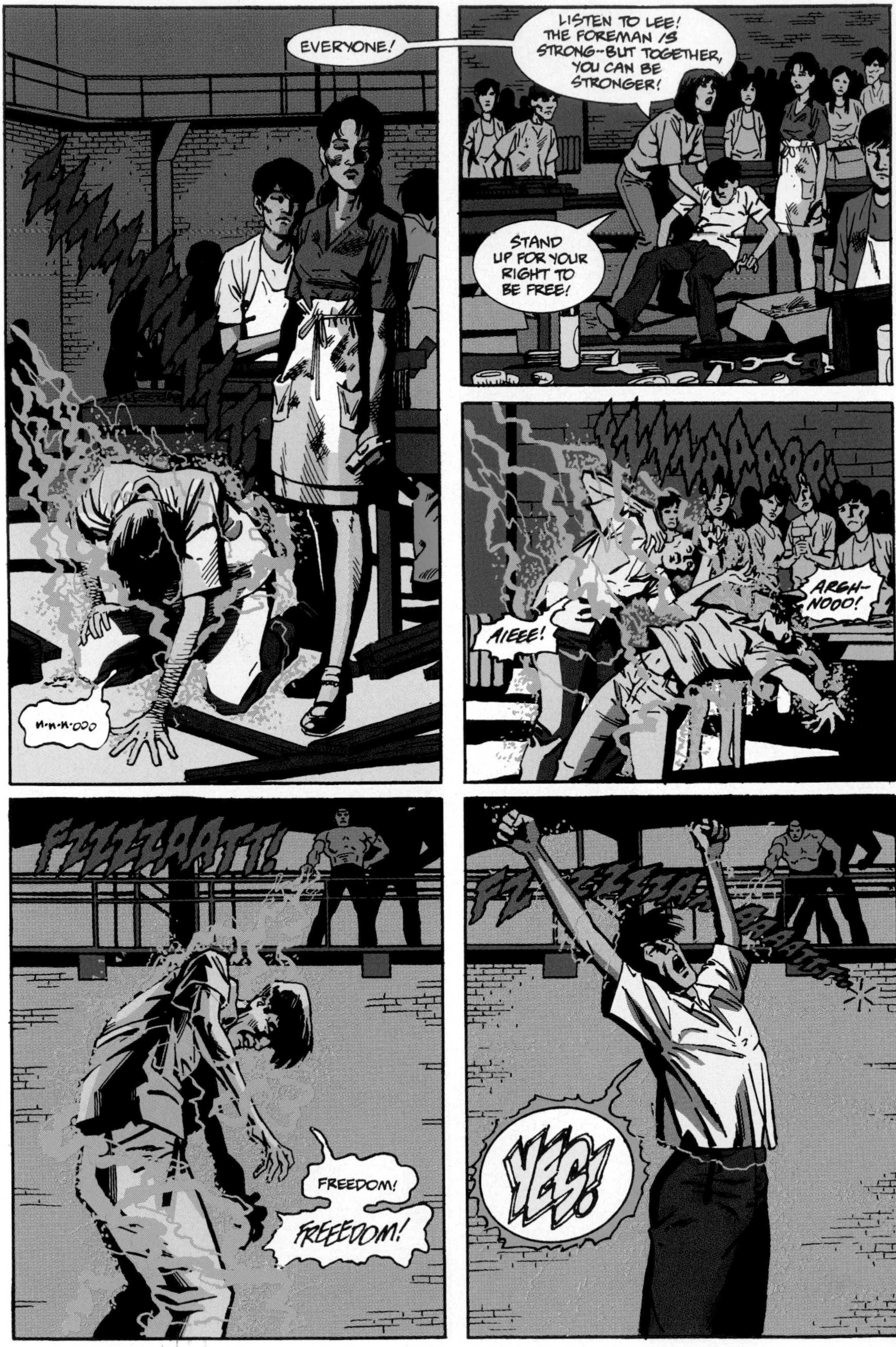
EVERYONE!
LISTEN TO LEE! THE FOREMAN IS STRONG--BUT TOGETHER, YOU CAN BE STRONGER!
STAND UP FOR YOUR RIGHT TO BE FREE!
N-N-N-OOO
ARGH-NOOO!
AIEEE!
FZZZZAATT!
FREEDOM!
FREEEDOM!
YES!

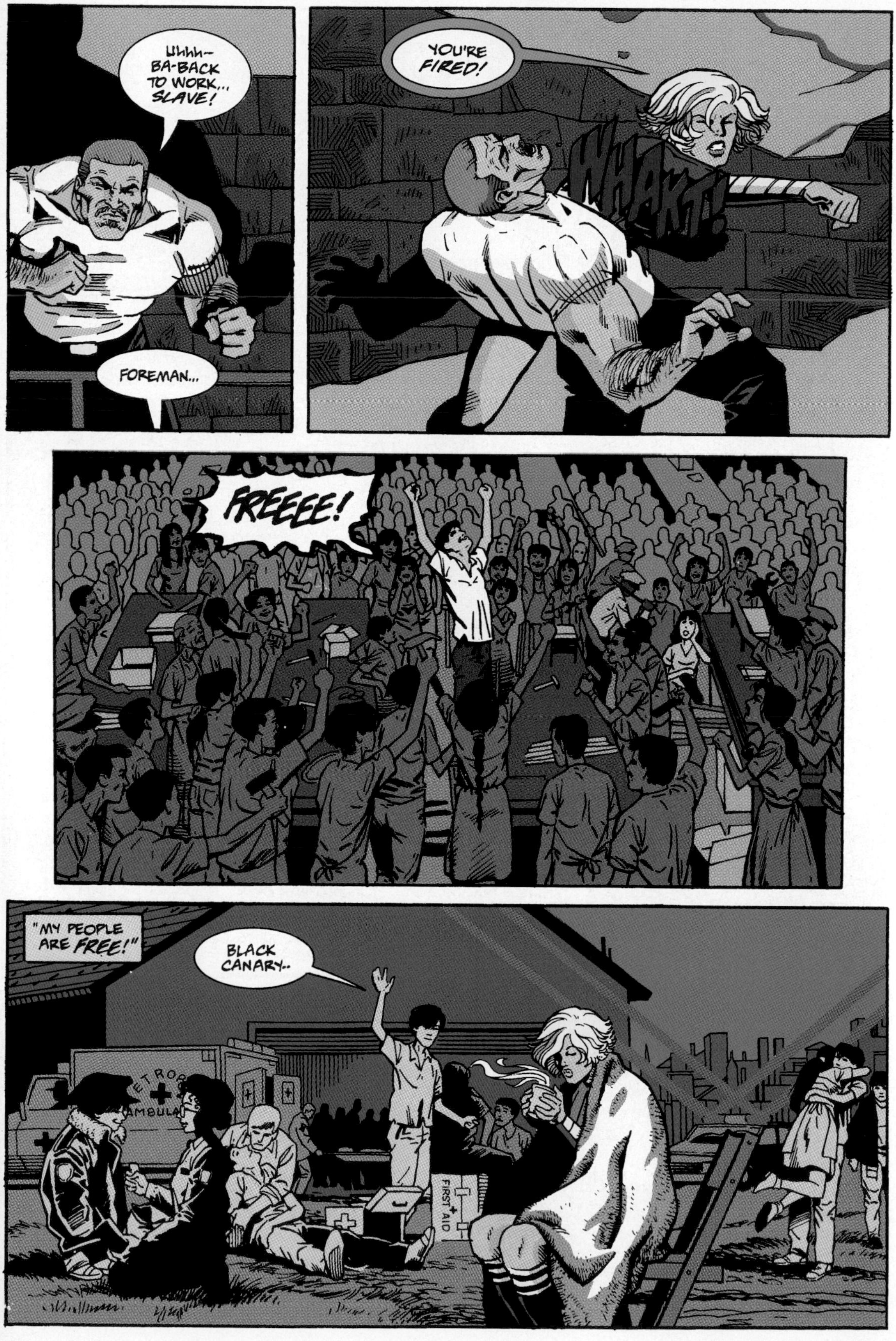
UHHH-
BA-BACK
TO WORK...
SLAVE!
FOREMAN...
YOU'RE
FIRED!
WHAKT!
FREEEEE!
"MY PEOPLE
ARE FREE!"
BLACK
CANARY..
FIRST AID

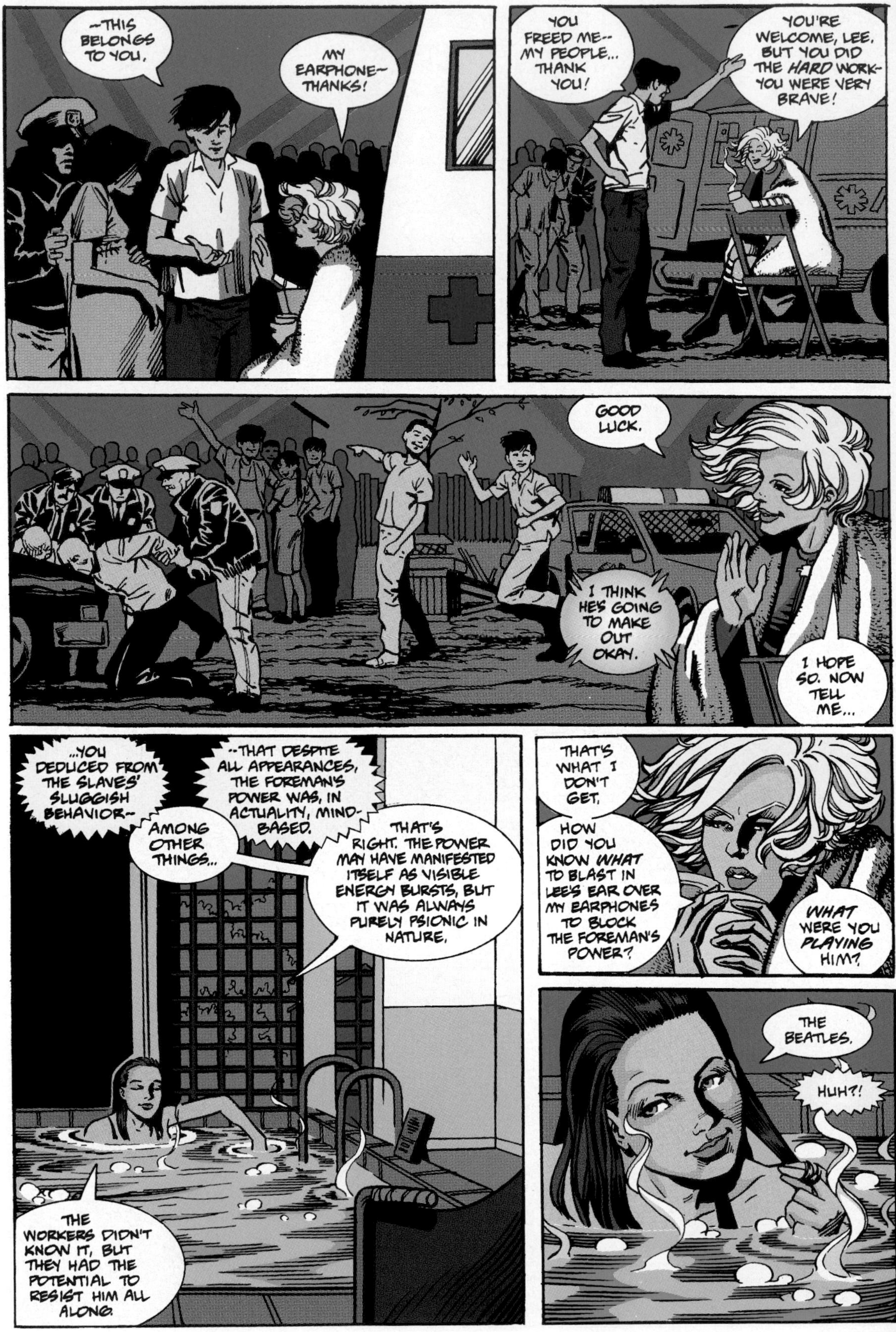
--THIS BELONGS TO YOU.
MY EARPHONE-- THANKS!
YOU FREED ME-- MY PEOPLE... THANK YOU!
YOU'RE WELCOME, LEE. BUT YOU DID THE *HARD* WORK-- YOU WERE VERY BRAVE!
GOOD LUCK.
I THINK HE'S GOING TO MAKE OUT OKAY.
I HOPE SO. NOW TELL ME...
...YOU DEDUCED FROM THE SLAVES' SLUGGISH BEHAVIOR--
--THAT DESPITE ALL APPEARANCES, THE FOREMAN'S POWER WAS, IN ACTUALITY, MIND-BASED.
AMONG OTHER THINGS...
THAT'S RIGHT. THE POWER MAY HAVE MANIFESTED ITSELF AS VISIBLE ENERGY BURSTS, BUT IT WAS ALWAYS PURELY PSIONIC IN NATURE.
THE WORKERS DIDN'T KNOW IT, BUT THEY HAD THE POTENTIAL TO RESIST HIM ALL ALONG.
THAT'S WHAT I DON'T GET.
HOW DID YOU KNOW *WHAT* TO BLAST IN LEE'S EAR OVER MY EARPHONES TO BLOCK THE FOREMAN'S POWER?
WHAT WERE YOU *PLAYING* HIM?
THE BEATLES.
HUH?!

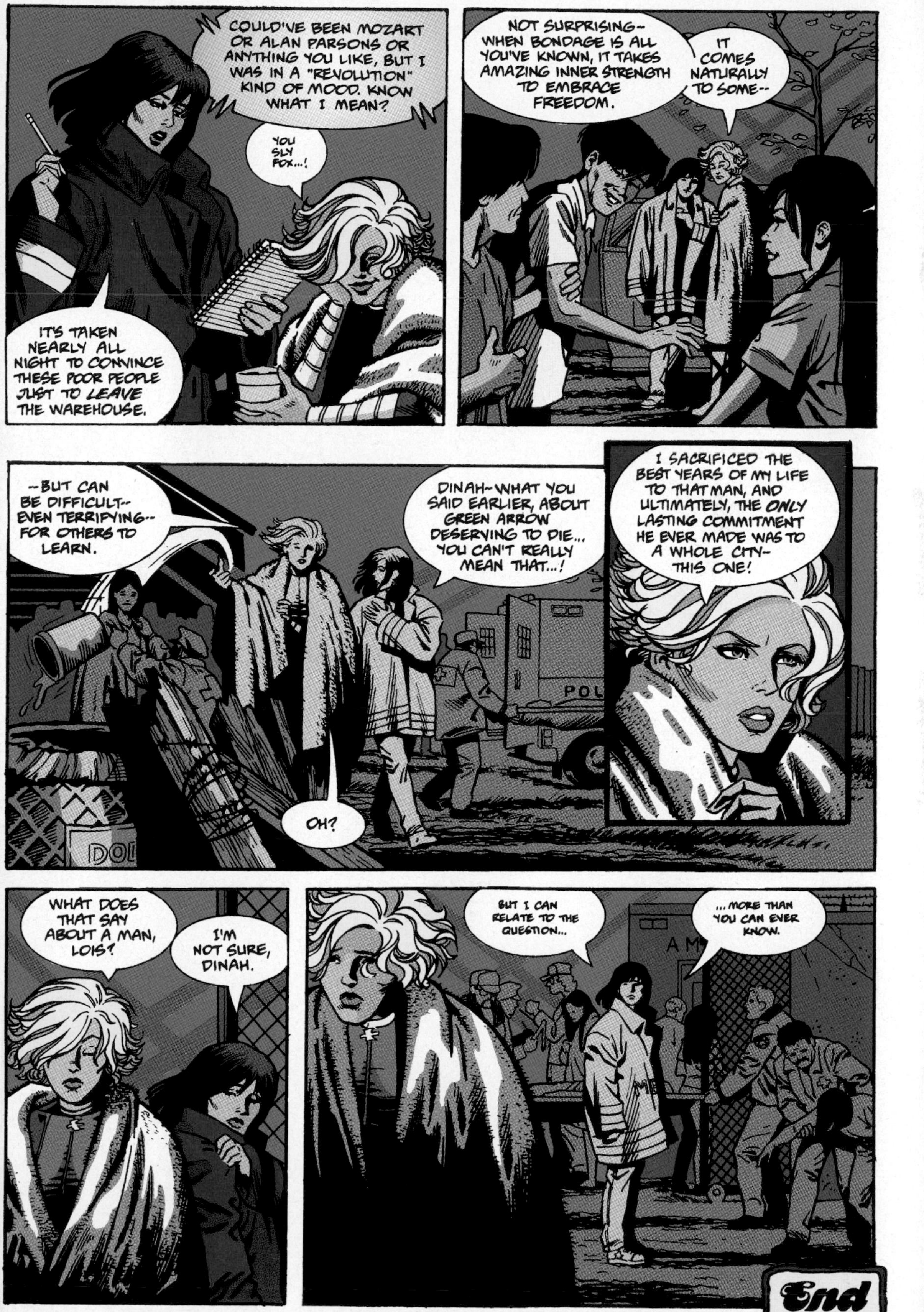
COULD'VE BEEN MOZART OR ALAN PARSONS OR ANYTHING YOU LIKE, BUT I WAS IN A "REVOLUTION" KIND OF MOOD. KNOW WHAT I MEAN?
YOU SLY FOX...!
IT'S TAKEN NEARLY ALL NIGHT TO CONVINCE THESE POOR PEOPLE JUST TO *LEAVE* THE WAREHOUSE.
NOT SURPRISING-- WHEN BONDAGE IS ALL YOU'VE KNOWN, IT TAKES AMAZING INNER STRENGTH TO EMBRACE FREEDOM.
IT COMES NATURALLY TO SOME--
--BUT CAN BE DIFFICULT-- EVEN TERRIFYING-- FOR OTHERS TO LEARN.
DINAH-- WHAT YOU SAID EARLIER, ABOUT GREEN ARROW DESERVING TO DIE... YOU CAN'T REALLY MEAN THAT...!
OH?
I SACRIFICED THE BEST YEARS OF MY LIFE TO THAT MAN, AND ULTIMATELY, THE *ONLY* LASTING COMMITMENT HE EVER MADE WAS TO A WHOLE CITY-- THIS ONE!
WHAT DOES THAT SAY ABOUT A MAN, LOIS?
I'M NOT SURE, DINAH.
BUT I CAN RELATE TO THE QUESTION...
...MORE THAN YOU CAN EVER KNOW.
End

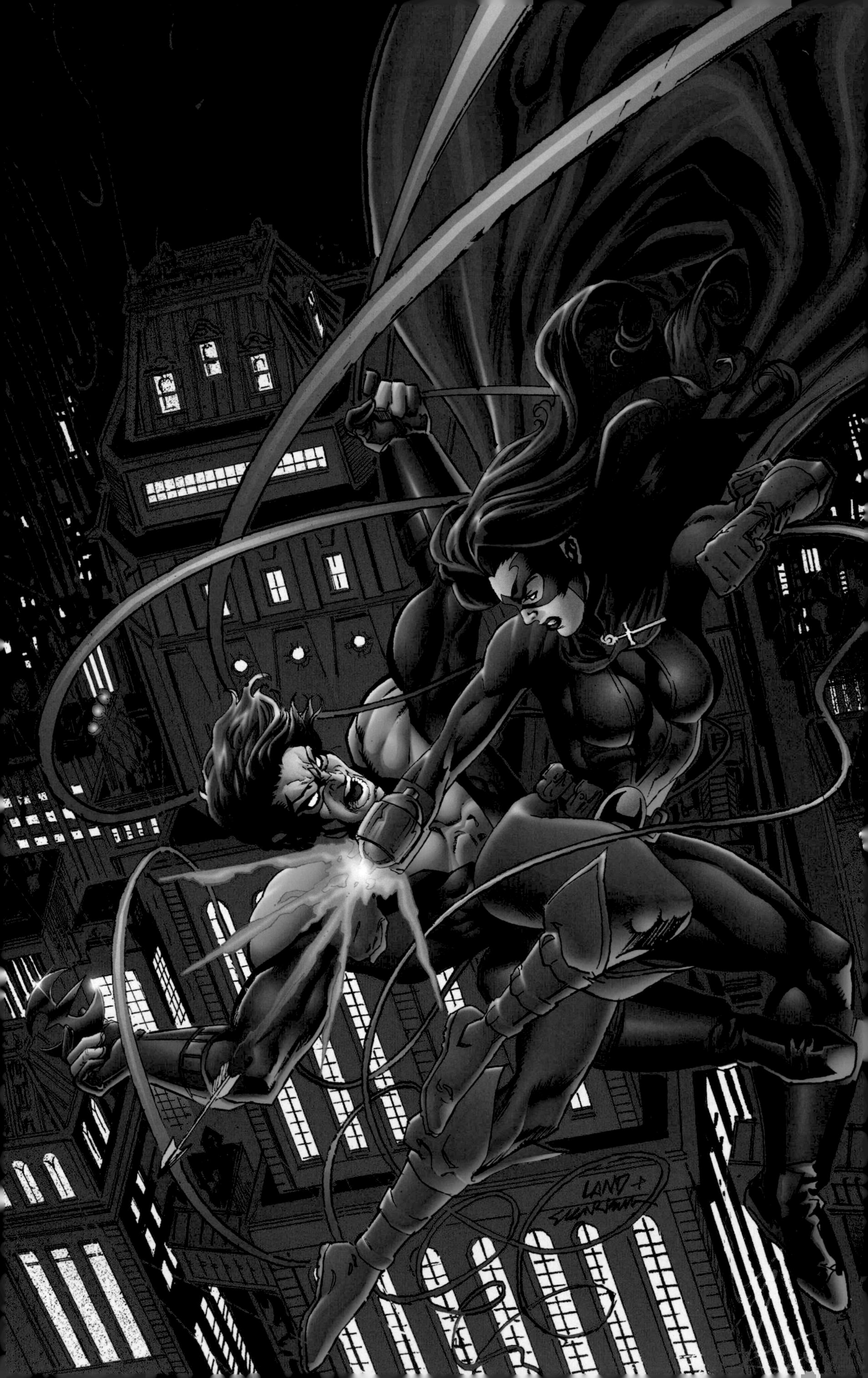

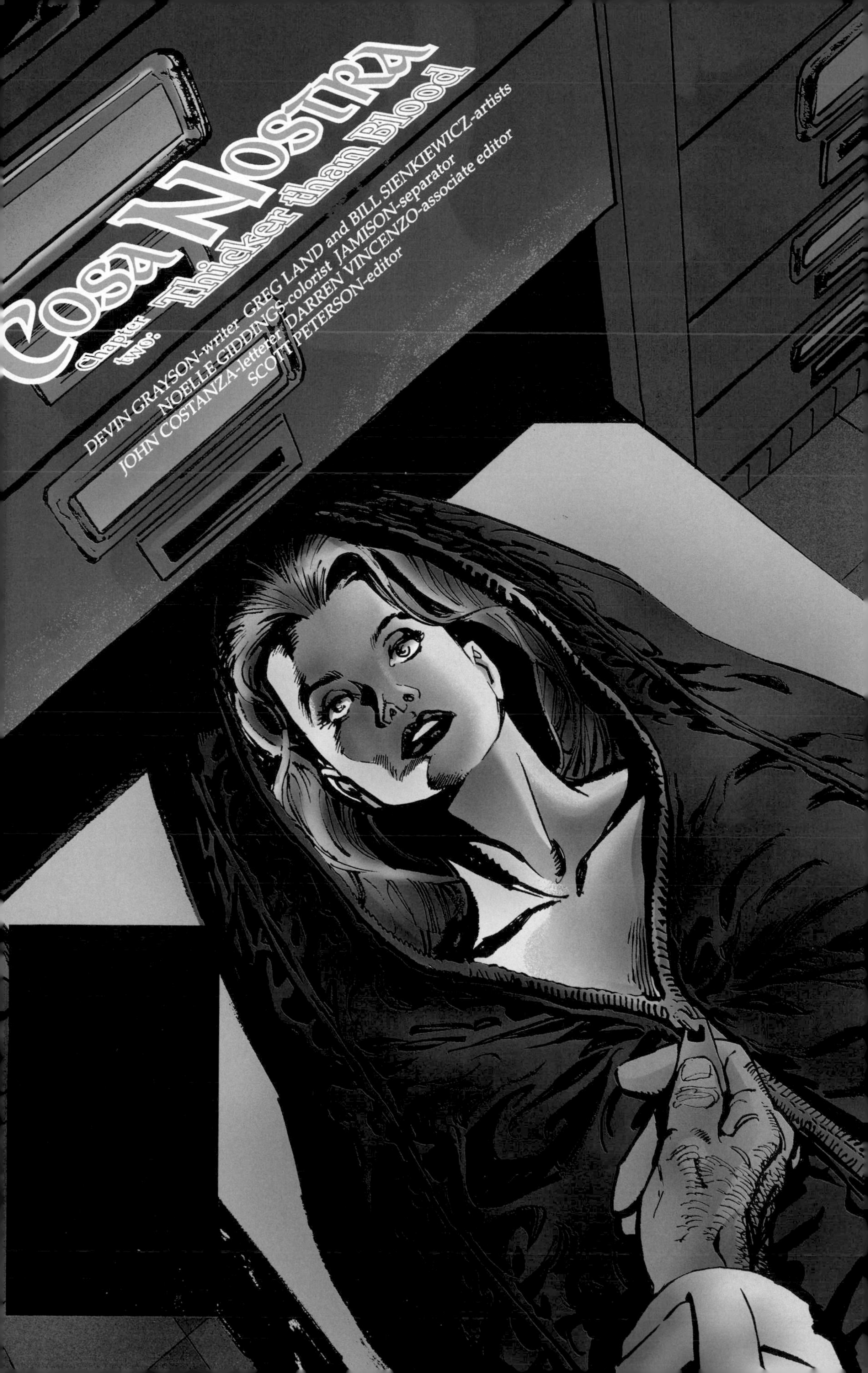
Cosa Nostra
Chapter two: Thicker than Blood
DEVIN GRAYSON-writer GREG LAND and BILL SIENKIEWICZ-artists
NOELLE GIDDINGS-colorist JAMISON-separator
JOHN COSTANZA-letterer DARREN VINCENZO-associate editor
SCOTT PETERSON-editor

WELL?

YEAH, IT'S CAITLYN, SO TELL ME--

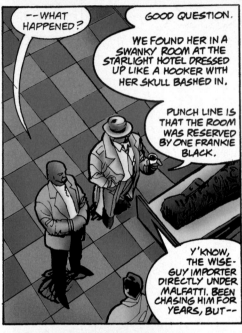

--WHAT HAPPENED?

GOOD QUESTION.

WE FOUND HER IN A SWANKY ROOM AT THE STARLIGHT HOTEL DRESSED UP LIKE A HOOKER WITH HER SKULL BASHED IN.

PUNCH LINE IS THAT THE ROOM WAS RESERVED BY ONE FRANKIE BLACK.

Y'KNOW, THE WISE-GUY IMPORTER DIRECTLY UNDER MALFATTI. BEEN CHASING HIM FOR YEARS, BUT--

I KNOW WHO FRANKIE BLACK IS, SERGEANT BULLOCK.

OKAY, WELL, THEN WHY DON'TCHA TELL US WHAT ELSE YOU KNOW, LIEUTENANT?

LIKE MAYBE WHAT YOUR PARTNER WAS DOING UNDERCOVER IN THE SUITE OF A MAJOR GUN RUNNER WITHOUT AUDIO CONTACT, A PIECE, ID, OR BACKUP?

CAITLYN WAS OBSESSED. WITH FRANKIE BLACK, MALFATTI, THE WHOLE FAMILIA. SHE MUST HAVE HEARD THAT FRANKIE WAS AT THE STARLIGHT AND REPLACED THE REQUESTED CALL GIRL.

IT...WASN'T AN OFFICIAL STING, SHE--WASN'T CLEARED...

OH, GOOD. 'CAUSE, YA KNOW, IF THERE'S ONE THING THIS CITY NEEDS--

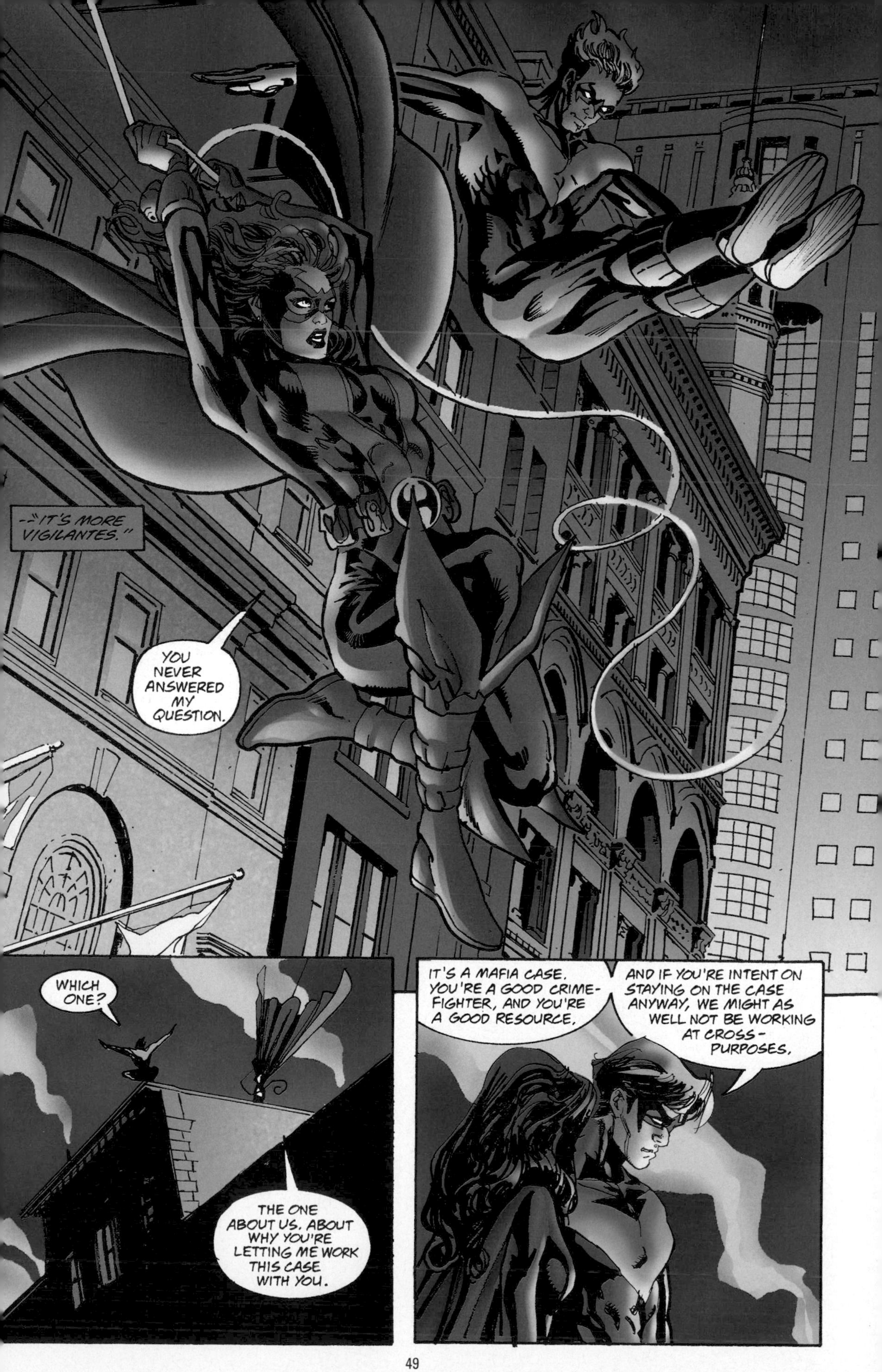

--"IT'S MORE VIGILANTES."
YOU NEVER ANSWERED MY QUESTION.
WHICH ONE?
THE ONE ABOUT US. ABOUT WHY YOU'RE LETTING ME WORK THIS CASE WITH YOU.
IT'S A MAFIA CASE. YOU'RE A GOOD CRIME-FIGHTER, AND YOU'RE A GOOD RESOURCE.
AND IF YOU'RE INTENT ON STAYING ON THE CASE ANYWAY, WE MIGHT AS WELL NOT BE WORKING AT CROSS-PURPOSES.

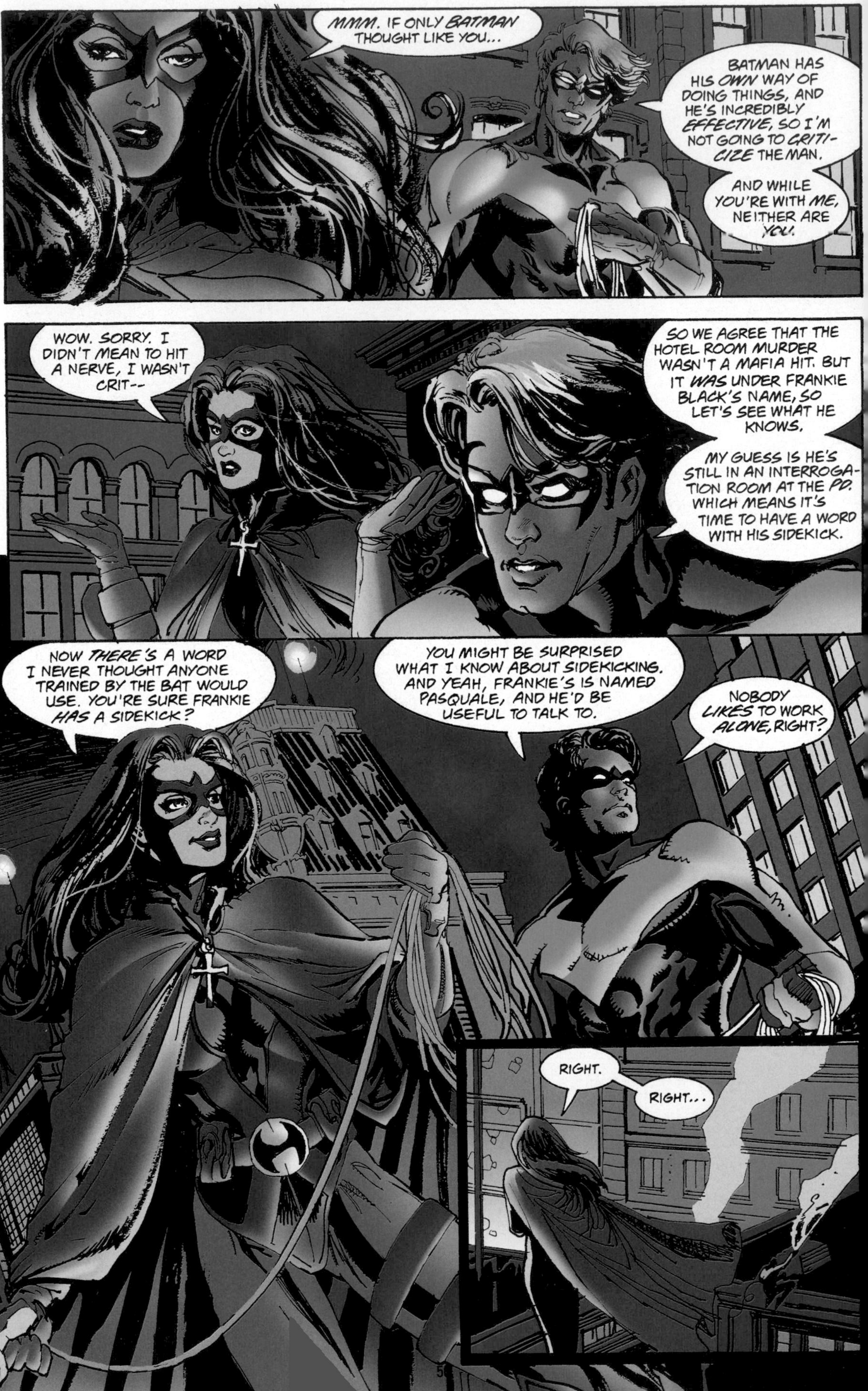
MMM. IF ONLY BATMAN THOUGHT LIKE YOU...
BATMAN HAS HIS OWN WAY OF DOING THINGS, AND HE'S INCREDIBLY EFFECTIVE, SO I'M NOT GOING TO CRITICIZE THE MAN.
AND WHILE YOU'RE WITH ME, NEITHER ARE YOU.
WOW. SORRY. I DIDN'T MEAN TO HIT A NERVE, I WASN'T CRIT--
SO WE AGREE THAT THE HOTEL ROOM MURDER WASN'T A MAFIA HIT. BUT IT WAS UNDER FRANKIE BLACK'S NAME, SO LET'S SEE WHAT HE KNOWS.
MY GUESS IS HE'S STILL IN AN INTERROGATION ROOM AT THE PD. WHICH MEANS IT'S TIME TO HAVE A WORD WITH HIS SIDEKICK.
NOW THERE'S A WORD I NEVER THOUGHT ANYONE TRAINED BY THE BAT WOULD USE. YOU'RE SURE FRANKIE HAS A SIDEKICK?
YOU MIGHT BE SURPRISED WHAT I KNOW ABOUT SIDEKICKING. AND YEAH, FRANKIE'S IS NAMED PASQUALE, AND HE'D BE USEFUL TO TALK TO.
NOBODY LIKES TO WORK ALONE, RIGHT?
RIGHT.
RIGHT...

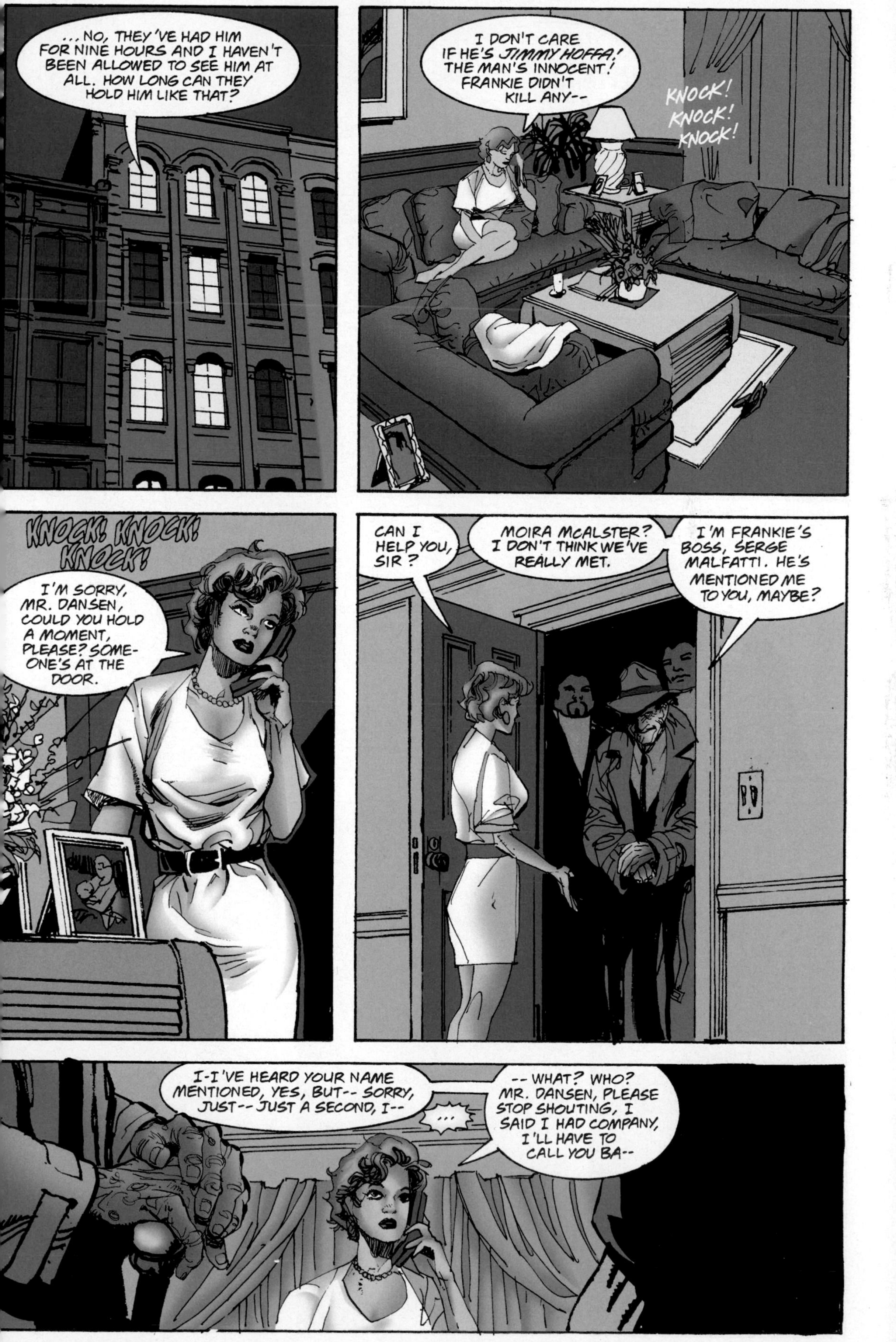
...NO, THEY'VE HAD HIM FOR NINE HOURS AND I HAVEN'T BEEN ALLOWED TO SEE HIM AT ALL. HOW LONG CAN THEY HOLD HIM LIKE THAT?
I DON'T CARE IF HE'S JIMMY HOFFA! THE MAN'S INNOCENT! FRANKIE DIDN'T KILL ANY--
KNOCK! KNOCK! KNOCK!
KNOCK! KNOCK! KNOCK!
I'M SORRY, MR. DANSEN, COULD YOU HOLD A MOMENT, PLEASE? SOME-ONE'S AT THE DOOR.
CAN I HELP YOU, SIR?
MOIRA McALSTER? I DON'T THINK WE'VE REALLY MET.
I'M FRANKIE'S BOSS, SERGE MALFATTI. HE'S MENTIONED ME TO YOU, MAYBE?
I-I'VE HEARD YOUR NAME MENTIONED, YES, BUT-- SORRY, JUST-- JUST A SECOND, I--
...
-- WHAT? WHO? MR. DANSEN, PLEASE STOP SHOUTING, I SAID I HAD COMPANY, I'LL HAVE TO CALL YOU BA--

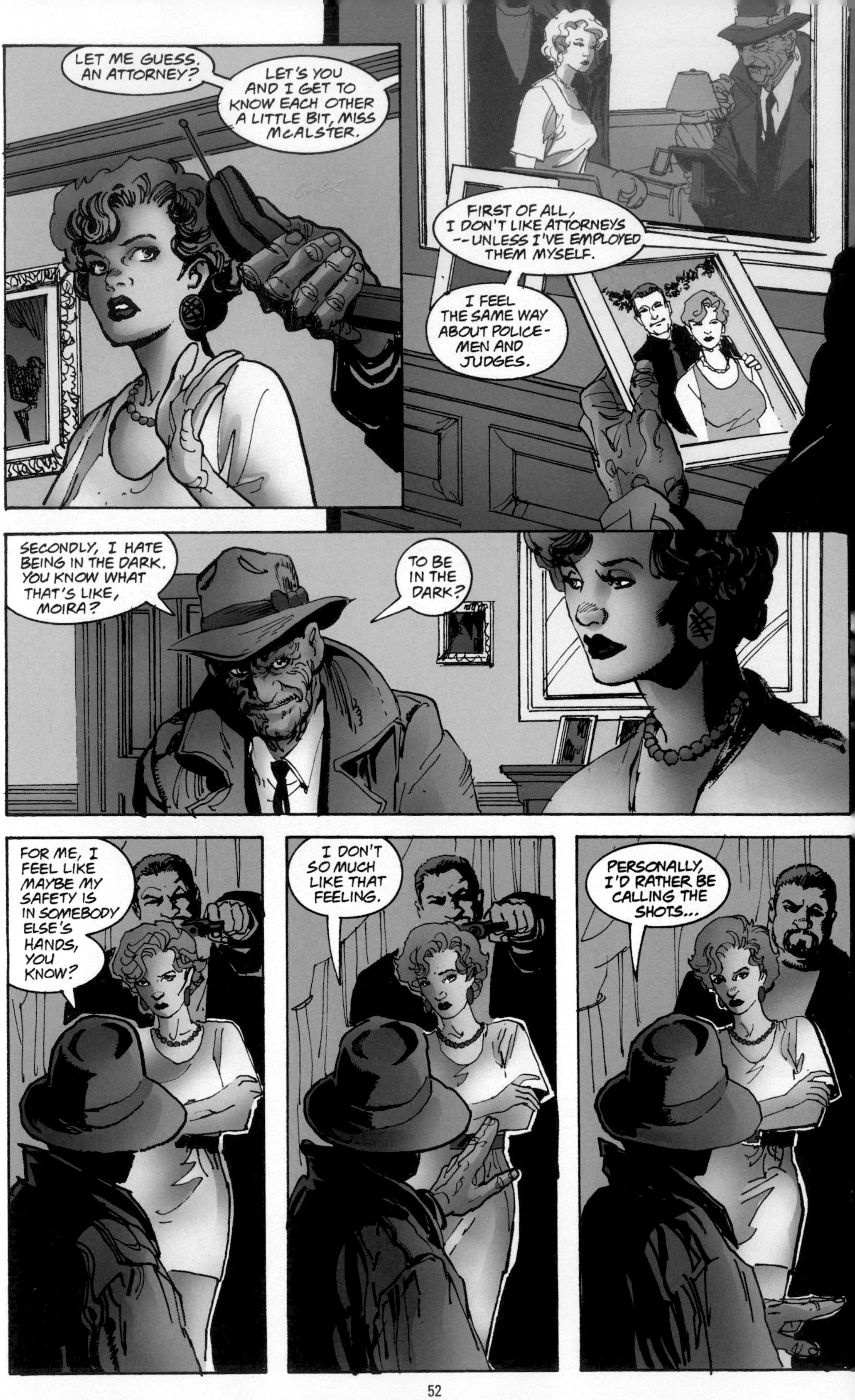
LET ME GUESS. AN ATTORNEY?
LET'S YOU AND I GET TO KNOW EACH OTHER A LITTLE BIT, MISS McALSTER.
FIRST OF ALL, I DON'T LIKE ATTORNEYS --UNLESS I'VE EMPLOYED THEM MYSELF.
I FEEL THE SAME WAY ABOUT POLICE-MEN AND JUDGES.
SECONDLY, I HATE BEING IN THE DARK. YOU KNOW WHAT THAT'S LIKE, MOIRA?
TO BE IN THE DARK?
FOR ME, I FEEL LIKE MAYBE MY SAFETY IS IN SOMEBODY ELSE'S HANDS, YOU KNOW?
I DON'T SO MUCH LIKE THAT FEELING.
PERSONALLY, I'D RATHER BE CALLING THE SHOTS...

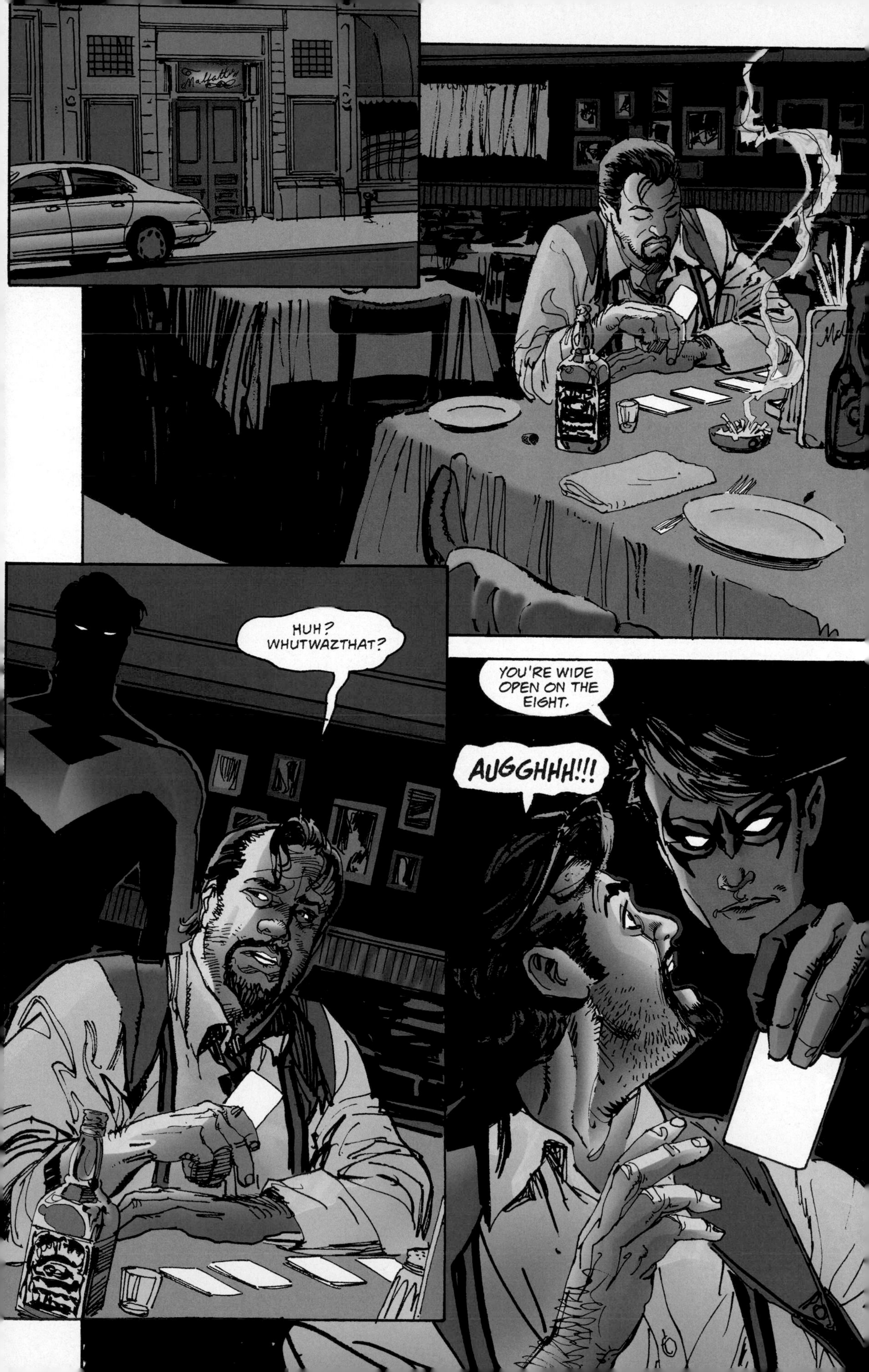
HUH? WHUTWAZTHAT?
YOU'RE WIDE OPEN ON THE EIGHT.
AUGGHHH!!!

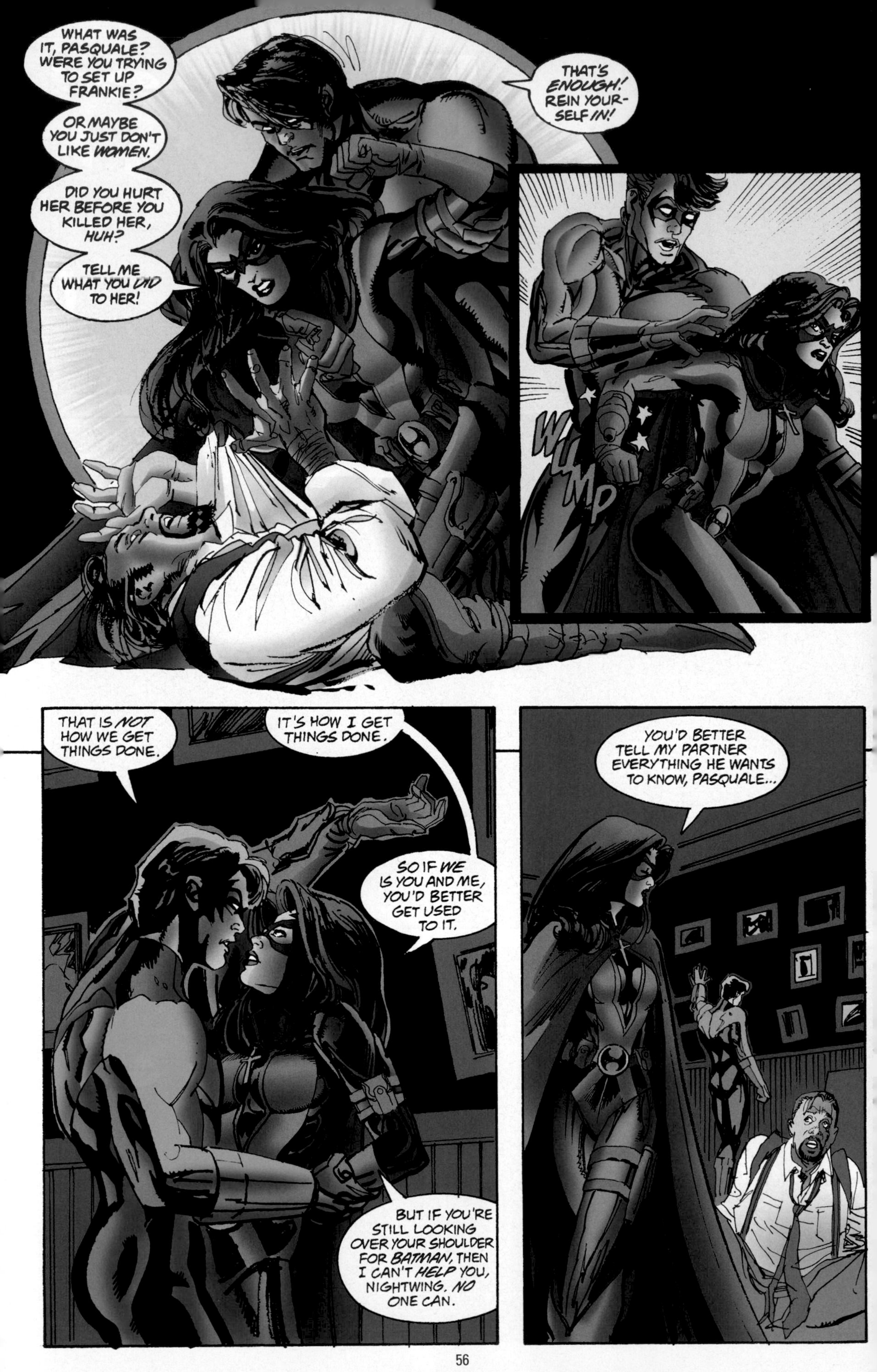
WHAT WAS IT, PASQUALE? WERE YOU TRYING TO SET UP FRANKIE?
OR MAYBE YOU JUST DON'T LIKE WOMEN.
DID YOU HURT HER BEFORE YOU KILLED HER, HUH?
TELL ME WHAT YOU DID TO HER!
THAT'S ENOUGH! REIN YOURSELF IN!
WUMP
THAT IS NOT HOW WE GET THINGS DONE.
IT'S HOW I GET THINGS DONE.
SO IF WE IS YOU AND ME, YOU'D BETTER GET USED TO IT.
BUT IF YOU'RE STILL LOOKING OVER YOUR SHOULDER FOR BATMAN, THEN I CAN'T HELP YOU, NIGHTWING. NO ONE CAN.
YOU'D BETTER TELL MY PARTNER EVERYTHING HE WANTS TO KNOW, PASQUALE...

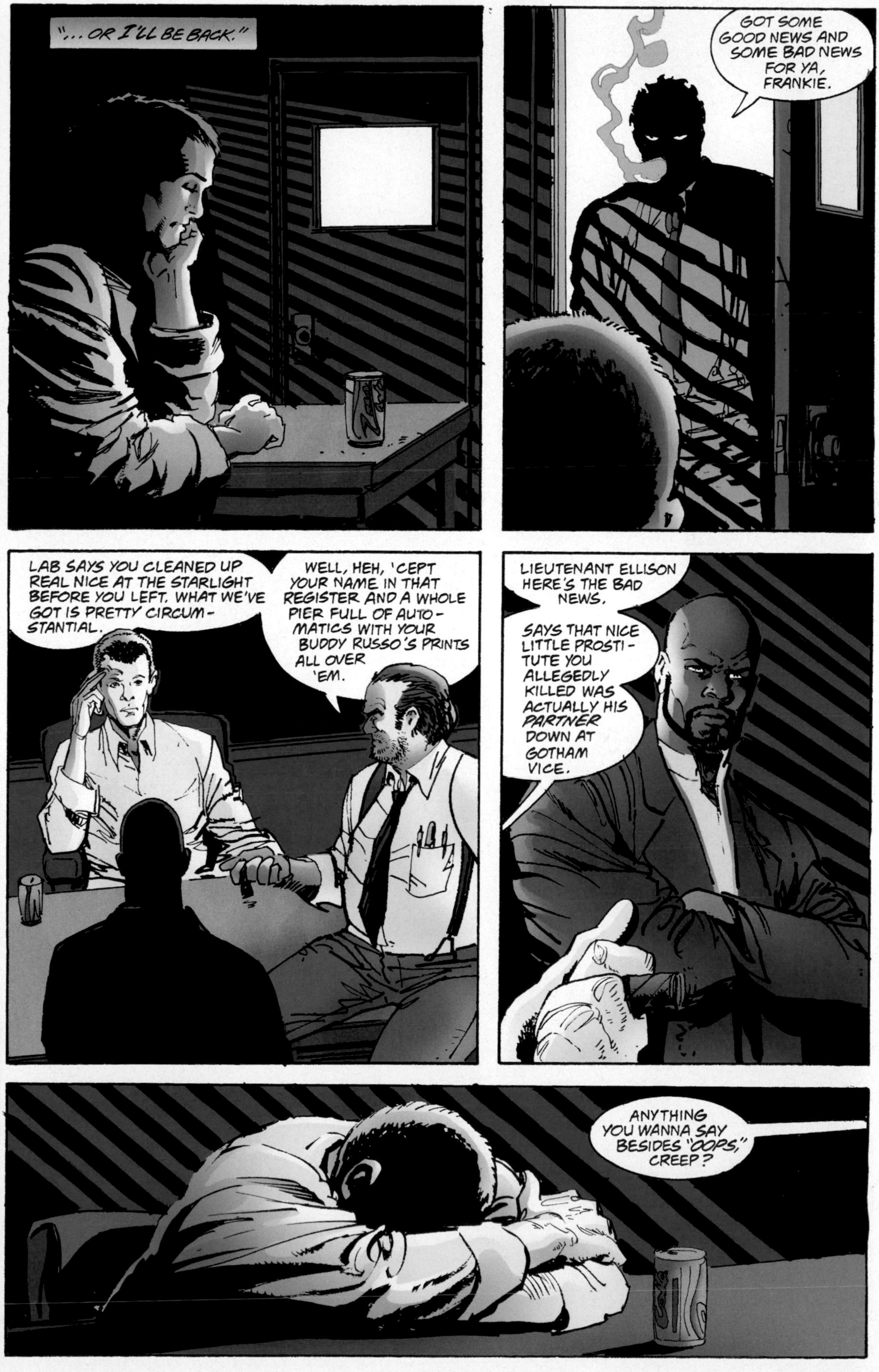
"...OR I'LL BE BACK."
GOT SOME GOOD NEWS AND SOME BAD NEWS FOR YA, FRANKIE.
LAB SAYS YOU CLEANED UP REAL NICE AT THE STARLIGHT BEFORE YOU LEFT. WHAT WE'VE GOT IS PRETTY CIRCUM-STANTIAL.
WELL, HEH, 'CEPT YOUR NAME IN THAT REGISTER AND A WHOLE PIER FULL OF AUTO-MATICS WITH YOUR BUDDY RUSSO'S PRINTS ALL OVER 'EM.
LIEUTENANT ELLISON HERE'S THE BAD NEWS.
SAYS THAT NICE LITTLE PROSTI-TUTE YOU ALLEGEDLY KILLED WAS ACTUALLY HIS PARTNER DOWN AT GOTHAM VICE.
ANYTHING YOU WANNA SAY BESIDES "OOPS," CREEP?

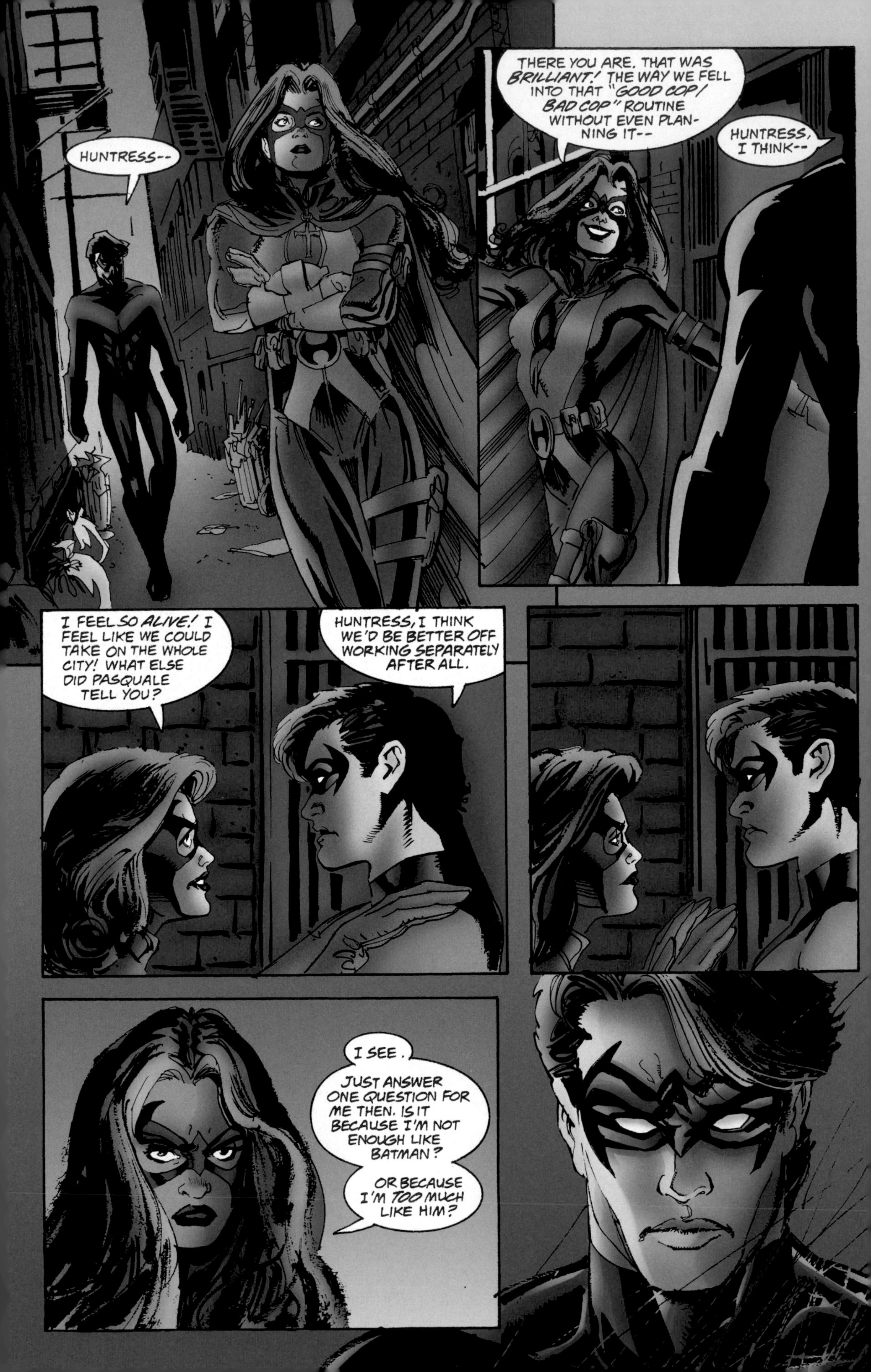
HUNTRESS--
THERE YOU ARE. THAT WAS BRILLIANT! THE WAY WE FELL INTO THAT "GOOD COP/ BAD COP" ROUTINE WITHOUT EVEN PLANNING IT--
HUNTRESS, I THINK--
I FEEL SO ALIVE! I FEEL LIKE WE COULD TAKE ON THE WHOLE CITY! WHAT ELSE DID PASQUALE TELL YOU?
HUNTRESS, I THINK WE'D BE BETTER OFF WORKING SEPARATELY AFTER ALL.
I SEE.
JUST ANSWER ONE QUESTION FOR ME THEN. IS IT BECAUSE I'M NOT ENOUGH LIKE BATMAN?
OR BECAUSE I'M TOO MUCH LIKE HIM?

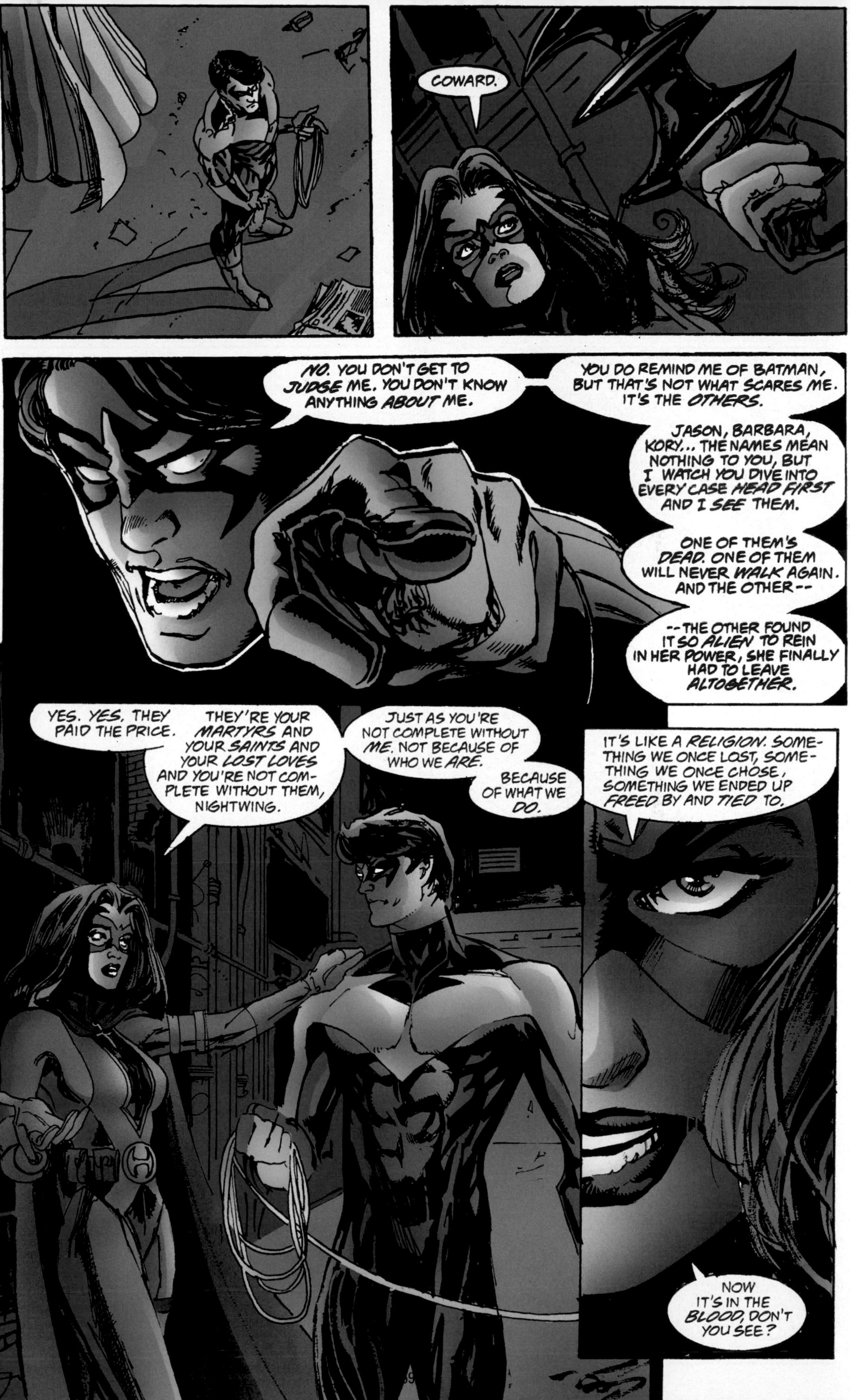

COWARD.
NO. YOU DON'T GET TO JUDGE ME. YOU DON'T KNOW ANYTHING ABOUT ME.
YOU DO REMIND ME OF BATMAN, BUT THAT'S NOT WHAT SCARES ME. IT'S THE OTHERS.
JASON, BARBARA, KORY... THE NAMES MEAN NOTHING TO YOU, BUT I WATCH YOU DIVE INTO EVERY CASE HEAD FIRST AND I SEE THEM.
ONE OF THEM'S DEAD. ONE OF THEM WILL NEVER WALK AGAIN. AND THE OTHER--
--THE OTHER FOUND IT SO ALIEN TO REIN IN HER POWER, SHE FINALLY HAD TO LEAVE ALTOGETHER.
YES. YES, THEY PAID THE PRICE.
THEY'RE YOUR MARTYRS AND YOUR SAINTS AND YOUR LOST LOVES AND YOU'RE NOT COMPLETE WITHOUT THEM, NIGHTWING.
JUST AS YOU'RE NOT COMPLETE WITHOUT ME. NOT BECAUSE OF WHO WE ARE.
BECAUSE OF WHAT WE DO.
IT'S LIKE A RELIGION. SOMETHING WE ONCE LOST, SOMETHING WE ONCE CHOSE, SOMETHING WE ENDED UP FREED BY AND TIED TO.
NOW IT'S IN THE BLOOD, DON'T YOU SEE?

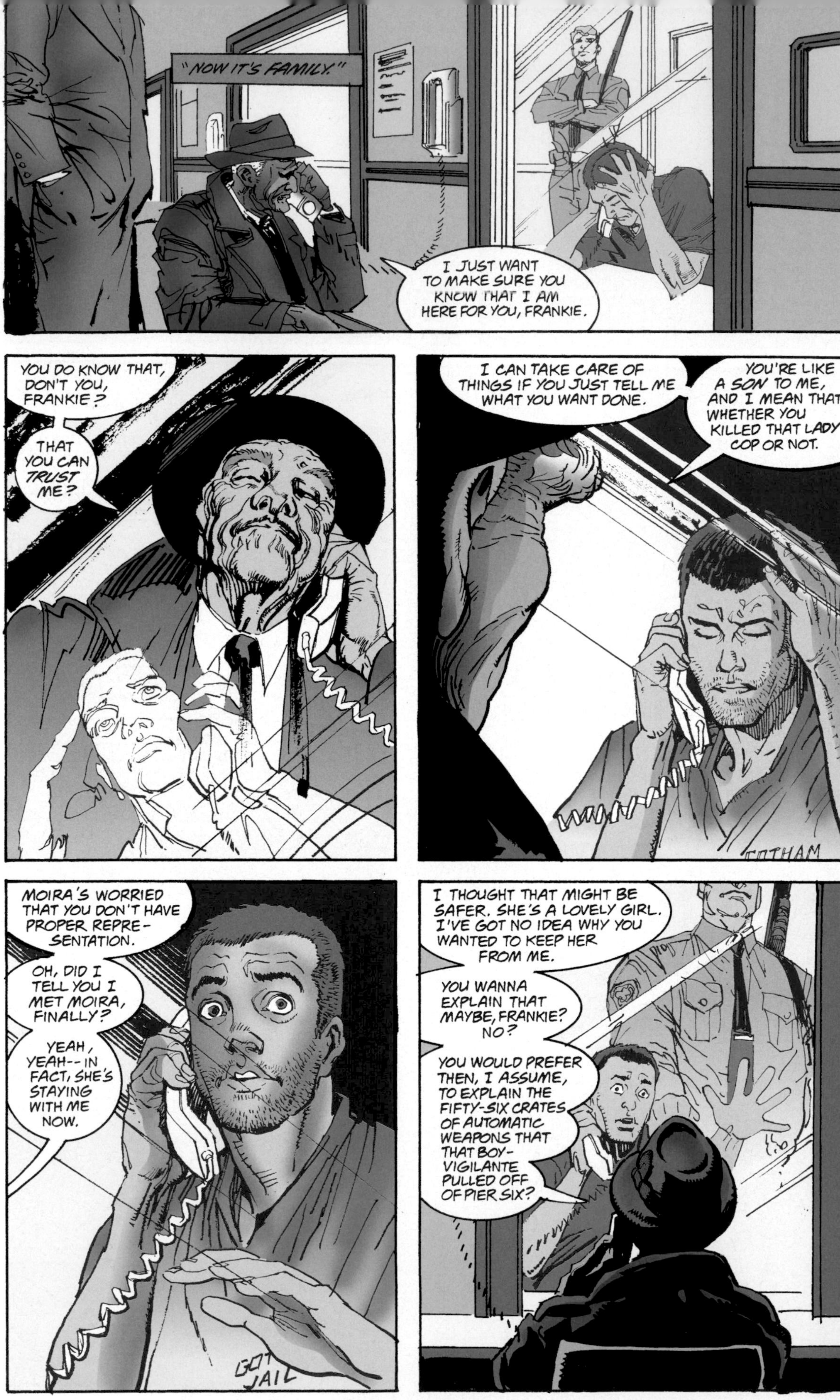
"NOW IT'S FAMILY."
I JUST WANT TO MAKE SURE YOU KNOW THAT I AM HERE FOR YOU, FRANKIE.
YOU DO KNOW THAT, DON'T YOU, FRANKIE?
THAT YOU CAN TRUST ME?
I CAN TAKE CARE OF THINGS IF YOU JUST TELL ME WHAT YOU WANT DONE.
YOU'RE LIKE A SON TO ME, AND I MEAN THAT WHETHER YOU KILLED THAT LADY COP OR NOT.
MOIRA'S WORRIED THAT YOU DON'T HAVE PROPER REPRE-SENTATION.
OH, DID I TELL YOU I MET MOIRA, FINALLY?
YEAH, YEAH-- IN FACT, SHE'S STAYING WITH ME NOW.
I THOUGHT THAT MIGHT BE SAFER. SHE'S A LOVELY GIRL. I'VE GOT NO IDEA WHY YOU WANTED TO KEEP HER FROM ME.
YOU WANNA EXPLAIN THAT MAYBE, FRANKIE? NO?
YOU WOULD PREFER THEN, I ASSUME, TO EXPLAIN THE FIFTY-SIX CRATES OF AUTOMATIC WEAPONS THAT THAT BOY-VIGILANTE PULLED OFF OF PIER SIX?

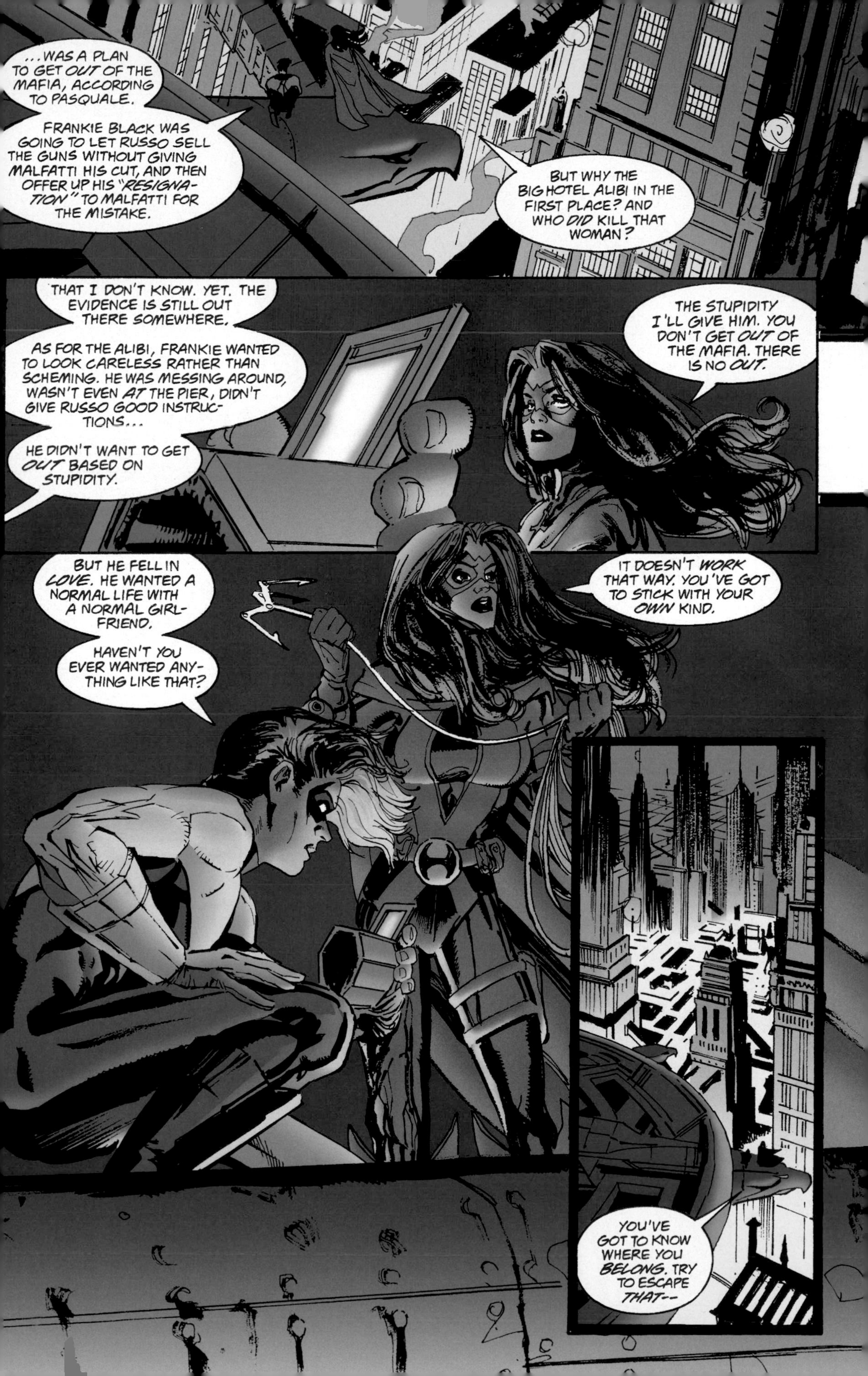
...WAS A PLAN TO GET OUT OF THE MAFIA, ACCORDING TO PASQUALE.
FRANKIE BLACK WAS GOING TO LET RUSSO SELL THE GUNS WITHOUT GIVING MALFATTI HIS CUT, AND THEN OFFER UP HIS "RESIGNATION" TO MALFATTI FOR THE MISTAKE.
BUT WHY THE BIG HOTEL ALIBI IN THE FIRST PLACE? AND WHO DID KILL THAT WOMAN?
THAT I DON'T KNOW. YET. THE EVIDENCE IS STILL OUT THERE SOMEWHERE.
AS FOR THE ALIBI, FRANKIE WANTED TO LOOK CARELESS RATHER THAN SCHEMING. HE WAS MESSING AROUND, WASN'T EVEN AT THE PIER, DIDN'T GIVE RUSSO GOOD INSTRUCTIONS...
HE DIDN'T WANT TO GET OUT BASED ON STUPIDITY.
THE STUPIDITY I'LL GIVE HIM. YOU DON'T GET OUT OF THE MAFIA. THERE IS NO OUT.
BUT HE FELL IN LOVE. HE WANTED A NORMAL LIFE WITH A NORMAL GIRLFRIEND.
HAVEN'T YOU EVER WANTED ANYTHING LIKE THAT?
IT DOESN'T WORK THAT WAY. YOU'VE GOT TO STICK WITH YOUR OWN KIND.
YOU'VE GOT TO KNOW WHERE YOU BELONG. TRY TO ESCAPE THAT--

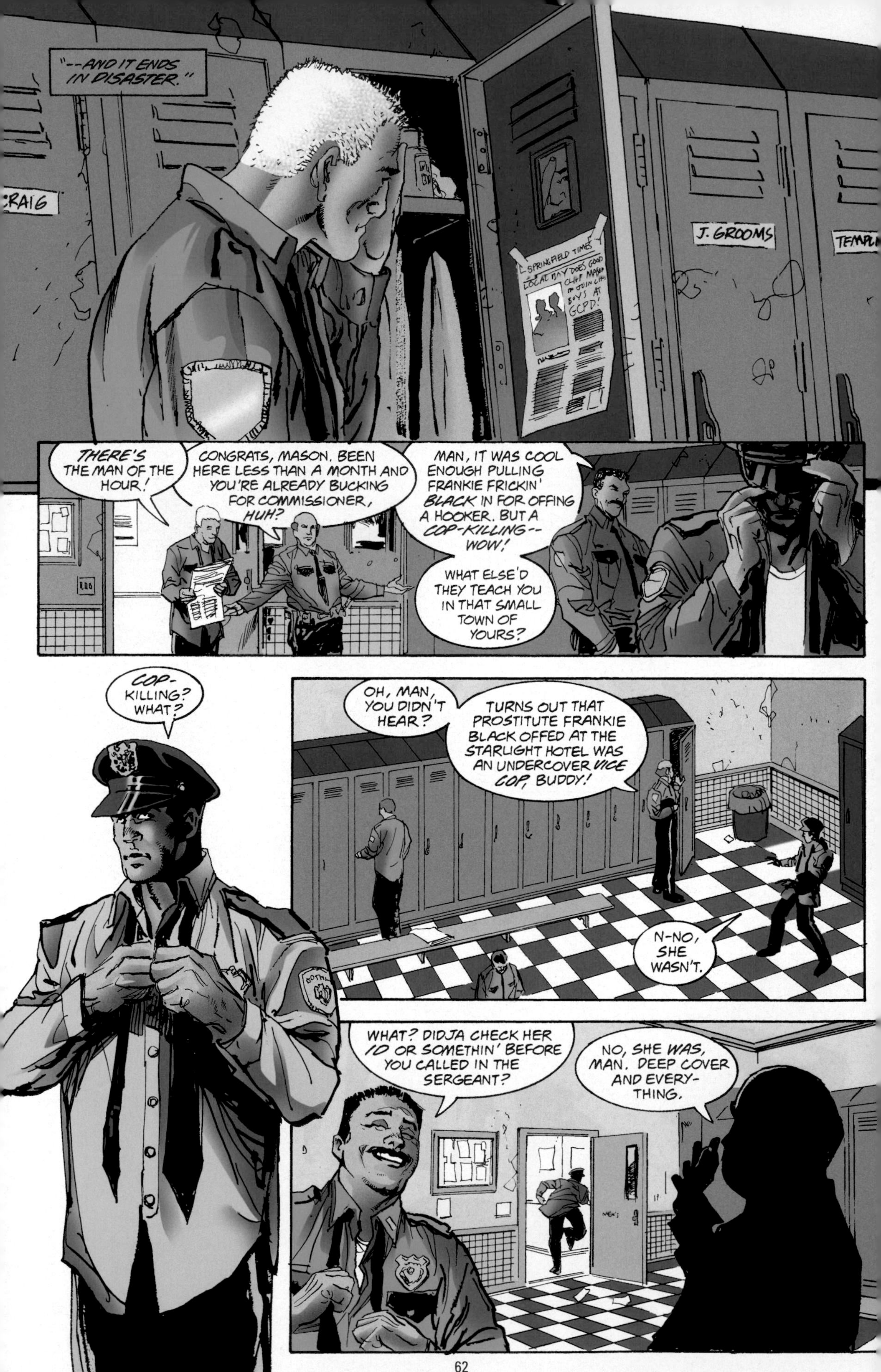
"--AND IT ENDS IN DISASTER."
CRAIG
J. GROOMS
SPRINGFIELD TIMES
LOCAL BOY DOES GOOD
THERE'S THE MAN OF THE HOUR!
CONGRATS, MASON. BEEN HERE LESS THAN A MONTH AND YOU'RE ALREADY BUCKING FOR COMMISSIONER, HUH?
MAN, IT WAS COOL ENOUGH PULLING FRANKIE FRICKIN' BLACK IN FOR OFFING A HOOKER. BUT A COP-KILLING--WOW!
WHAT ELSE'D THEY TEACH YOU IN THAT SMALL TOWN OF YOURS?
COP-KILLING? WHAT?
OH, MAN, YOU DIDN'T HEAR?
TURNS OUT THAT PROSTITUTE FRANKIE BLACK OFFED AT THE STARLIGHT HOTEL WAS AN UNDERCOVER VICE COP, BUDDY!
N-NO, SHE WASN'T.
WHAT? DIDJA CHECK HER ID OR SOMETHIN' BEFORE YOU CALLED IN THE SERGEANT?
NO, SHE WAS, MAN. DEEP COVER AND EVERY-THING.

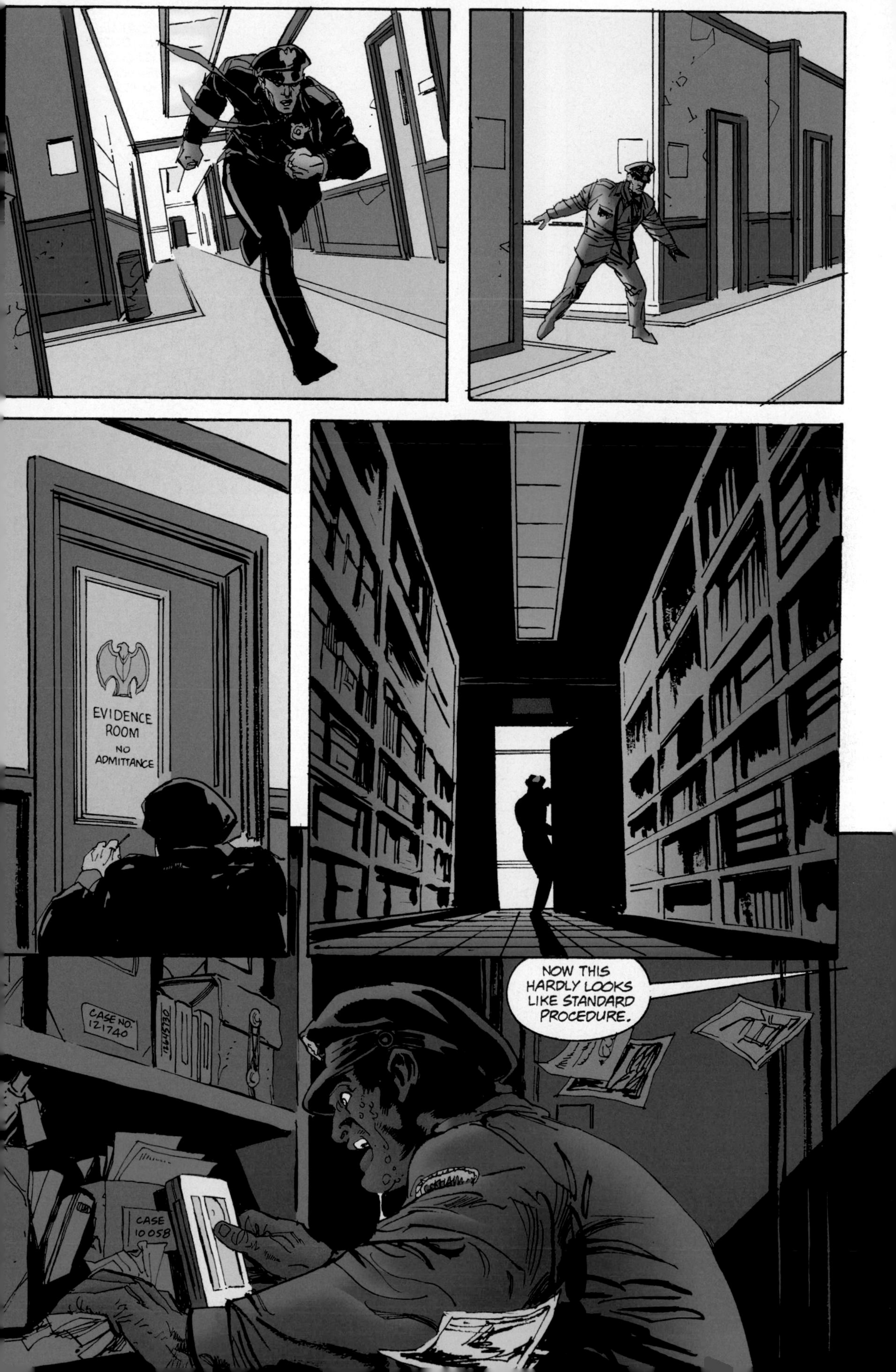

EVIDENCE
ROOM
NO
ADMITTANCE
CASE NO.
121740
CASE
10058
NOW THIS HARDLY LOOKS LIKE STANDARD PROCEDURE.

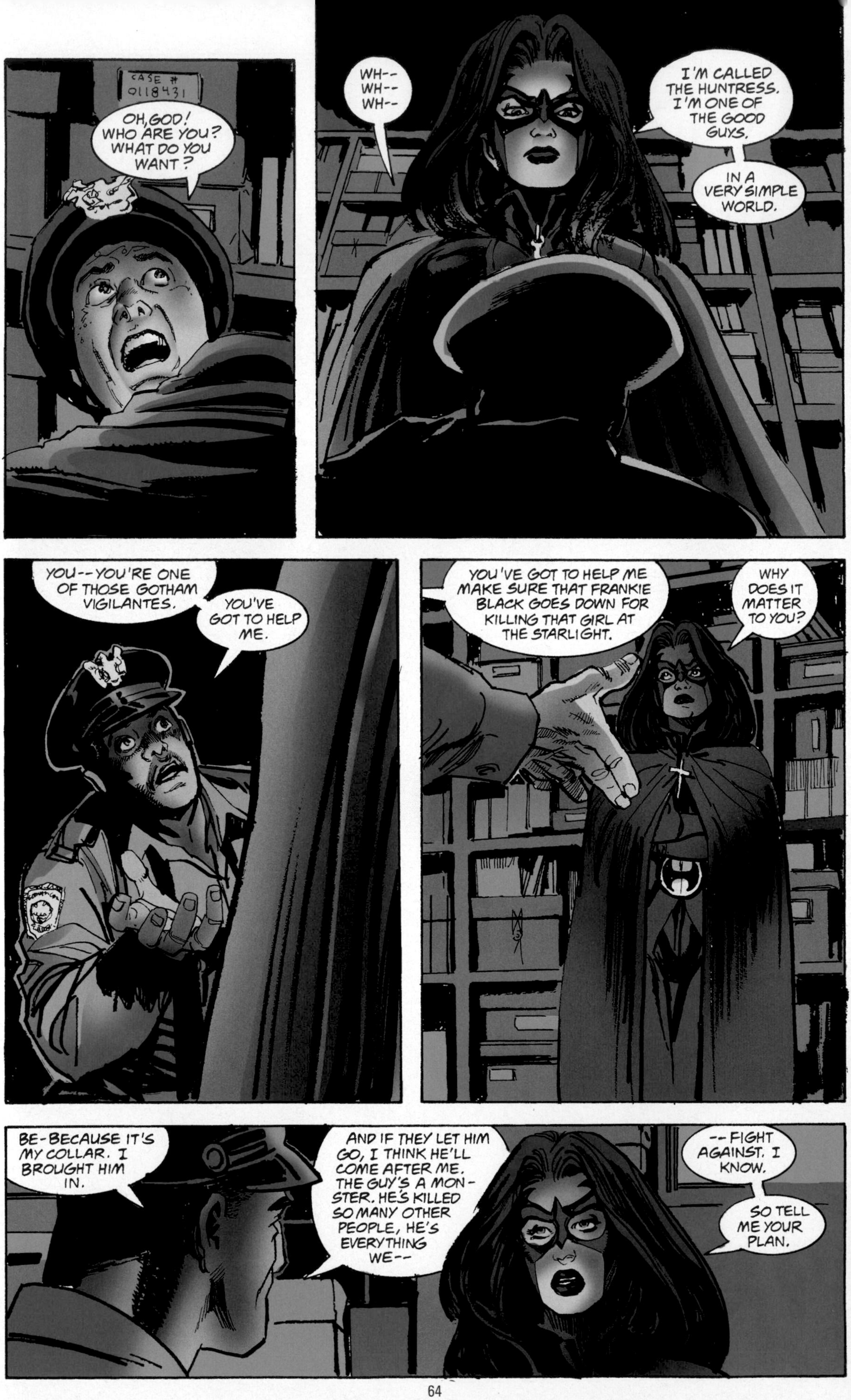
CASE # 0118431
OH, GOD! WHO ARE YOU? WHAT DO YOU WANT?
WH-- WH-- WH--
I'M CALLED THE HUNTRESS. I'M ONE OF THE GOOD GUYS.
IN A VERY SIMPLE WORLD.
YOU--YOU'RE ONE OF THOSE GOTHAM VIGILANTES.
YOU'VE GOT TO HELP ME.
YOU'VE GOT TO HELP ME MAKE SURE THAT FRANKIE BLACK GOES DOWN FOR KILLING THAT GIRL AT THE STARLIGHT.
WHY DOES IT MATTER TO YOU?
BE-BECAUSE IT'S MY COLLAR. I BROUGHT HIM IN.
AND IF THEY LET HIM GO, I THINK HE'LL COME AFTER ME. THE GUY'S A MON-STER. HE'S KILLED SO MANY OTHER PEOPLE, HE'S EVERYTHING WE--
--FIGHT AGAINST. I KNOW.
SO TELL ME YOUR PLAN.

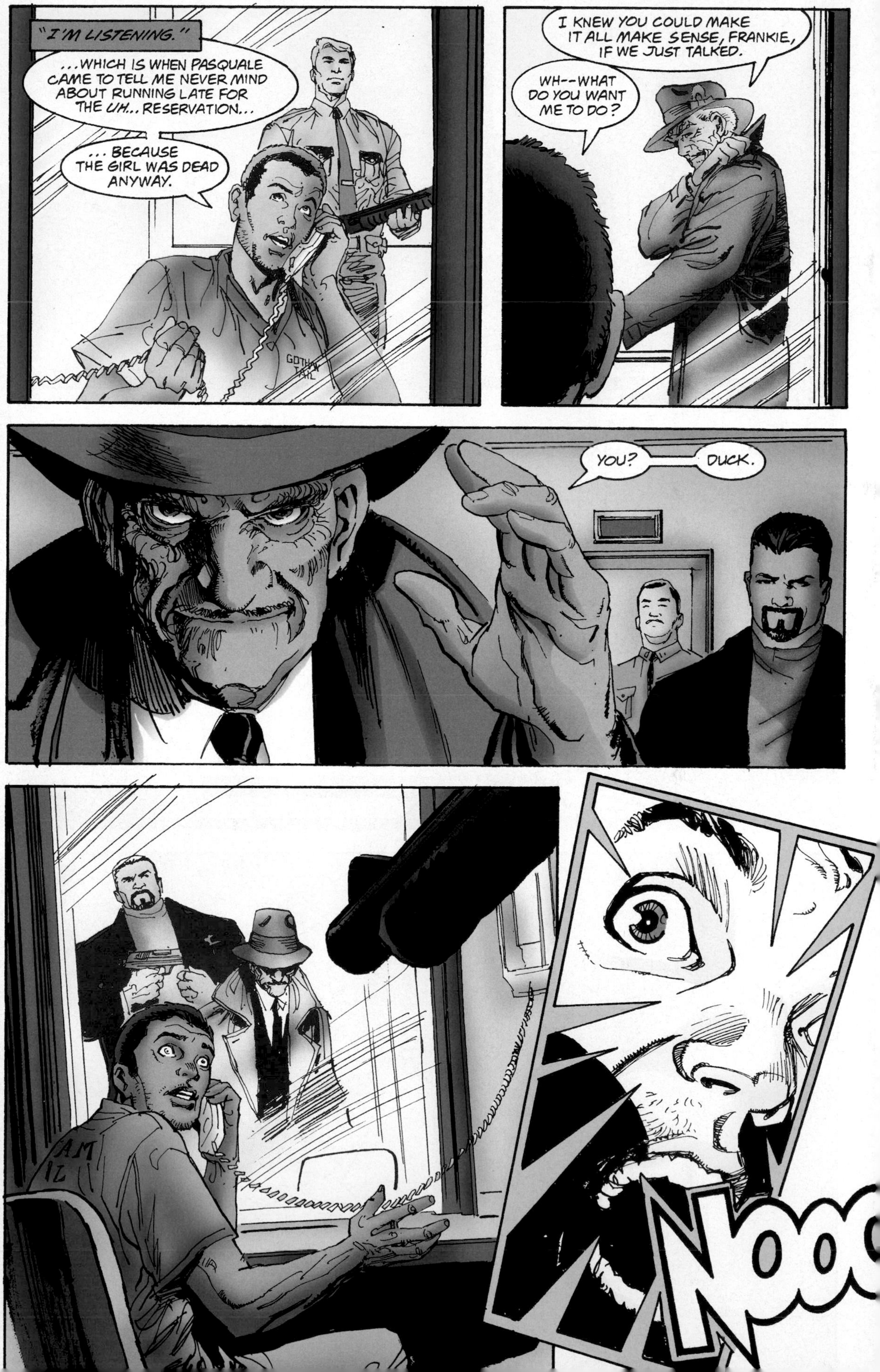
"I'M LISTENING."
...WHICH IS WHEN PASQUALE CAME TO TELL ME NEVER MIND ABOUT RUNNING LATE FOR THE UH... RESERVATION...
...BECAUSE THE GIRL WAS DEAD ANYWAY.
I KNEW YOU COULD MAKE IT ALL MAKE SENSE, FRANKIE, IF WE JUST TALKED.
WH--WHAT DO YOU WANT ME TO DO?
YOU?
DUCK.
NOOO

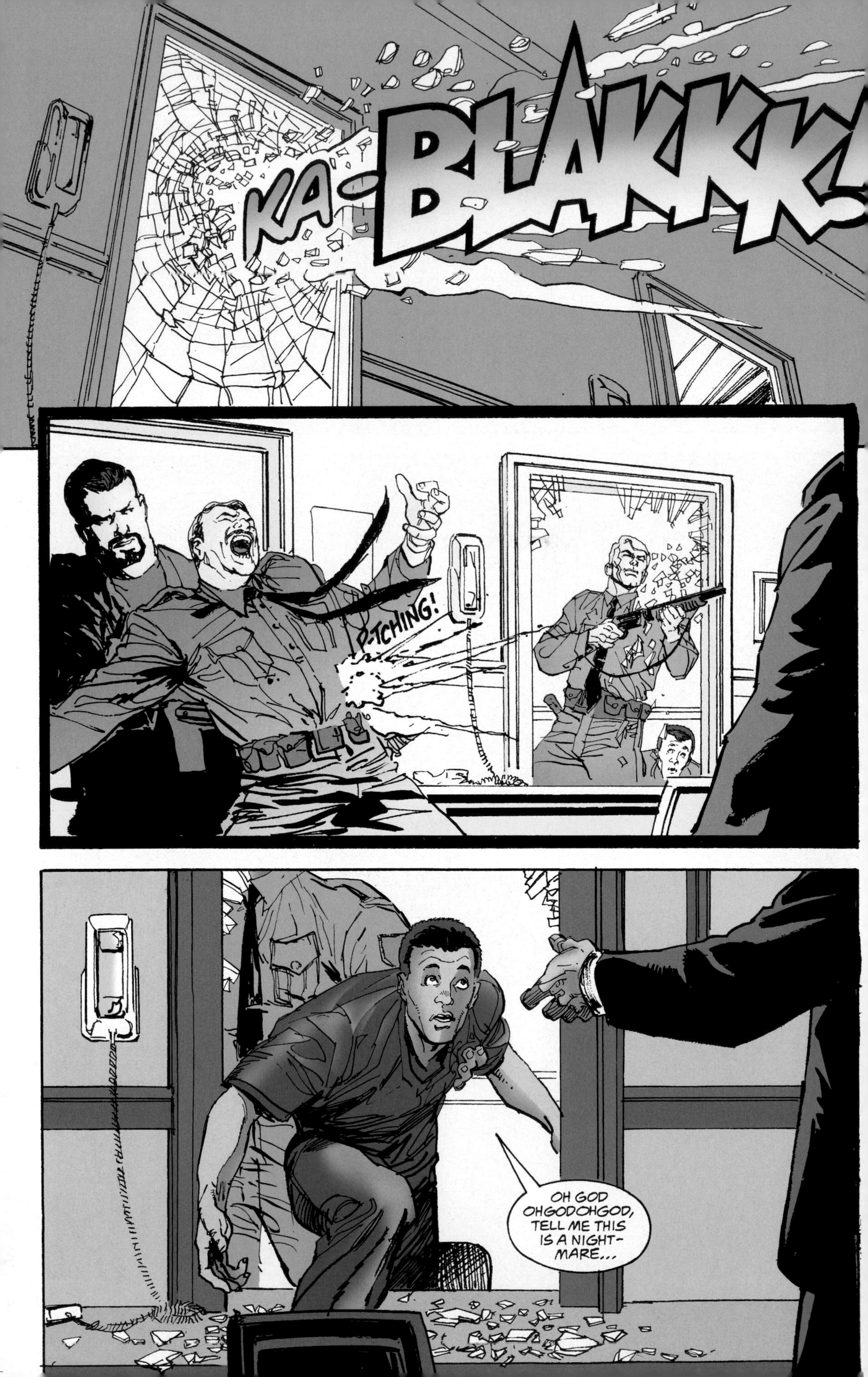
KA-BLAKKK!
P-TCHING!
OH GOD OHGODOHGOD, TELL ME THIS IS A NIGHT-MARE...

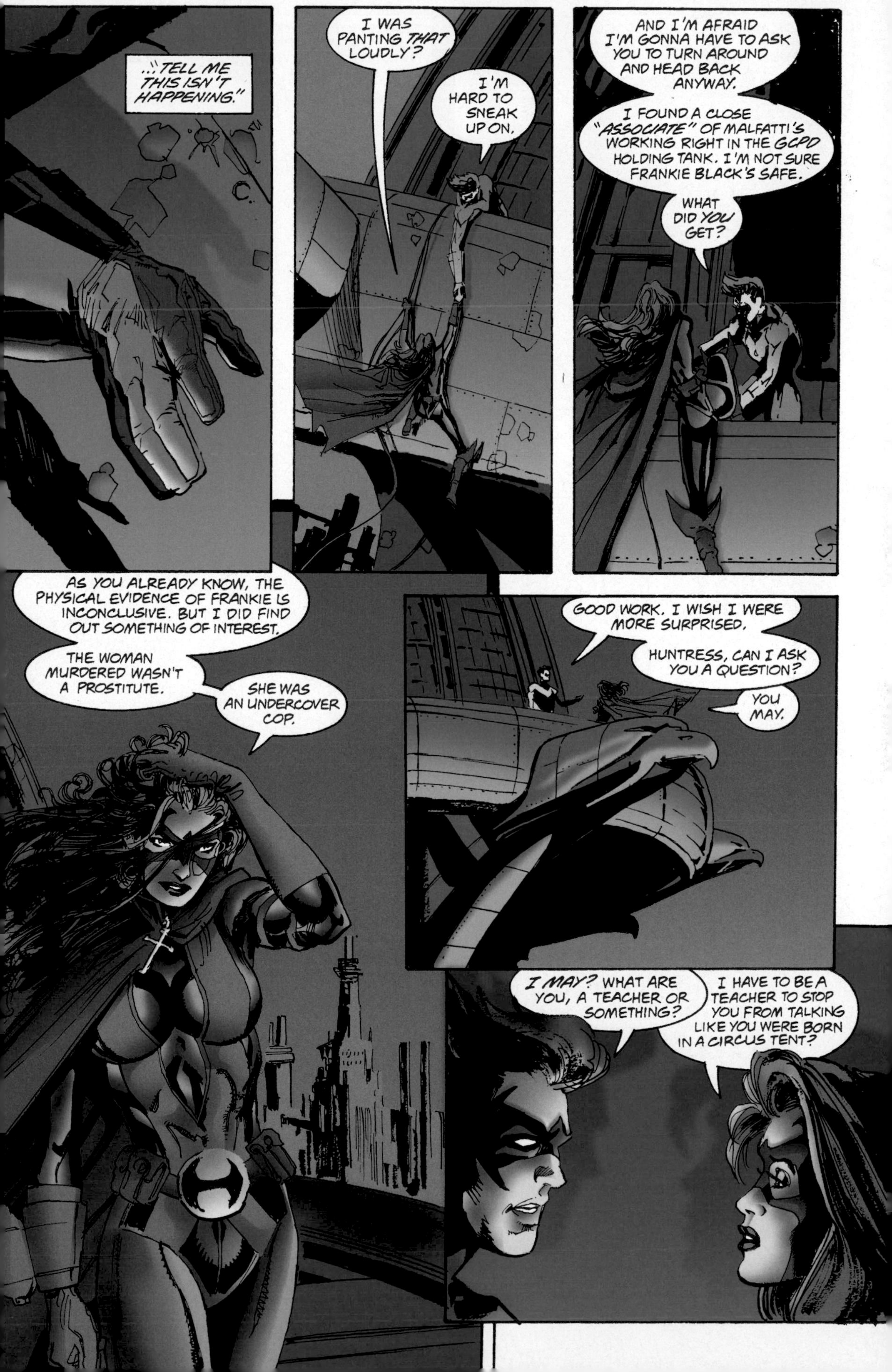
...!"TELL ME THIS ISN'T HAPPENING."
I WAS PANTING THAT LOUDLY?
I'M HARD TO SNEAK UP ON.
AND I'M AFRAID I'M GONNA HAVE TO ASK YOU TO TURN AROUND AND HEAD BACK ANYWAY.
I FOUND A CLOSE "ASSOCIATE" OF MALFATTI'S WORKING RIGHT IN THE GCPD HOLDING TANK. I'M NOT SURE FRANKIE BLACK'S SAFE.
WHAT DID YOU GET?
AS YOU ALREADY KNOW, THE PHYSICAL EVIDENCE OF FRANKIE IS INCONCLUSIVE. BUT I DID FIND OUT SOMETHING OF INTEREST.
THE WOMAN MURDERED WASN'T A PROSTITUTE.
SHE WAS AN UNDERCOVER COP.
GOOD WORK. I WISH I WERE MORE SURPRISED.
HUNTRESS, CAN I ASK YOU A QUESTION?
YOU MAY.
I MAY? WHAT ARE YOU, A TEACHER OR SOMETHING?
I HAVE TO BE A TEACHER TO STOP YOU FROM TALKING LIKE YOU WERE BORN IN A CIRCUS TENT?

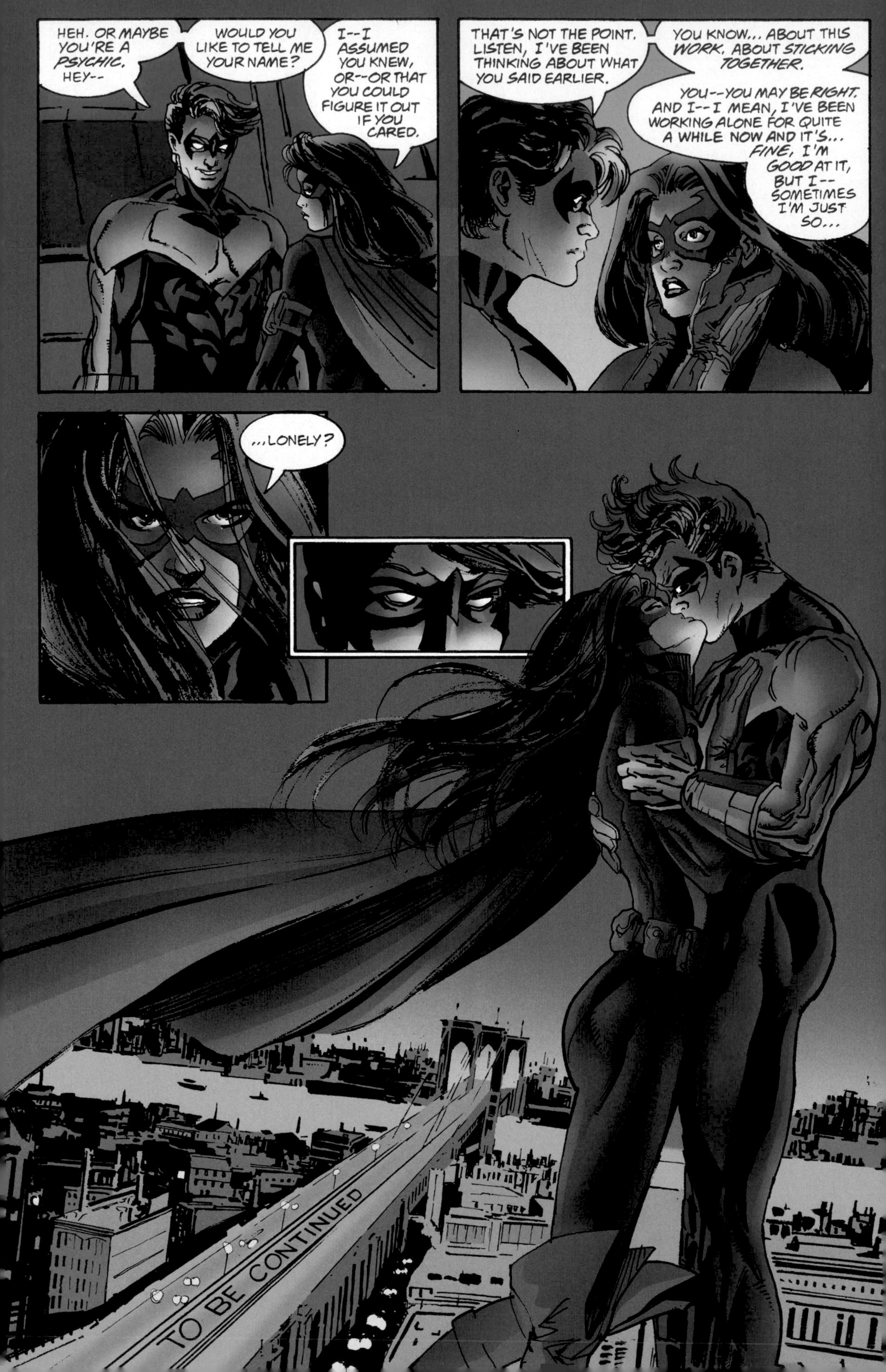
HEH. OR MAYBE YOU'RE A PSYCHIC. HEY--
WOULD YOU LIKE TO TELL ME YOUR NAME?
I--I ASSUMED YOU KNEW, OR--OR THAT YOU COULD FIGURE IT OUT IF YOU CARED.
THAT'S NOT THE POINT. LISTEN, I'VE BEEN THINKING ABOUT WHAT YOU SAID EARLIER.
YOU KNOW... ABOUT THIS WORK. ABOUT STICKING TOGETHER.
YOU--YOU MAY BE RIGHT. AND I-- I MEAN, I'VE BEEN WORKING ALONE FOR QUITE A WHILE NOW AND IT'S... FINE, I'M GOOD AT IT, BUT I-- SOMETIMES I'M JUST SO...
...LONELY?
TO BE CONTINUED

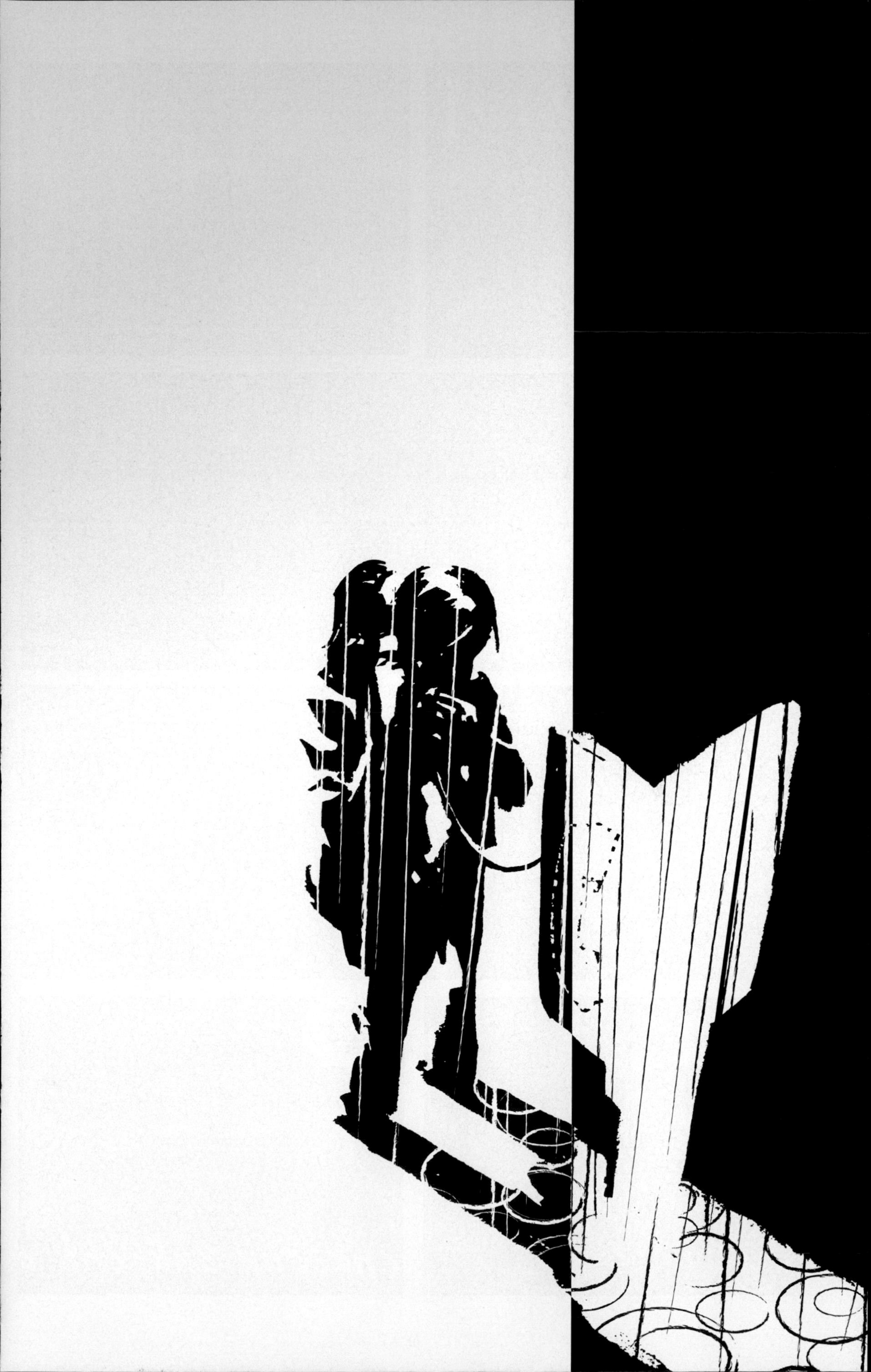

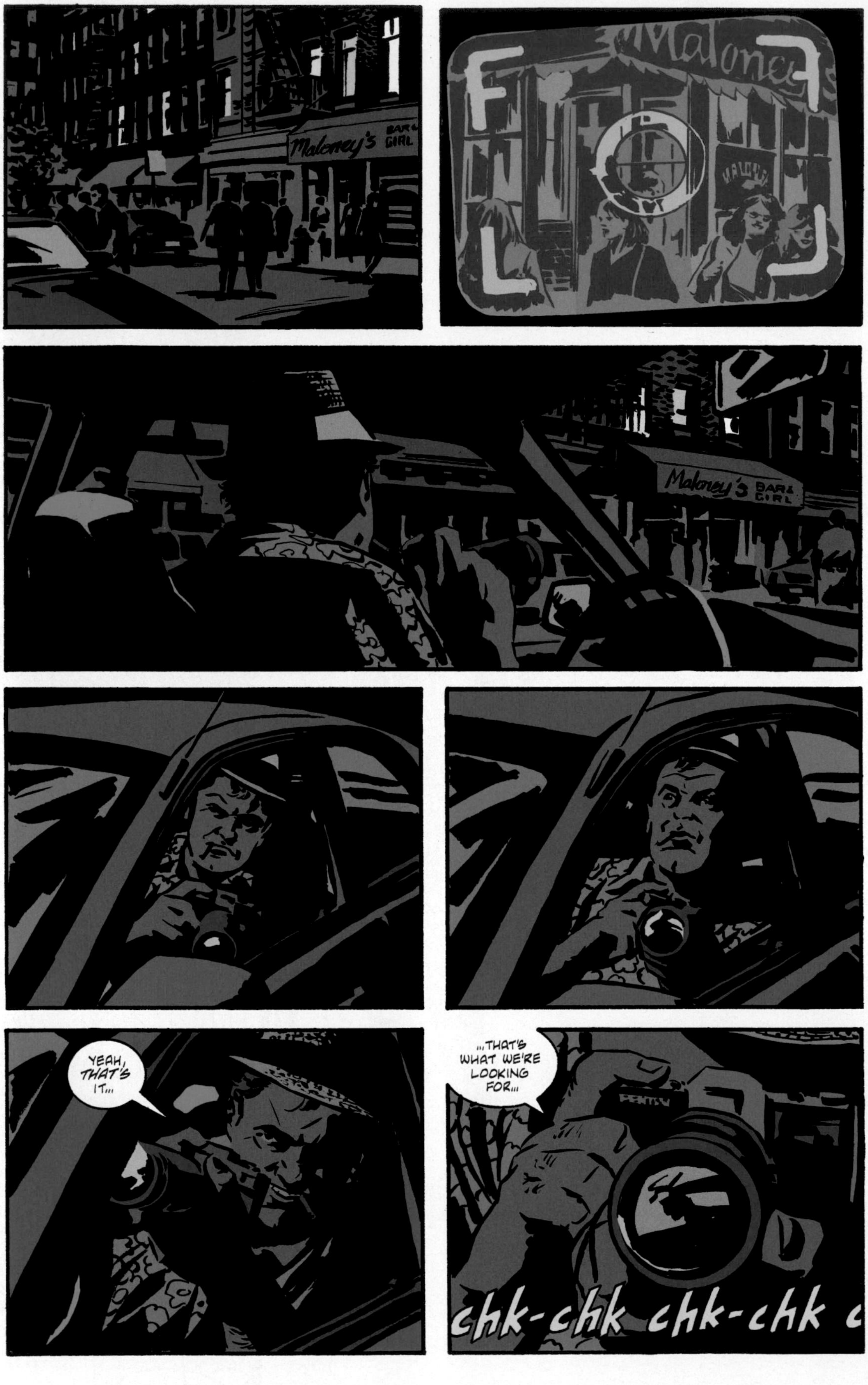
Maloney's BAR & GRILL
YEAH, THAT'S IT...
...THAT'S WHAT WE'RE LOOKING FOR...
chk-chk chk-chk

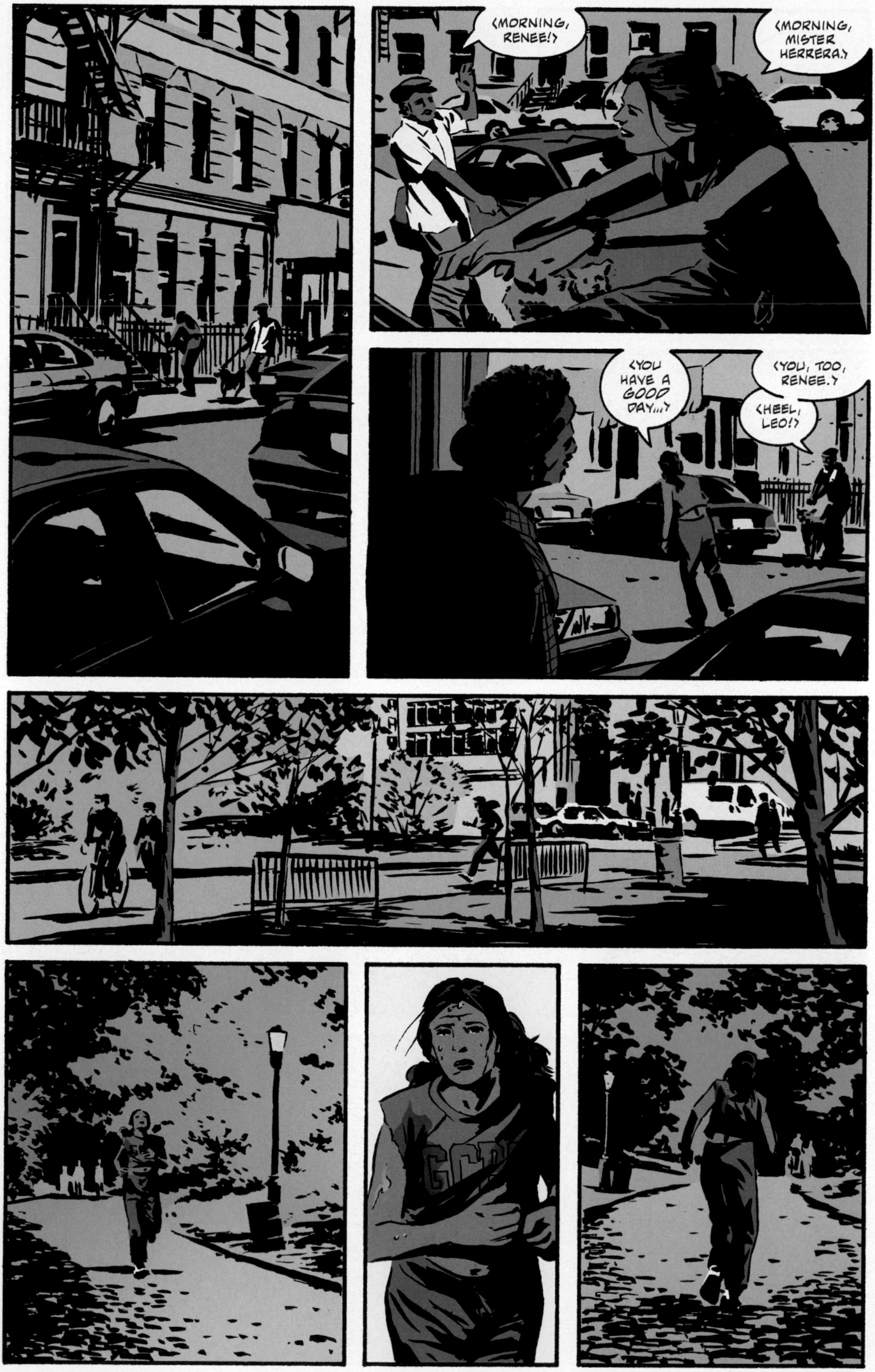

<MORNING, RENEE!>
<MORNING, MISTER HERRERA.>
<YOU HAVE A GOOD DAY...>
<YOU, TOO, RENEE.>
<HEEL, LEO!>

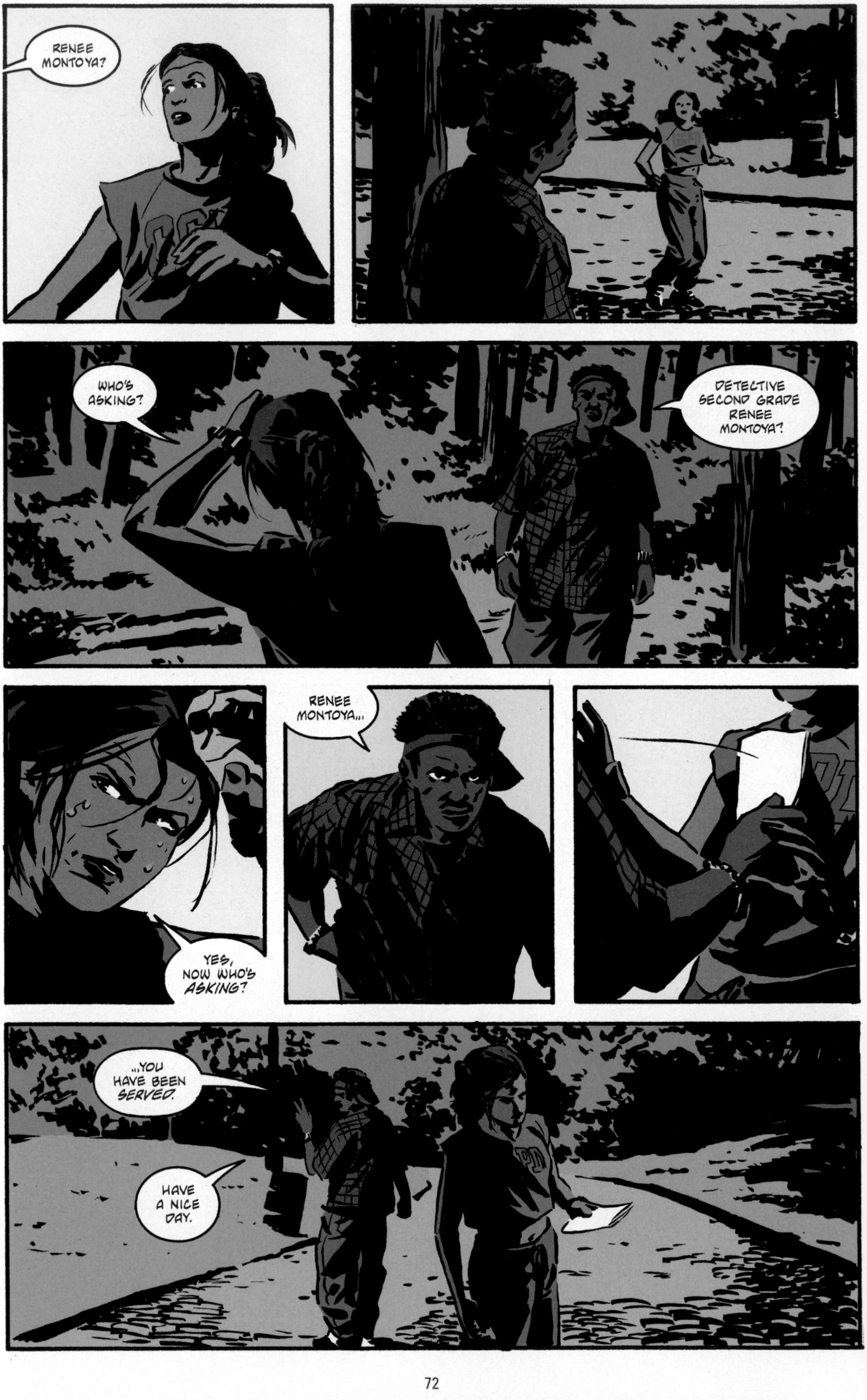
RENEE MONTOYA?
WHO'S ASKING?
DETECTIVE SECOND GRADE RENEE MONTOYA?
YES, NOW WHO'S ASKING?
RENEE MONTOYA...
...YOU HAVE BEEN SERVED.
HAVE A NICE DAY.

Half a Life

Part One

words GREG RUCKA
art MICHAEL LARK
letters WILLIE SCHUBERT
colors MATT HOLLINGSWORTH
assistant edits NACHIE CASTRO edits MATT IDELSON

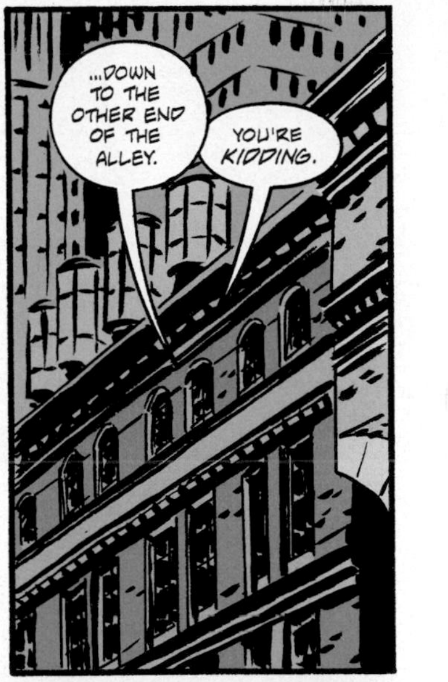
...DOWN TO THE OTHER END OF THE ALLEY.
YOU'RE KIDDING.

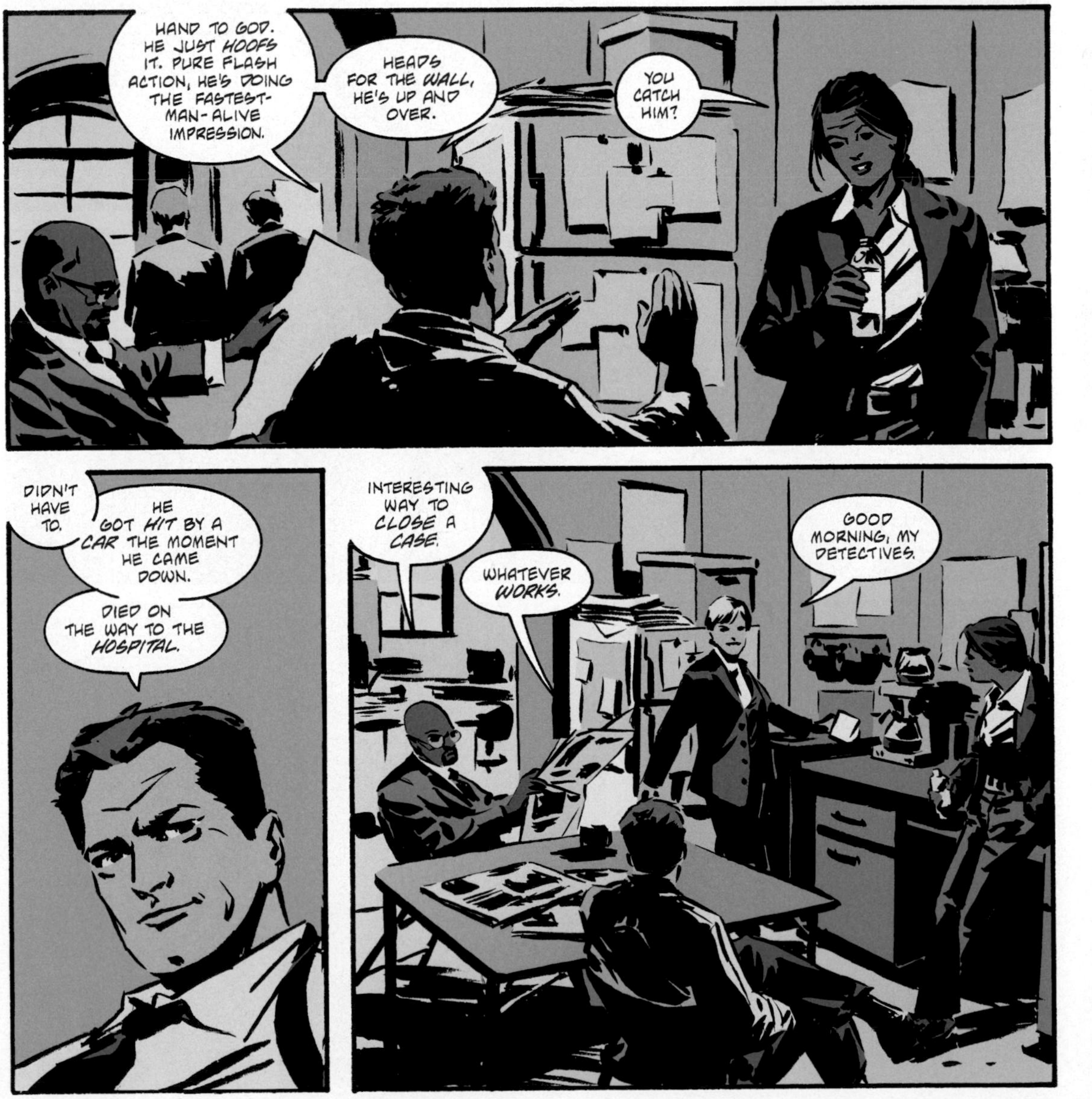
HAND TO GOD. HE JUST HOOFS IT. PURE FLASH ACTION, HE'S DOING THE FASTEST-MAN-ALIVE IMPRESSION.
HEADS FOR THE WALL, HE'S UP AND OVER.
YOU CATCH HIM?
DIDN'T HAVE TO.
HE GOT HIT BY A CAR THE MOMENT HE CAME DOWN.
DIED ON THE WAY TO THE HOSPITAL.
INTERESTING WAY TO CLOSE A CASE.
WHATEVER WORKS.
GOOD MORNING, MY DETECTIVES.

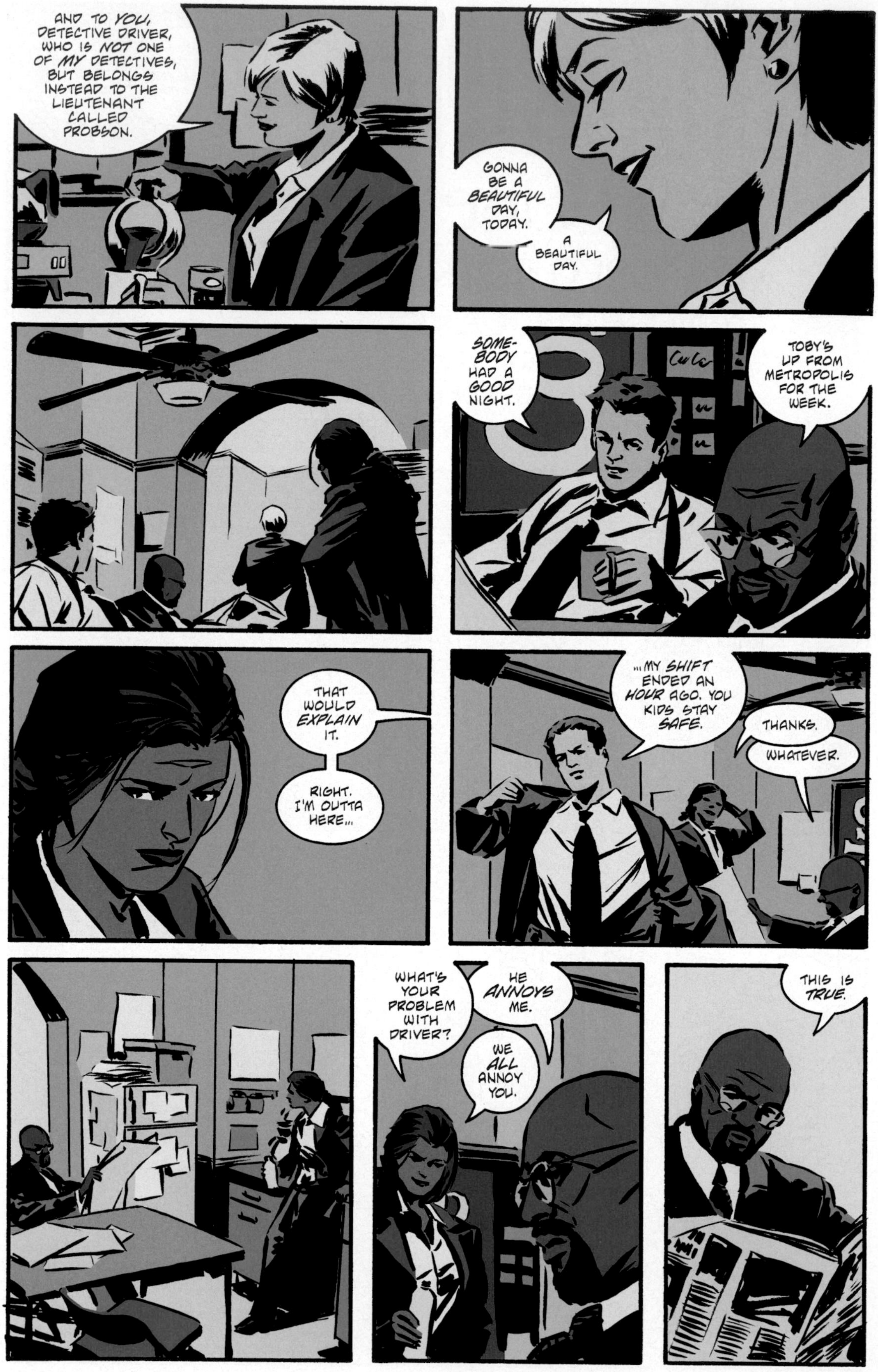
AND TO YOU, DETECTIVE DRIVER, WHO IS NOT ONE OF MY DETECTIVES, BUT BELONGS INSTEAD TO THE LIEUTENANT CALLED PROBSON.
GONNA BE A BEAUTIFUL DAY, TODAY.
A BEAUTIFUL DAY.
SOME-BODY HAD A GOOD NIGHT.
TOBY'S UP FROM METROPOLIS FOR THE WEEK.
THAT WOULD EXPLAIN IT.
RIGHT. I'M OUTTA HERE...
...MY SHIFT ENDED AN HOUR AGO. YOU KIDS STAY SAFE.
THANKS.
WHATEVER.
WHAT'S YOUR PROBLEM WITH DRIVER?
HE ANNOYS ME.
WE ALL ANNOY YOU.
THIS IS TRUE.

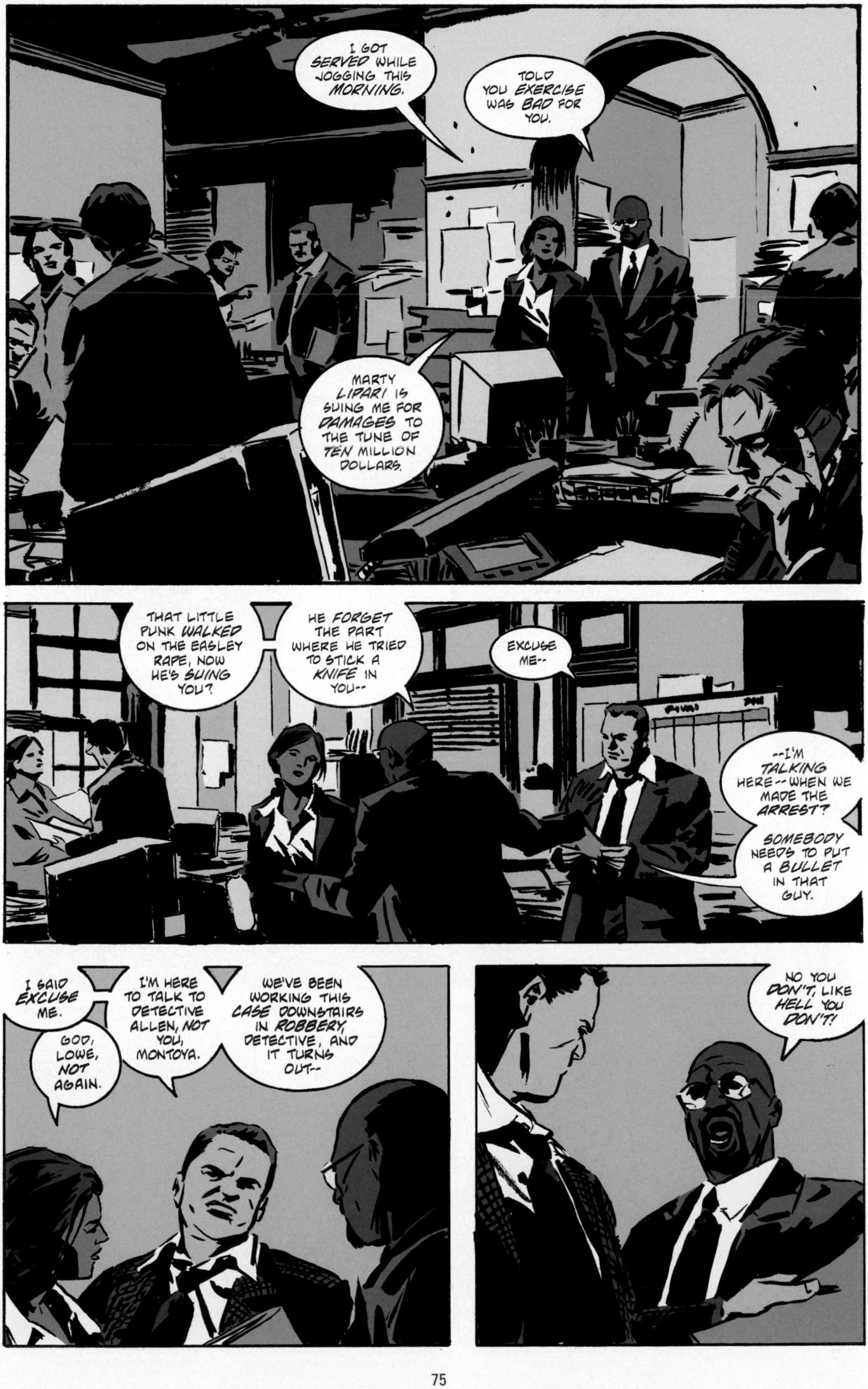
I GOT SERVED WHILE JOGGING THIS MORNING.
TOLD YOU EXERCISE WAS BAD FOR YOU.
MARTY LIPARI IS SUING ME FOR DAMAGES TO THE TUNE OF TEN MILLION DOLLARS.
THAT LITTLE PUNK WALKED ON THE EASLEY RAPE, NOW HE'S SUING YOU?
HE FORGET THE PART WHERE HE TRIED TO STICK A KNIFE IN YOU--
EXCUSE ME--
--I'M TALKING HERE--WHEN WE MADE THE ARREST?
SOMEBODY NEEDS TO PUT A BULLET IN THAT GUY.
I SAID EXCUSE ME.
GOD, LOWE, NOT AGAIN.
I'M HERE TO TALK TO DETECTIVE ALLEN, NOT YOU, MONTOYA.
WE'VE BEEN WORKING THIS CASE DOWNSTAIRS IN ROBBERY, DETECTIVE, AND IT TURNS OUT--
NO YOU DON'T, LIKE HELL YOU DON'T!

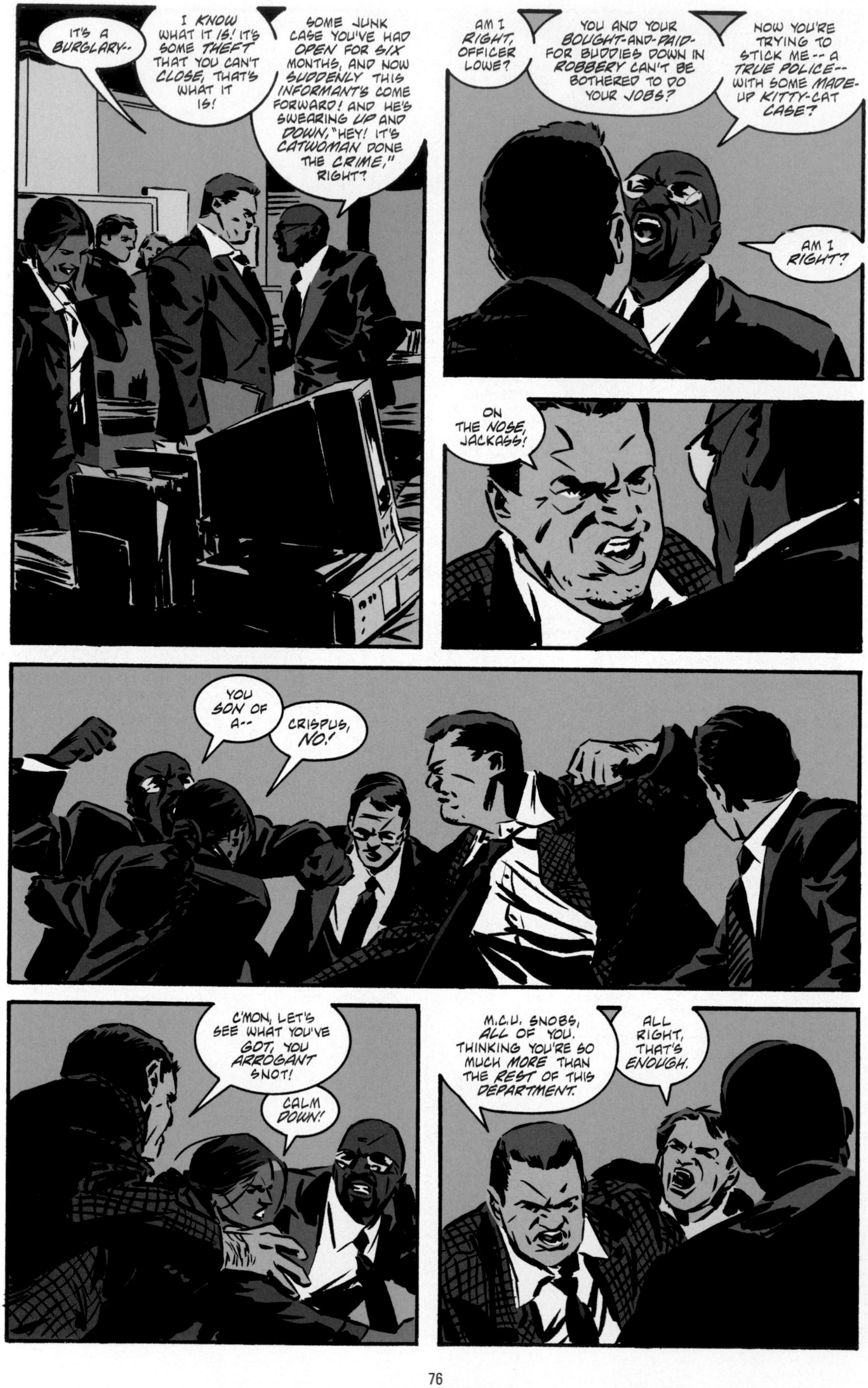
IT'S A BURGLARY--
I KNOW WHAT IT IS! IT'S SOME THEFT THAT YOU CAN'T CLOSE, THAT'S WHAT IT IS!
SOME JUNK CASE YOU'VE HAD OPEN FOR SIX MONTHS, AND NOW SUDDENLY THIS INFORMANT'S COME FORWARD! AND HE'S SWEARING UP AND DOWN, "HEY! IT'S CATWOMAN DONE THE CRIME," RIGHT?
AM I RIGHT, OFFICER LOWE?
YOU AND YOUR BOUGHT-AND-PAID-FOR BUDDIES DOWN IN ROBBERY CAN'T BE BOTHERED TO DO YOUR JOBS?
NOW YOU'RE TRYING TO STICK ME-- A TRUE POLICE-- WITH SOME MADE-UP KITTY-CAT CASE?
AM I RIGHT?
ON THE NOSE, JACKASS!
YOU SON OF A--
CRISPUS, NO!
C'MON, LET'S SEE WHAT YOU'VE GOT, YOU ARROGANT SNOT!
CALM DOWN!
M.C.U. SNOBS, ALL OF YOU. THINKING YOU'RE SO MUCH MORE THAN THE REST OF THIS DEPARTMENT.
ALL RIGHT, THAT'S ENOUGH.

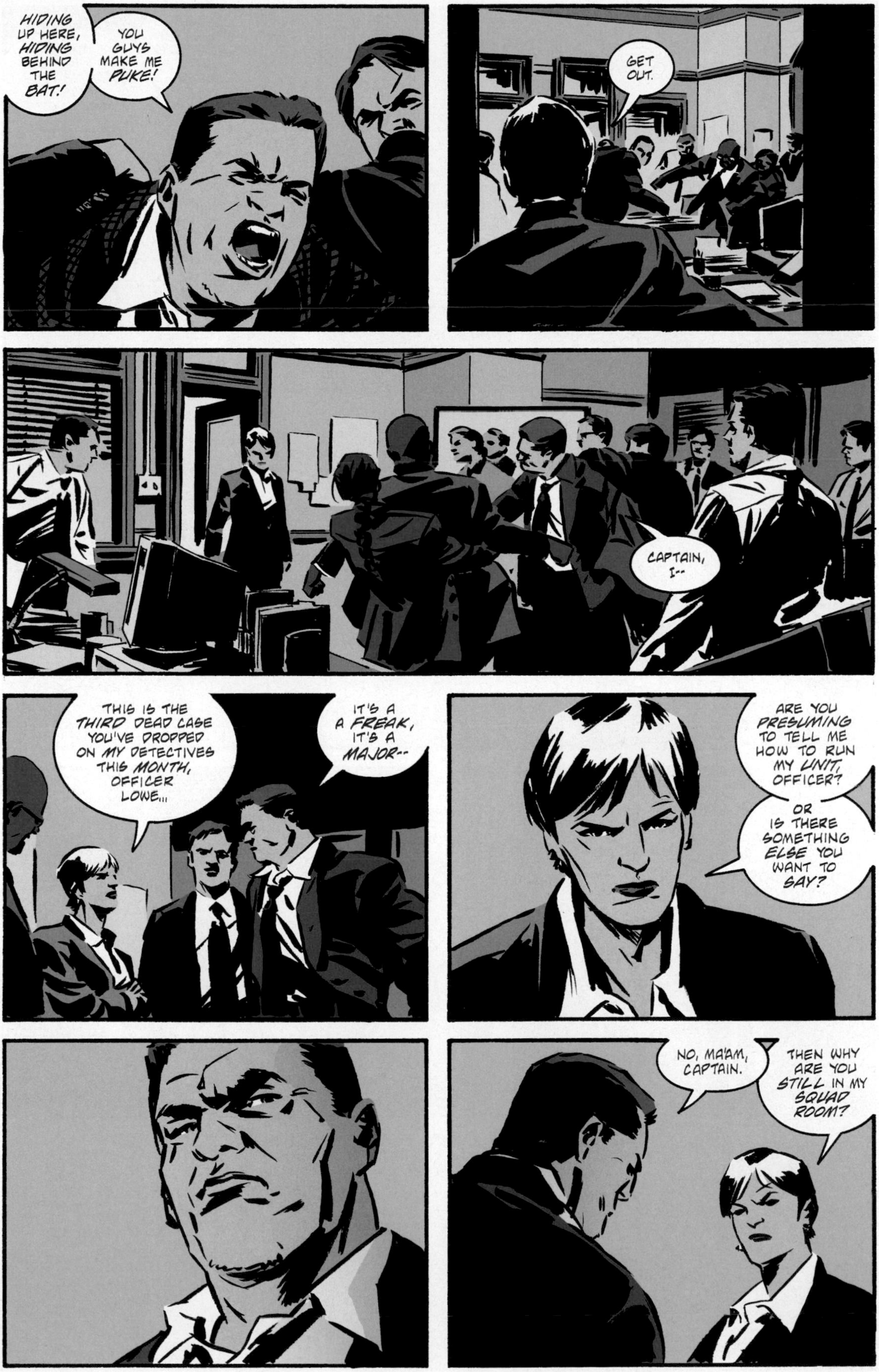
HIDING UP HERE, HIDING BEHIND THE BAT!
YOU GUYS MAKE ME PUKE!
GET OUT.
CAPTAIN, I--
THIS IS THE THIRD DEAD CASE YOU'VE DROPPED ON MY DETECTIVES THIS MONTH, OFFICER LOWE...
IT'S A FREAK, IT'S A MAJOR--
ARE YOU PRESUMING TO TELL ME HOW TO RUN MY UNIT, OFFICER?
OR IS THERE SOMETHING ELSE YOU WANT TO SAY?
NO, MA'AM, CAPTAIN.
THEN WHY ARE YOU STILL IN MY SQUAD ROOM?

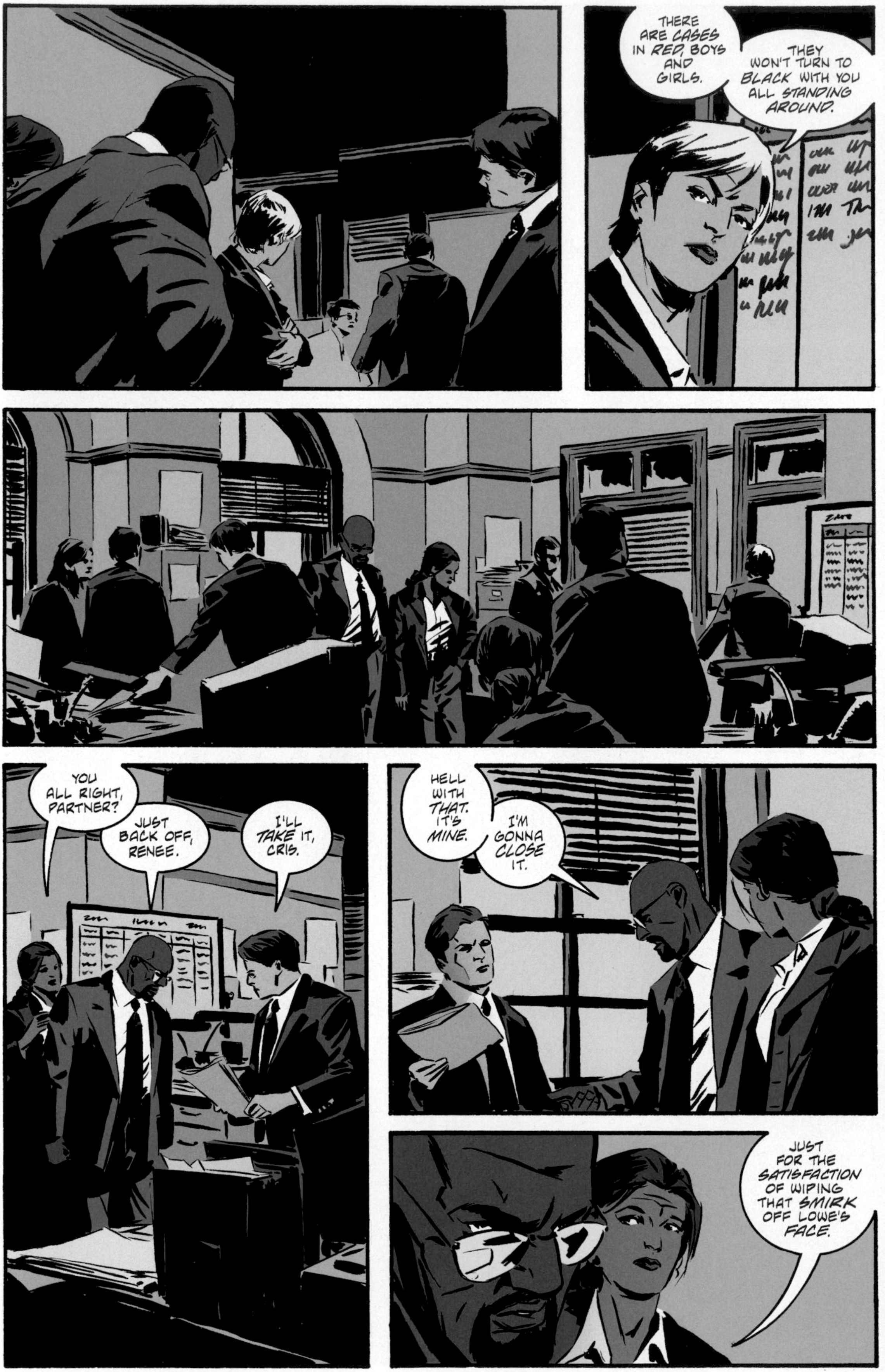
THERE ARE CASES IN RED, BOYS AND GIRLS.
THEY WON'T TURN TO BLACK WITH YOU ALL STANDING AROUND.
YOU ALL RIGHT, PARTNER?
JUST BACK OFF, RENEE.
I'LL TAKE IT, CRIS.
HELL WITH THAT. IT'S MINE.
I'M GONNA CLOSE IT.
JUST FOR THE SATISFACTION OF WIPING THAT SMIRK OFF LOWE'S FACE.

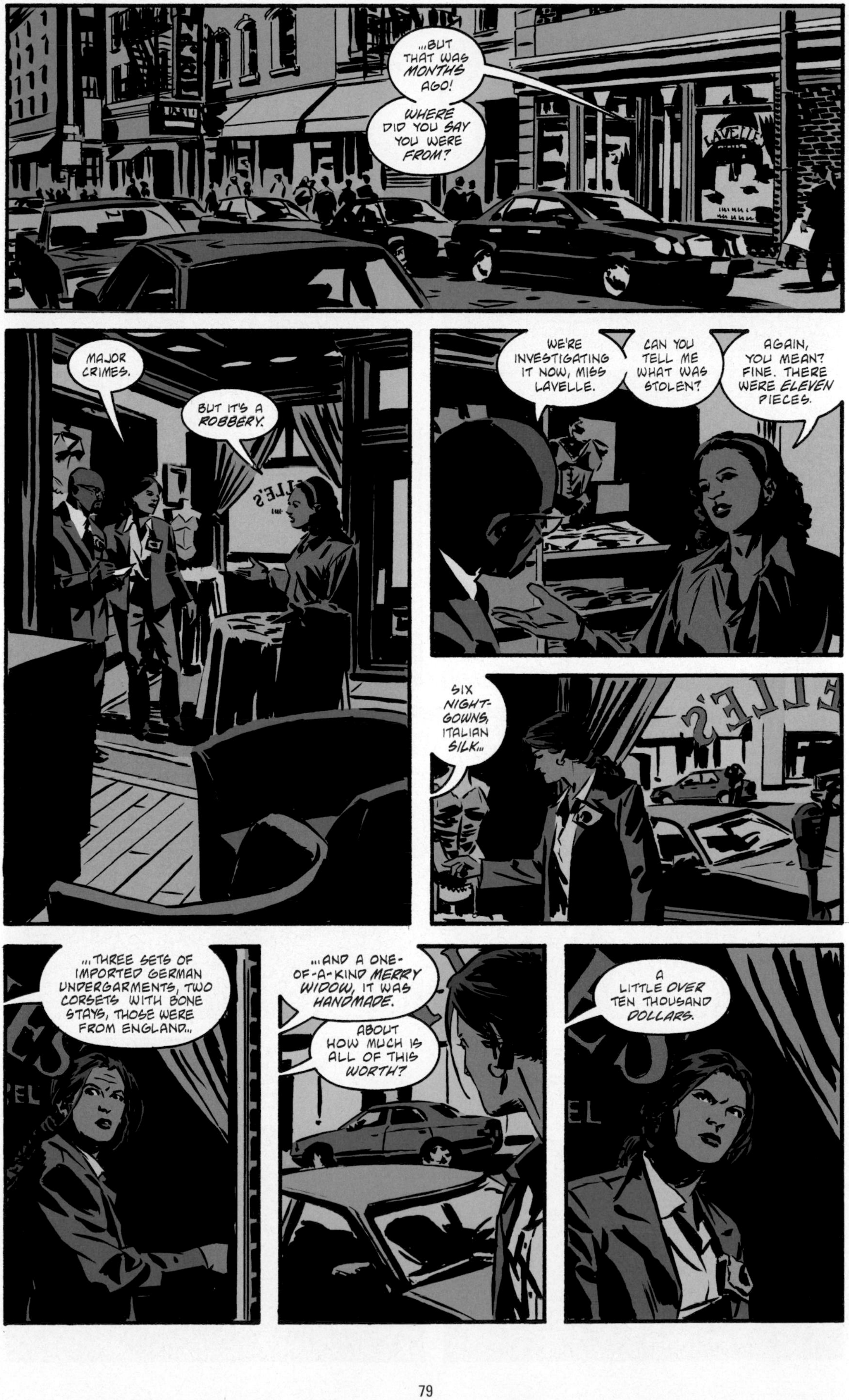
...BUT THAT WAS MONTHS AGO!
WHERE DID YOU SAY YOU WERE FROM?
MAJOR CRIMES.
BUT IT'S A ROBBERY.
WE'RE INVESTIGATING IT NOW, MISS LAVELLE.
CAN YOU TELL ME WHAT WAS STOLEN?
AGAIN, YOU MEAN? FINE. THERE WERE ELEVEN PIECES.
SIX NIGHT-GOWNS, ITALIAN SILK...
...THREE SETS OF IMPORTED GERMAN UNDERGARMENTS, TWO CORSETS WITH BONE STAYS, THOSE WERE FROM ENGLAND...
...AND A ONE-OF-A-KIND MERRY WIDOW, IT WAS HANDMADE.
ABOUT HOW MUCH IS ALL OF THIS WORTH?
A LITTLE OVER TEN THOUSAND DOLLARS.

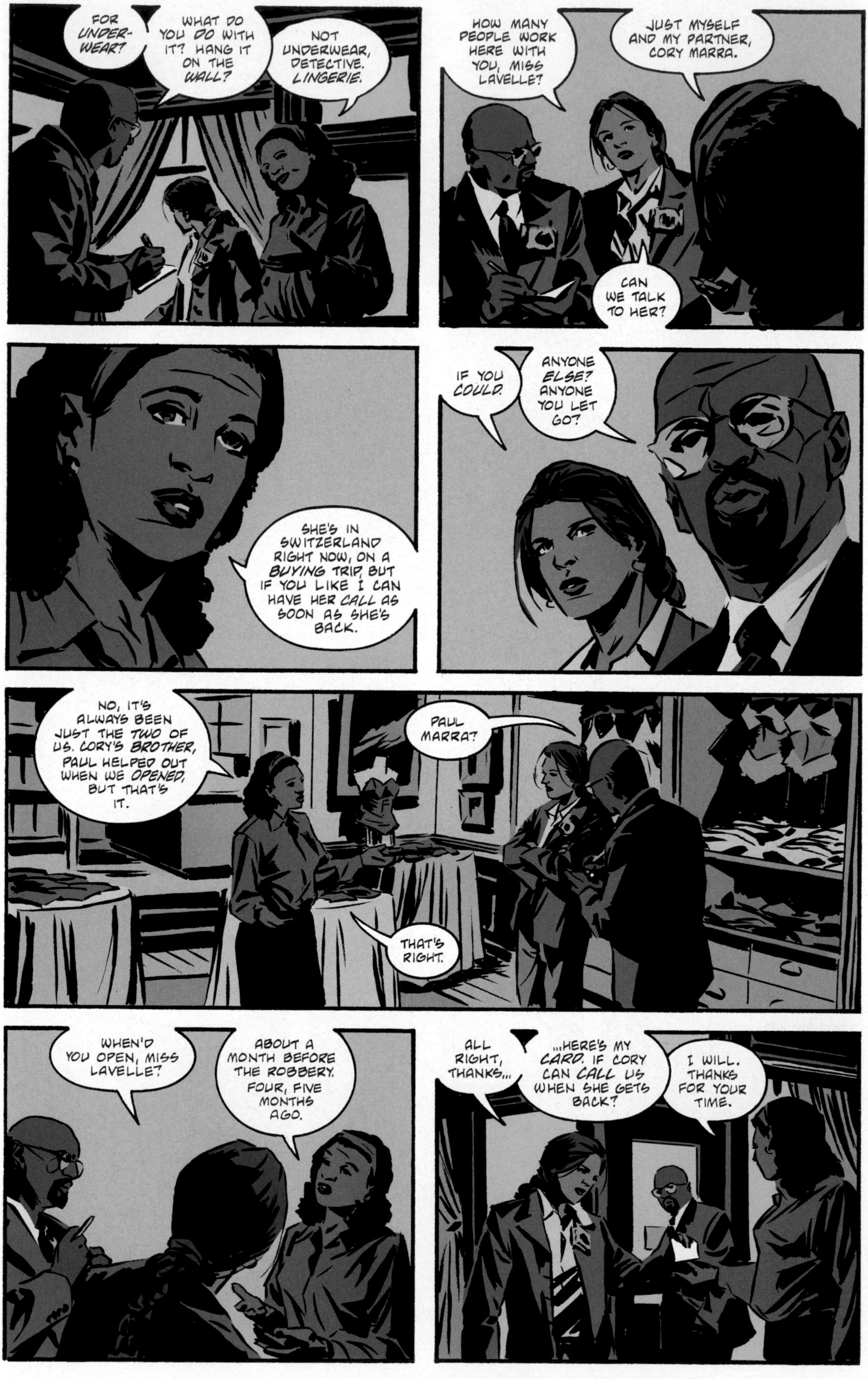
FOR UNDER-WEAR?
WHAT DO YOU DO WITH IT? HANG IT ON THE WALL?
NOT UNDERWEAR, DETECTIVE. LINGERIE.
HOW MANY PEOPLE WORK HERE WITH YOU, MISS LAVELLE?
JUST MYSELF AND MY PARTNER, CORY MARRA.
CAN WE TALK TO HER?
SHE'S IN SWITZERLAND RIGHT NOW, ON A BUYING TRIP, BUT IF YOU LIKE I CAN HAVE HER CALL AS SOON AS SHE'S BACK.
IF YOU COULD.
ANYONE ELSE? ANYONE YOU LET GO?
NO, IT'S ALWAYS BEEN JUST THE TWO OF US. CORY'S BROTHER, PAUL HELPED OUT WHEN WE OPENED, BUT THAT'S IT.
PAUL MARRA?
THAT'S RIGHT.
WHEN'D YOU OPEN, MISS LAVELLE?
ABOUT A MONTH BEFORE THE ROBBERY. FOUR, FIVE MONTHS AGO.
ALL RIGHT, THANKS...
...HERE'S MY CARD. IF CORY CAN CALL US WHEN SHE GETS BACK?
I WILL. THANKS FOR YOUR TIME.

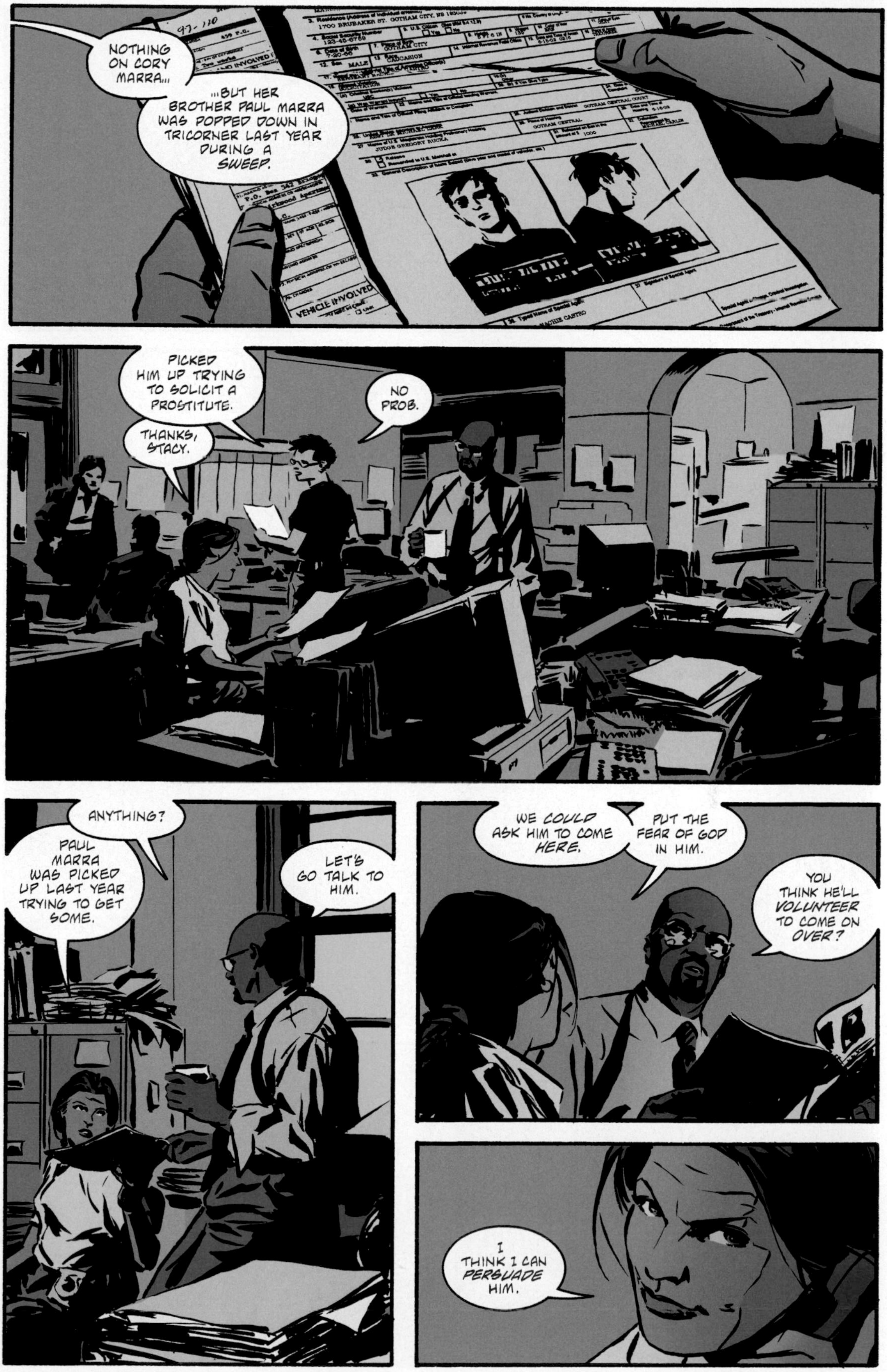
NOTHING ON CORY MARRA...
...BUT HER BROTHER PAUL MARRA WAS POPPED DOWN IN TRICORNER LAST YEAR DURING A SWEEP.
PICKED HIM UP TRYING TO SOLICIT A PROSTITUTE.
THANKS, STACY.
NO PROB.
ANYTHING?
PAUL MARRA WAS PICKED UP LAST YEAR TRYING TO GET SOME.
LET'S GO TALK TO HIM.
WE COULD ASK HIM TO COME HERE.
PUT THE FEAR OF GOD IN HIM.
YOU THINK HE'LL VOLUNTEER TO COME ON OVER?
I THINK I CAN PERSUADE HIM.

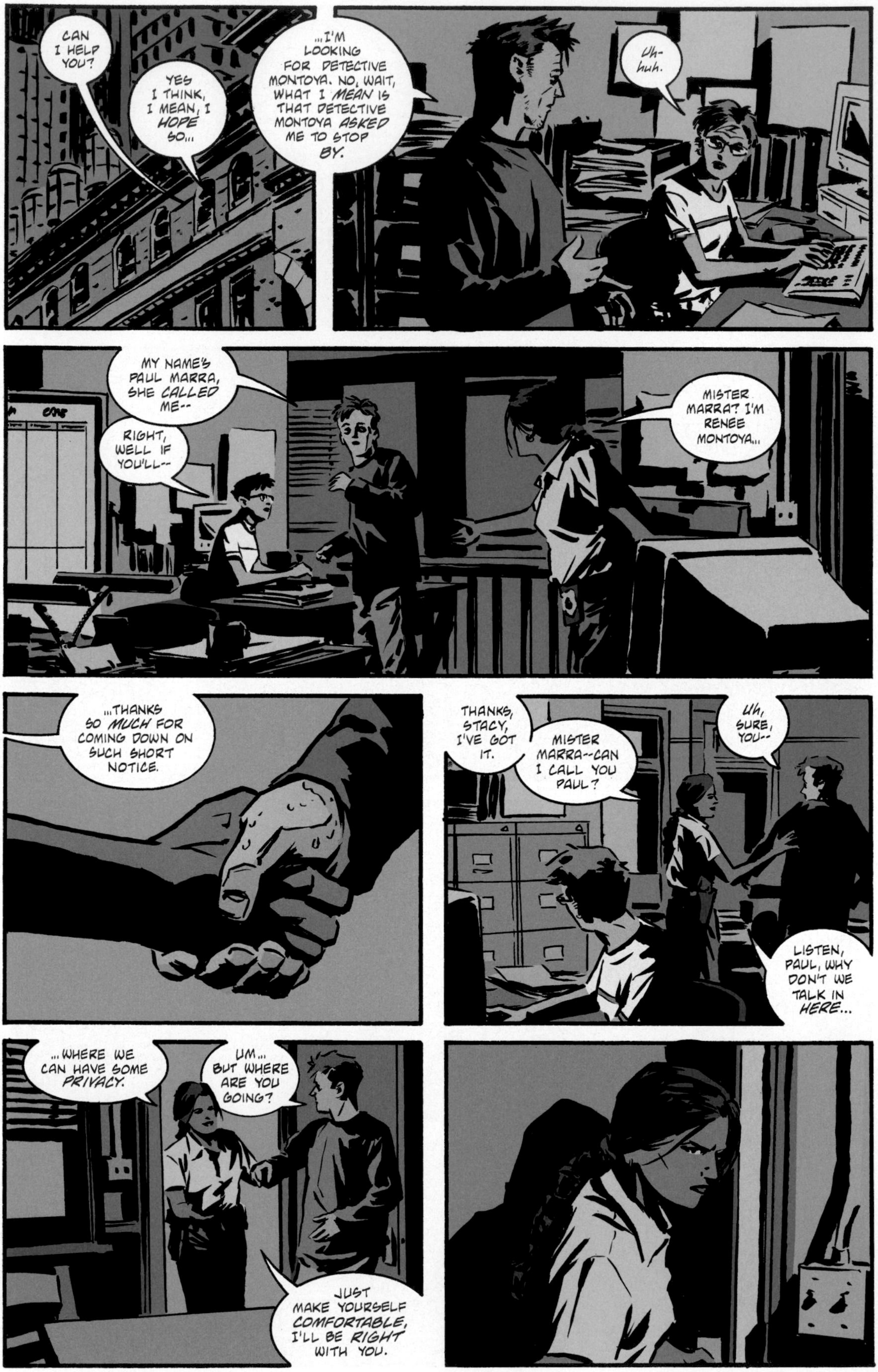
CAN I HELP YOU?
YES I THINK, I MEAN, I HOPE SO...
...I'M LOOKING FOR DETECTIVE MONTOYA. NO, WAIT, WHAT I MEAN IS THAT DETECTIVE MONTOYA ASKED ME TO STOP BY.
Uh-huh.
MY NAME'S PAUL MARRA, SHE CALLED ME--
RIGHT, WELL IF YOU'LL--
MISTER MARRA? I'M RENEE MONTOYA...
...THANKS SO MUCH FOR COMING DOWN ON SUCH SHORT NOTICE.
THANKS, STACY, I'VE GOT IT.
Uh, SURE, YOU--
MISTER MARRA--CAN I CALL YOU PAUL?
LISTEN, PAUL, WHY DON'T WE TALK IN HERE...
...WHERE WE CAN HAVE SOME PRIVACY.
UM... BUT WHERE ARE YOU GOING?
JUST MAKE YOURSELF COMFORTABLE, I'LL BE RIGHT WITH YOU.

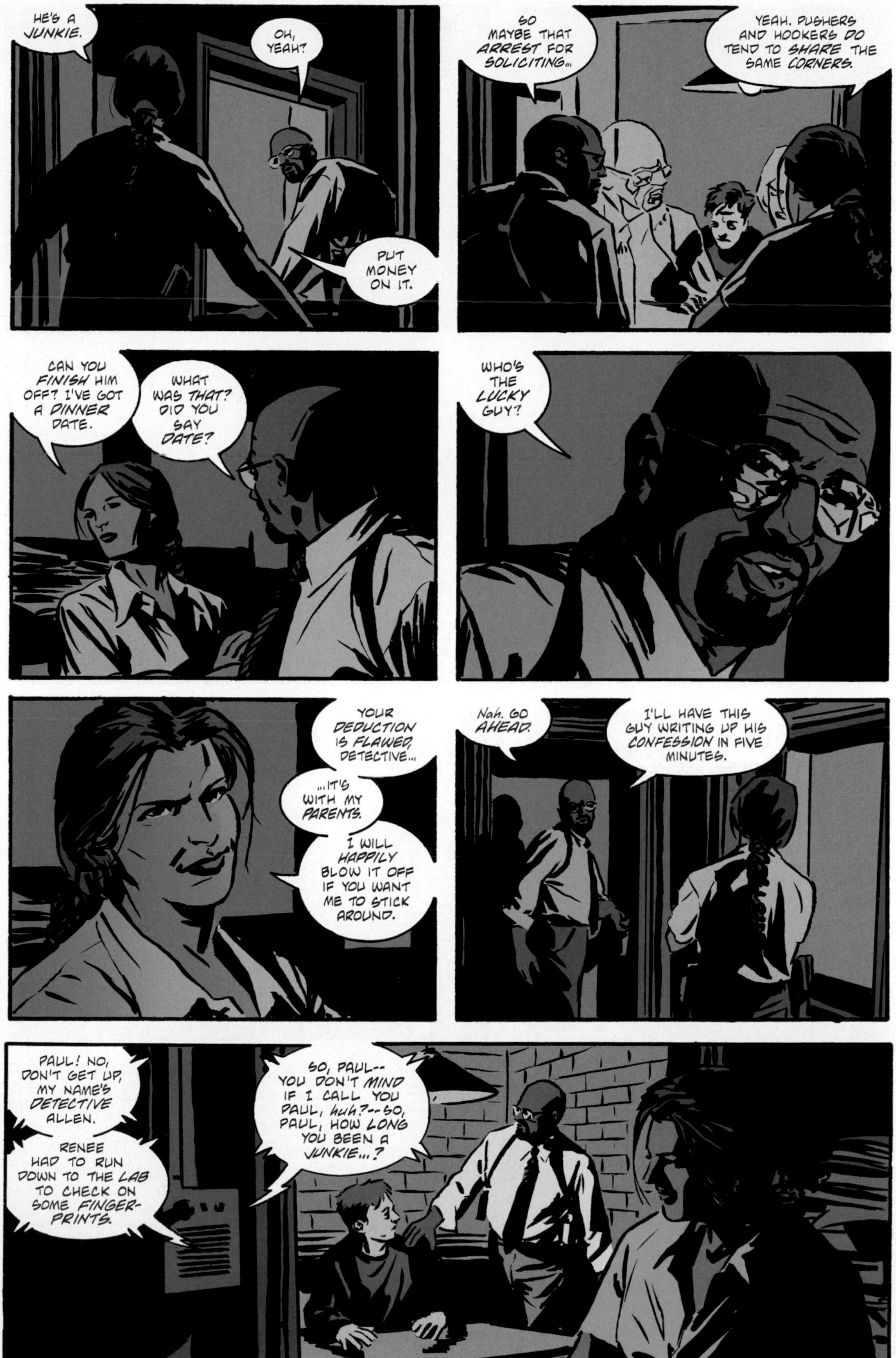

HE'S A JUNKIE.
OH, YEAH?
PUT MONEY ON IT.
SO MAYBE THAT ARREST FOR SOLICITING...
YEAH. PUSHERS AND HOOKERS DO TEND TO SHARE THE SAME CORNERS.
CAN YOU FINISH HIM OFF? I'VE GOT A DINNER DATE.
WHAT WAS THAT? DID YOU SAY DATE?
WHO'S THE LUCKY GUY?
YOUR DEDUCTION IS FLAWED, DETECTIVE...
...IT'S WITH MY PARENTS.
I WILL HAPPILY BLOW IT OFF IF YOU WANT ME TO STICK AROUND.
Nah. GO AHEAD.
I'LL HAVE THIS GUY WRITING UP HIS CONFESSION IN FIVE MINUTES.
PAUL! NO, DON'T GET UP, MY NAME'S DETECTIVE ALLEN.
RENEE HAD TO RUN DOWN TO THE LAB TO CHECK ON SOME FINGER-PRINTS.
SO, PAUL-- YOU DON'T MIND IF I CALL YOU PAUL, huh?-- SO, PAUL, HOW LONG YOU BEEN A JUNKIE...?

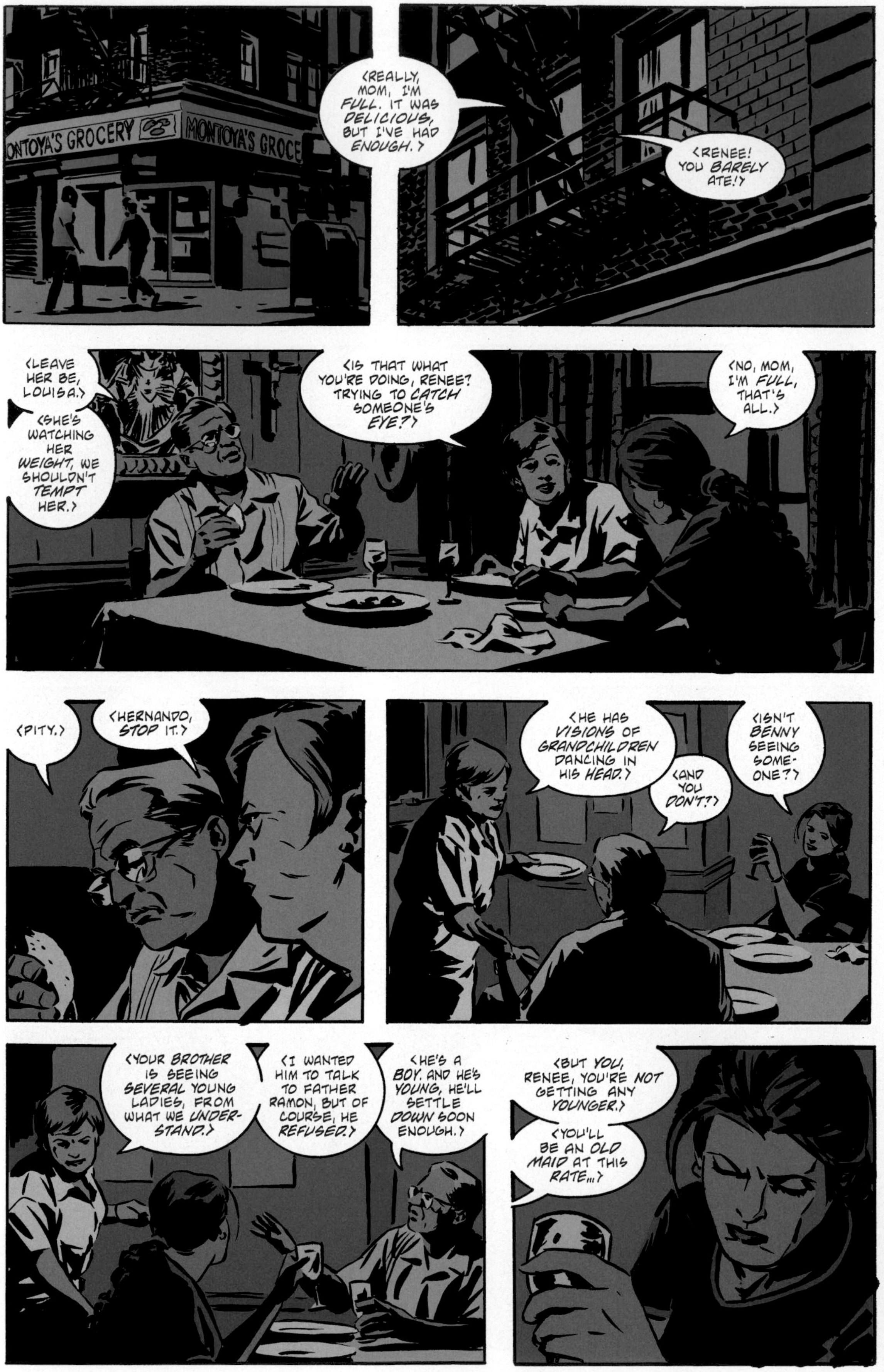
MONTOYA'S GROCERY
MONTOYA'S GROCE
<REALLY, MOM, I'M FULL. IT WAS DELICIOUS, BUT I'VE HAD ENOUGH.>
<RENEE! YOU BARELY ATE!>
<LEAVE HER BE, LOUISA.>
<SHE'S WATCHING HER WEIGHT, WE SHOULDN'T TEMPT HER.>
<IS THAT WHAT YOU'RE DOING, RENEE? TRYING TO CATCH SOMEONE'S EYE?>
<NO, MOM, I'M FULL, THAT'S ALL.>
<PITY.>
<HERNANDO, STOP IT.>
<HE HAS VISIONS OF GRANDCHILDREN DANCING IN HIS HEAD.>
<AND YOU DON'T?>
<ISN'T BENNY SEEING SOME-ONE?>
<YOUR BROTHER IS SEEING SEVERAL YOUNG LADIES, FROM WHAT WE UNDER-STAND.>
<I WANTED HIM TO TALK TO FATHER RAMON, BUT OF COURSE, HE REFUSED.>
<HE'S A BOY. AND HE'S YOUNG, HE'LL SETTLE DOWN SOON ENOUGH.>
<BUT YOU, RENEE, YOU'RE NOT GETTING ANY YOUNGER.>
<YOU'LL BE AN OLD MAID AT THIS RATE...>

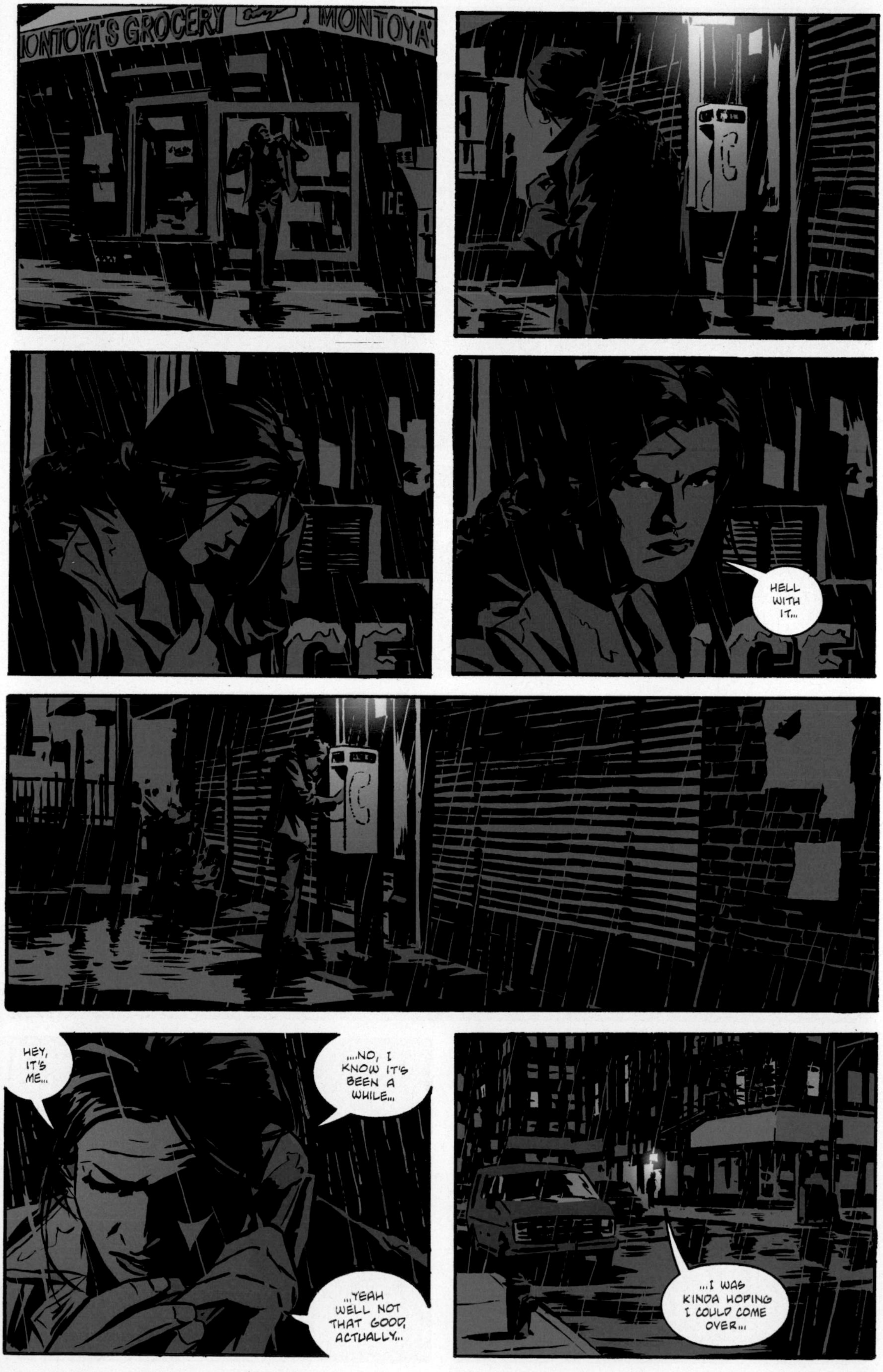
MONTOYA'S GROCERY
MONTOYA'S
ICE
HELL WITH IT...
HEY, IT'S ME...
...NO, I KNOW IT'S BEEN A WHILE...
...YEAH WELL NOT THAT GOOD, ACTUALLY...
...I WAS KINDA HOPING I COULD COME OVER...

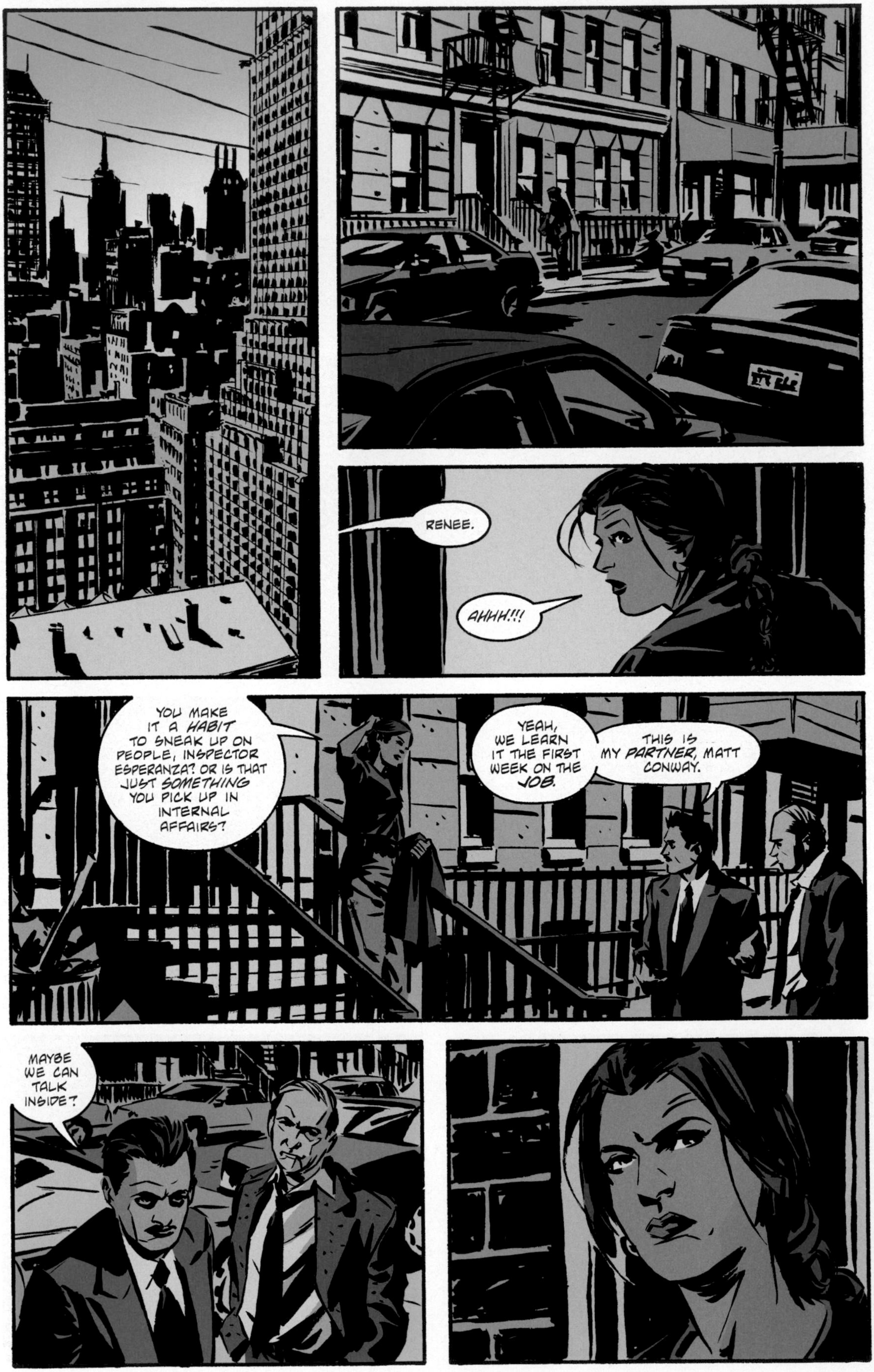
RENEE.
AHHH!!!
YOU MAKE IT A HABIT TO SNEAK UP ON PEOPLE, INSPECTOR ESPERANZA? OR IS THAT JUST SOMETHING YOU PICK UP IN INTERNAL AFFAIRS?
YEAH, WE LEARN IT THE FIRST WEEK ON THE JOB.
THIS IS MY PARTNER, MATT CONWAY.
MAYBE WE CAN TALK INSIDE?

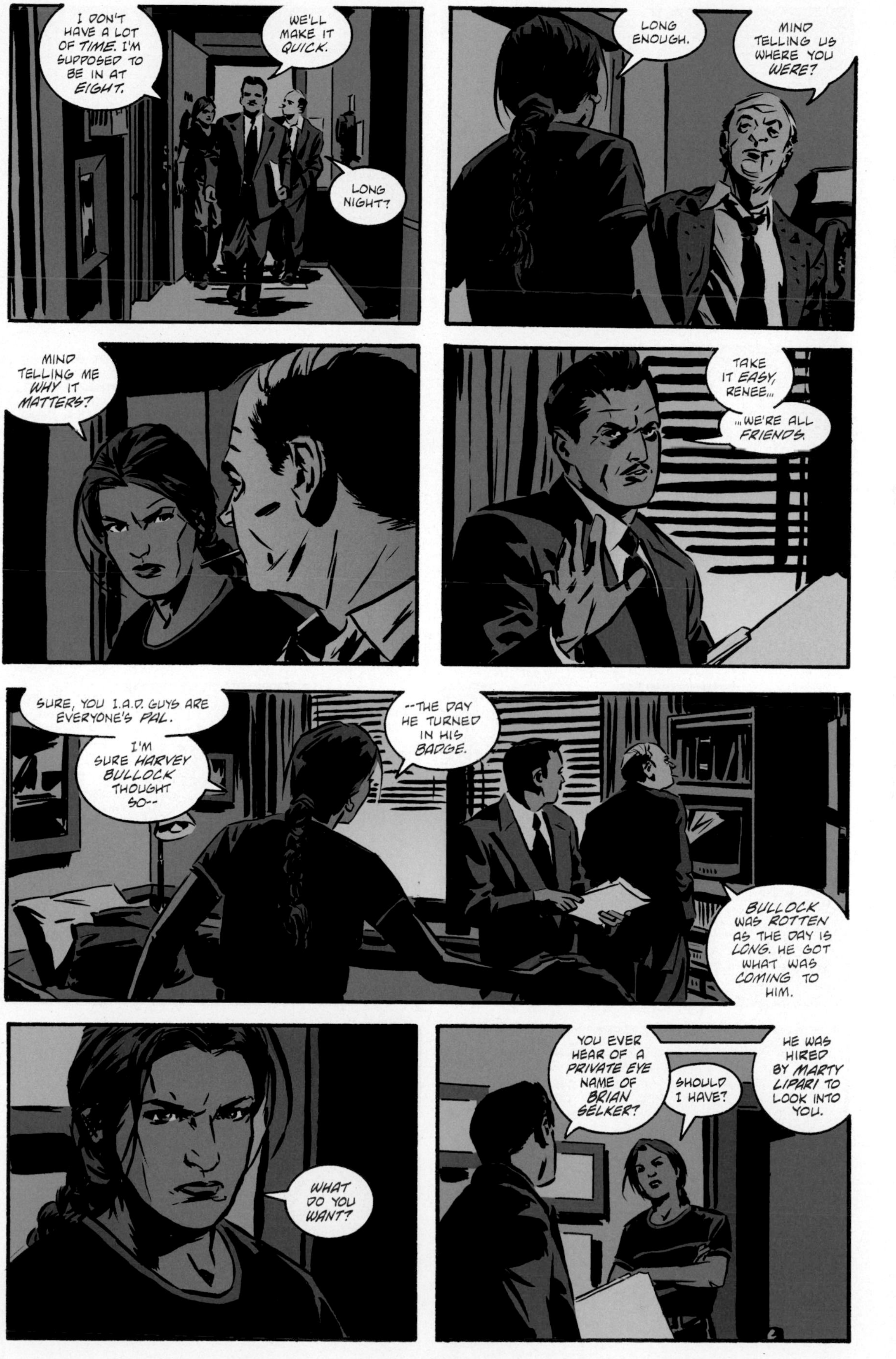
I DON'T HAVE A LOT OF TIME. I'M SUPPOSED TO BE IN AT EIGHT.
WE'LL MAKE IT QUICK.
LONG NIGHT?
LONG ENOUGH.
MIND TELLING US WHERE YOU WERE?
MIND TELLING ME WHY IT MATTERS?
TAKE IT EASY, RENEE...
...WE'RE ALL FRIENDS.
SURE, YOU I.A.D. GUYS ARE EVERYONE'S PAL.
I'M SURE HARVEY BULLOCK THOUGHT SO--
--THE DAY HE TURNED IN HIS BADGE.
BULLOCK WAS ROTTEN AS THE DAY IS LONG. HE GOT WHAT WAS COMING TO HIM.
WHAT DO YOU WANT?
YOU EVER HEAR OF A PRIVATE EYE NAME OF BRIAN SELKER?
SHOULD I HAVE?
HE WAS HIRED BY MARTY LIPARI TO LOOK INTO YOU.

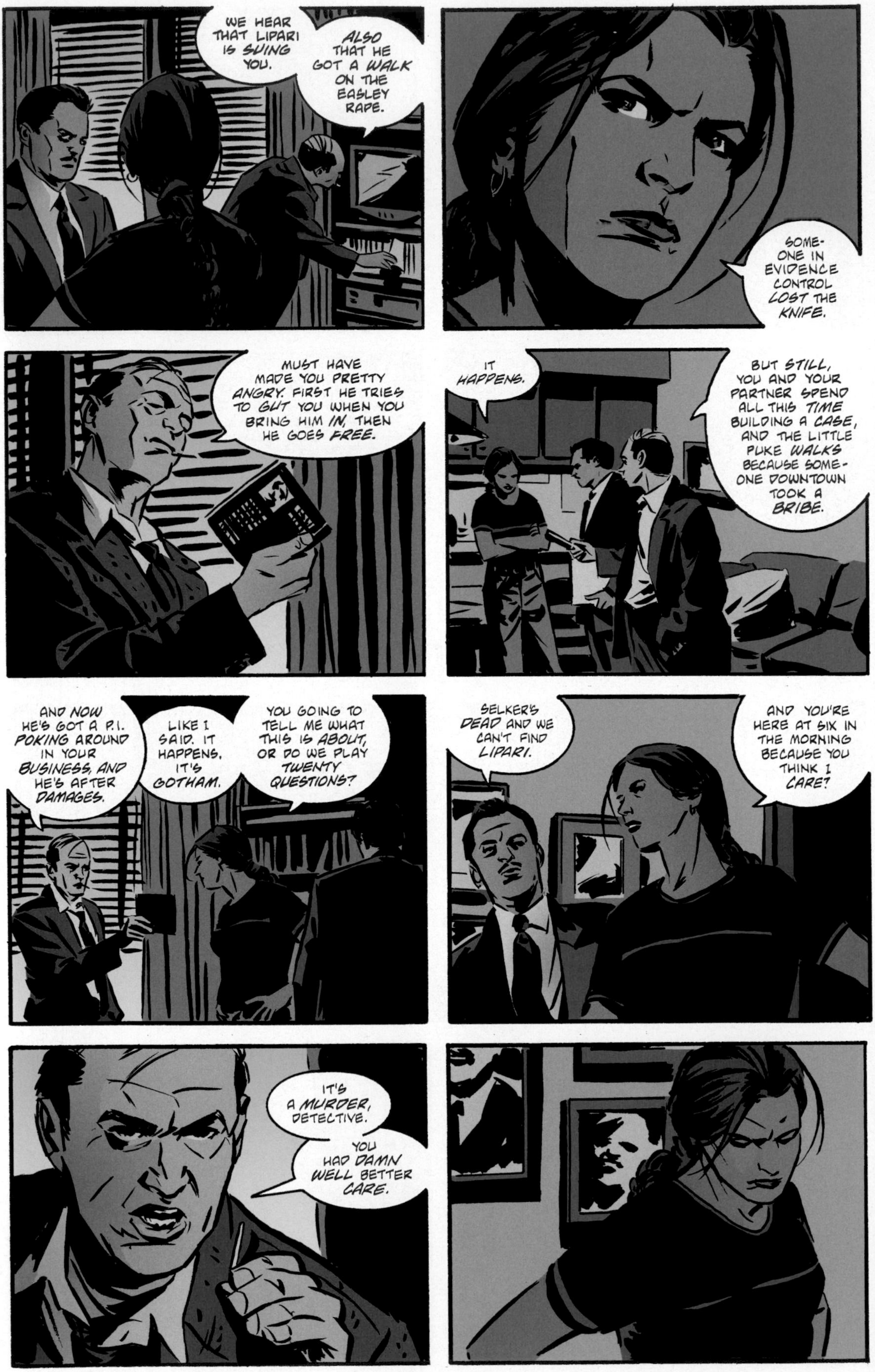
WE HEAR THAT LIPARI IS SUING YOU.
ALSO THAT HE GOT A WALK ON THE EASLEY RAPE.
SOME-ONE IN EVIDENCE CONTROL LOST THE KNIFE.
MUST HAVE MADE YOU PRETTY ANGRY. FIRST HE TRIES TO GUT YOU WHEN YOU BRING HIM IN, THEN HE GOES FREE.
IT HAPPENS.
BUT STILL, YOU AND YOUR PARTNER SPEND ALL THIS TIME BUILDING A CASE, AND THE LITTLE PUKE WALKS BECAUSE SOME-ONE DOWNTOWN TOOK A BRIBE.
AND NOW HE'S GOT A P.I. POKING AROUND IN YOUR BUSINESS, AND HE'S AFTER DAMAGES.
LIKE I SAID. IT HAPPENS. IT'S GOTHAM.
YOU GOING TO TELL ME WHAT THIS IS ABOUT, OR DO WE PLAY TWENTY QUESTIONS?
SELKER'S DEAD AND WE CAN'T FIND LIPARI.
AND YOU'RE HERE AT SIX IN THE MORNING BECAUSE YOU THINK I CARE?
IT'S A MURDER, DETECTIVE.
YOU HAD DAMN WELL BETTER CARE.

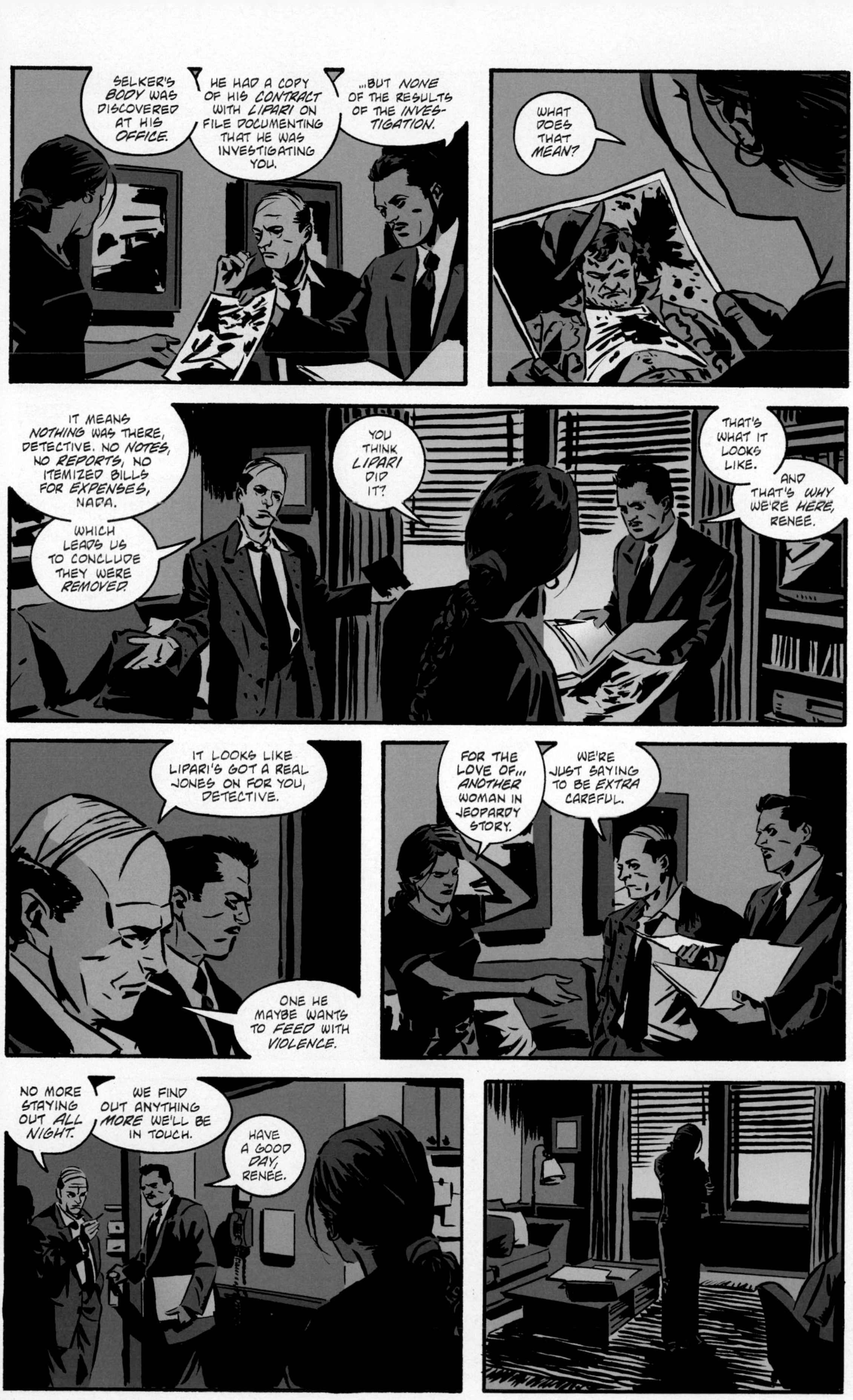
SELKER'S BODY WAS DISCOVERED AT HIS OFFICE.
HE HAD A COPY OF HIS CONTRACT WITH LIPARI ON FILE DOCUMENTING THAT HE WAS INVESTIGATING YOU.
...BUT NONE OF THE RESULTS OF THE INVESTIGATION.
WHAT DOES THAT MEAN?
IT MEANS NOTHING WAS THERE, DETECTIVE. NO NOTES, NO REPORTS, NO ITEMIZED BILLS FOR EXPENSES, NADA.
WHICH LEADS US TO CONCLUDE THEY WERE REMOVED.
YOU THINK LIPARI DID IT?
THAT'S WHAT IT LOOKS LIKE.
AND THAT'S WHY WE'RE HERE, RENEE.
IT LOOKS LIKE LIPARI'S GOT A REAL JONES ON FOR YOU, DETECTIVE.
ONE HE MAYBE WANTS TO FEED WITH VIOLENCE.
FOR THE LOVE OF... ANOTHER WOMAN IN JEOPARDY STORY.
WE'RE JUST SAYING TO BE EXTRA CAREFUL.
NO MORE STAYING OUT ALL NIGHT.
WE FIND OUT ANYTHING MORE WE'LL BE IN TOUCH.
HAVE A GOOD DAY, RENEE.

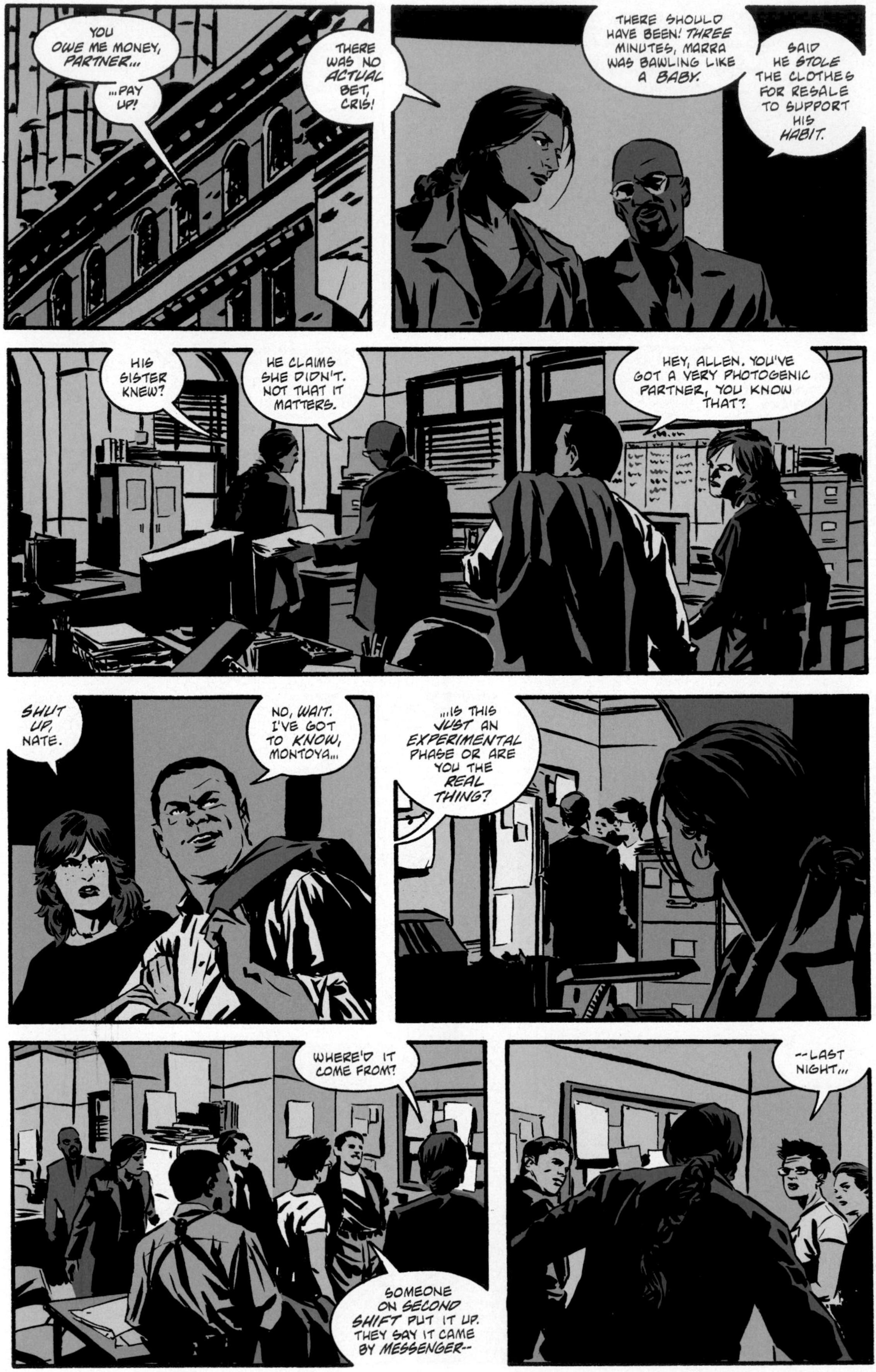

YOU OWE ME MONEY, PARTNER...
...PAY UP!
THERE WAS NO ACTUAL BET, CRIS!
THERE SHOULD HAVE BEEN! THREE MINUTES, MARRA WAS BAWLING LIKE A BABY.
SAID HE STOLE THE CLOTHES FOR RESALE TO SUPPORT HIS HABIT.
HIS SISTER KNEW?
HE CLAIMS SHE DIDN'T. NOT THAT IT MATTERS.
HEY, ALLEN. YOU'VE GOT A VERY PHOTOGENIC PARTNER, YOU KNOW THAT?
SHUT UP, NATE.
NO, WAIT. I'VE GOT TO KNOW, MONTOYA...
...IS THIS JUST AN EXPERIMENTAL PHASE OR ARE YOU THE REAL THING?
WHERE'D IT COME FROM?
SOMEONE ON SECOND SHIFT PUT IT UP. THEY SAY IT CAME BY MESSENGER--
--LAST NIGHT...

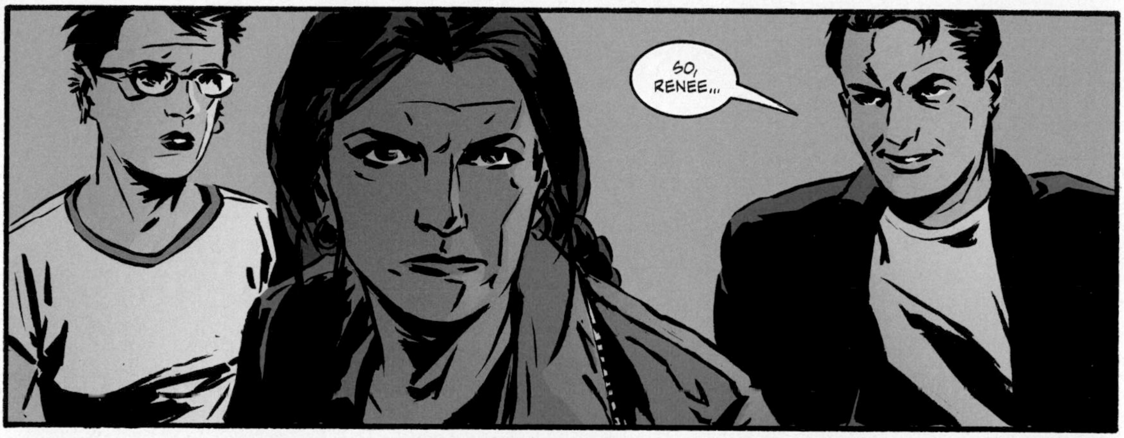
SO, RENEE...

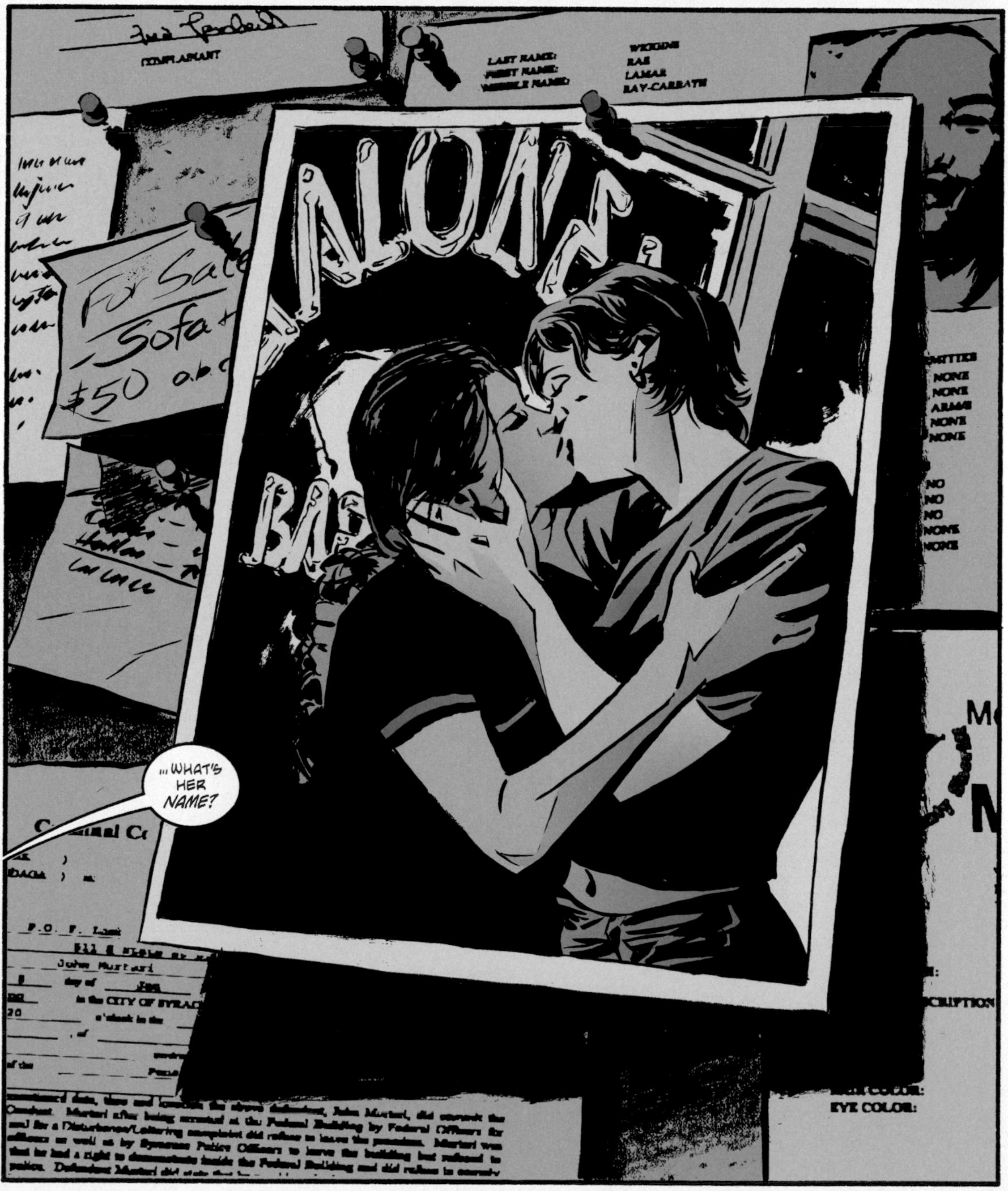
...WHAT'S HER NAME?

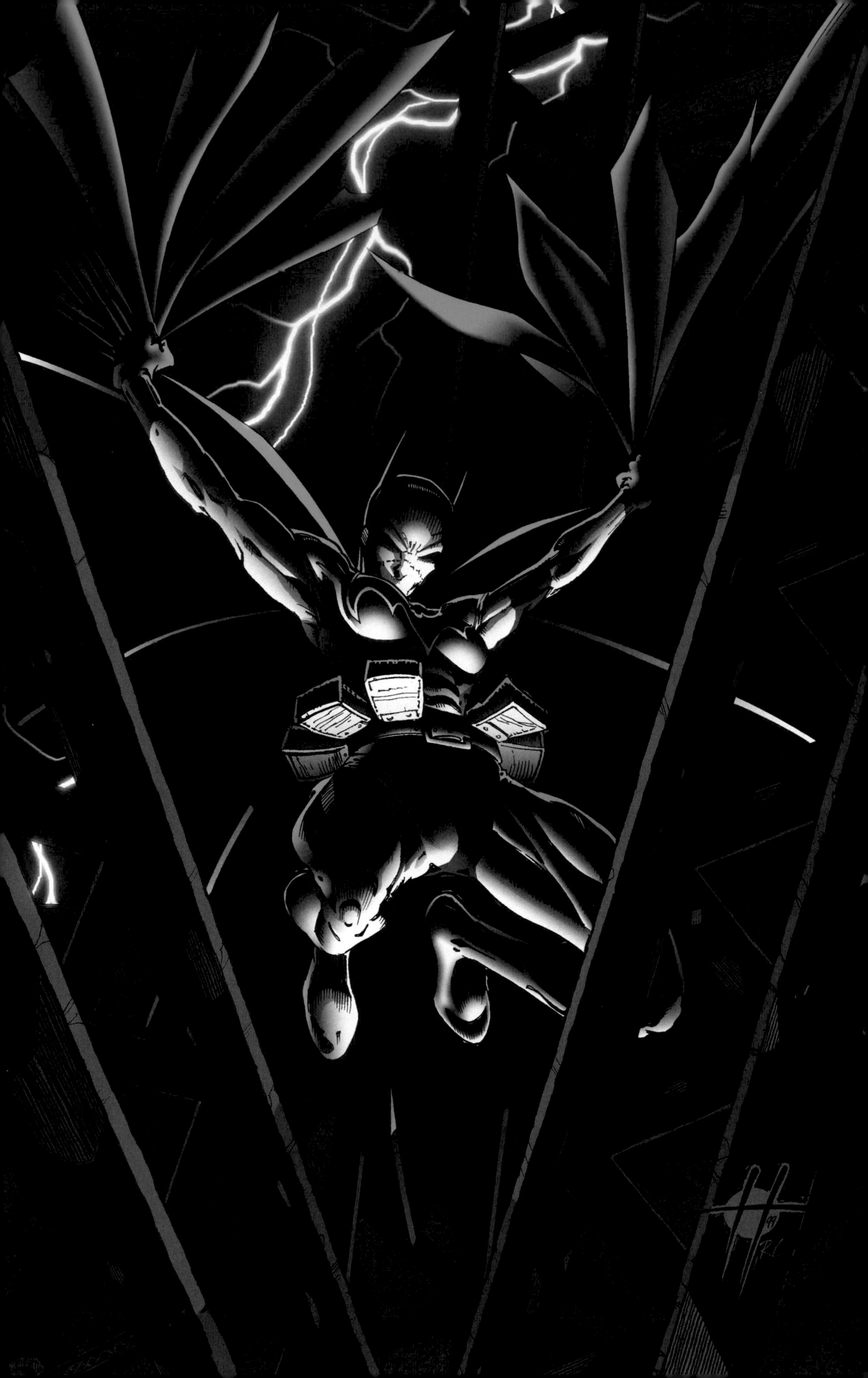

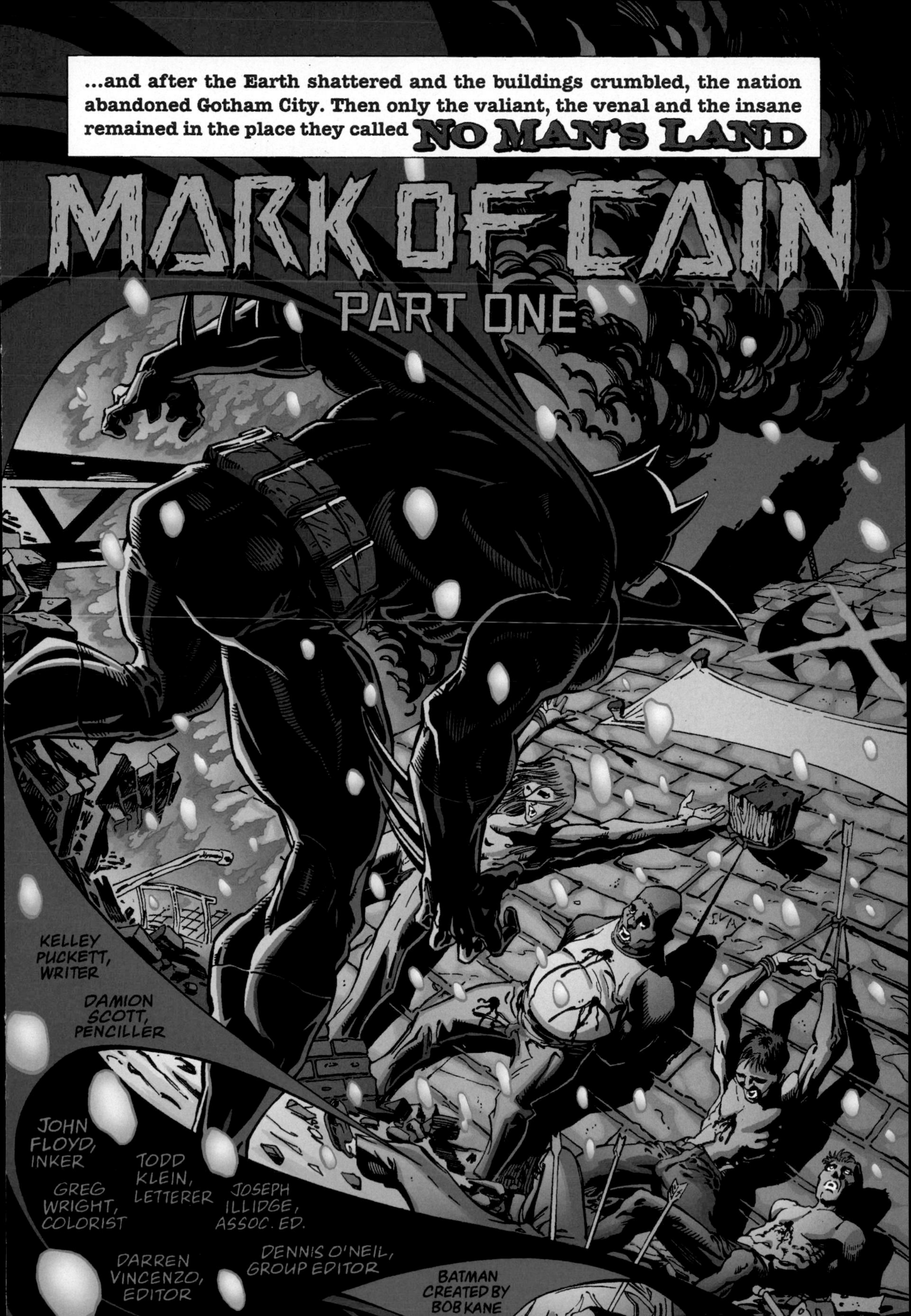
...and after the Earth shattered and the buildings crumbled, the nation abandoned Gotham City. Then only the valiant, the venal and the insane remained in the place they called NO MAN'S LAND
MARK OF CAIN
PART ONE
KELLEY PUCKETT, WRITER
DAMION SCOTT, PENCILLER
JOHN FLOYD, INKER
TODD KLEIN, LETTERER
GREG WRIGHT, COLORIST
JOSEPH ILLIDGE, ASSOC. ED.
DARREN VINCENZO, EDITOR
DENNIS O'NEIL, GROUP EDITOR
BATMAN CREATED BY BOB KANE

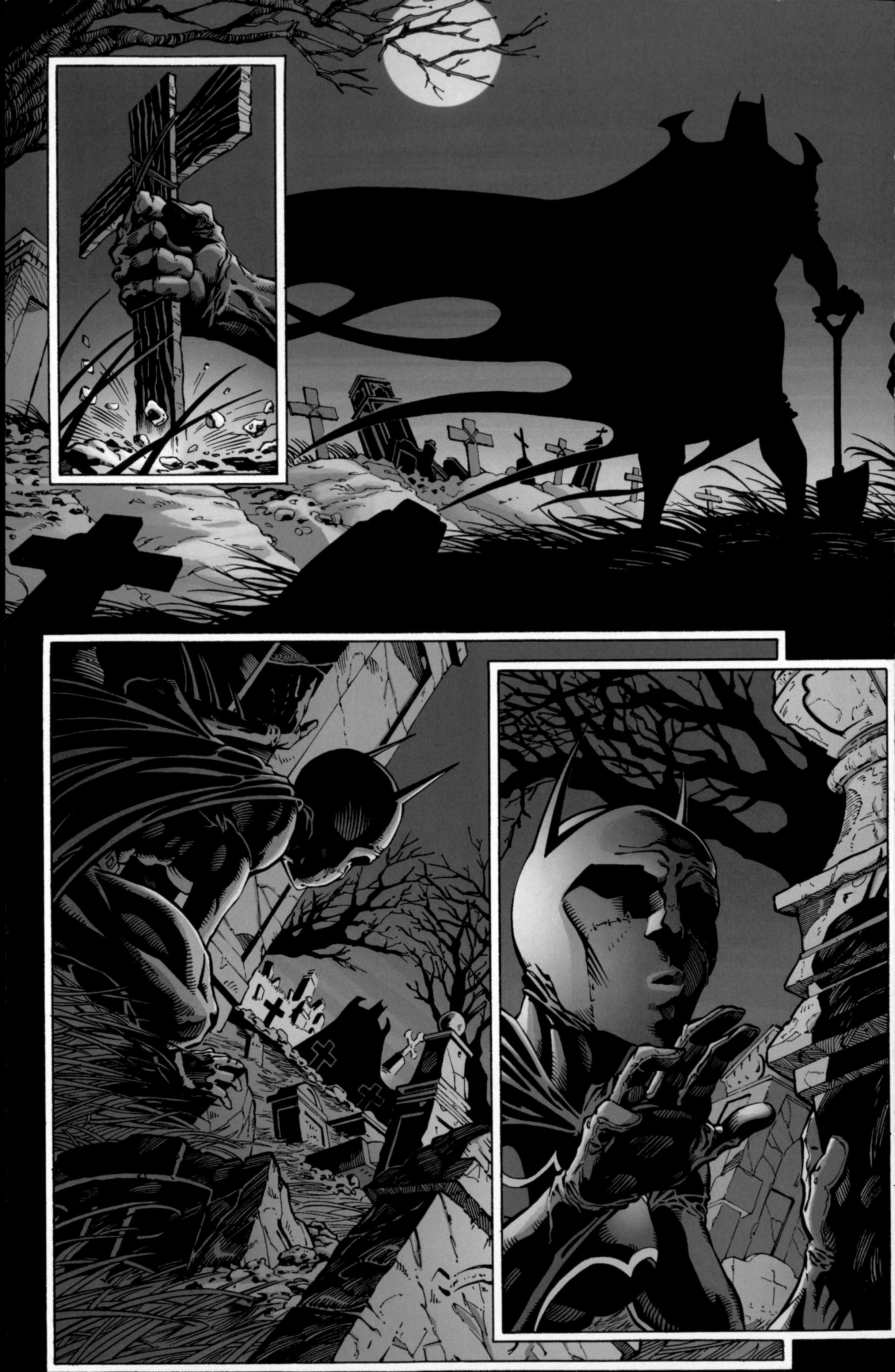

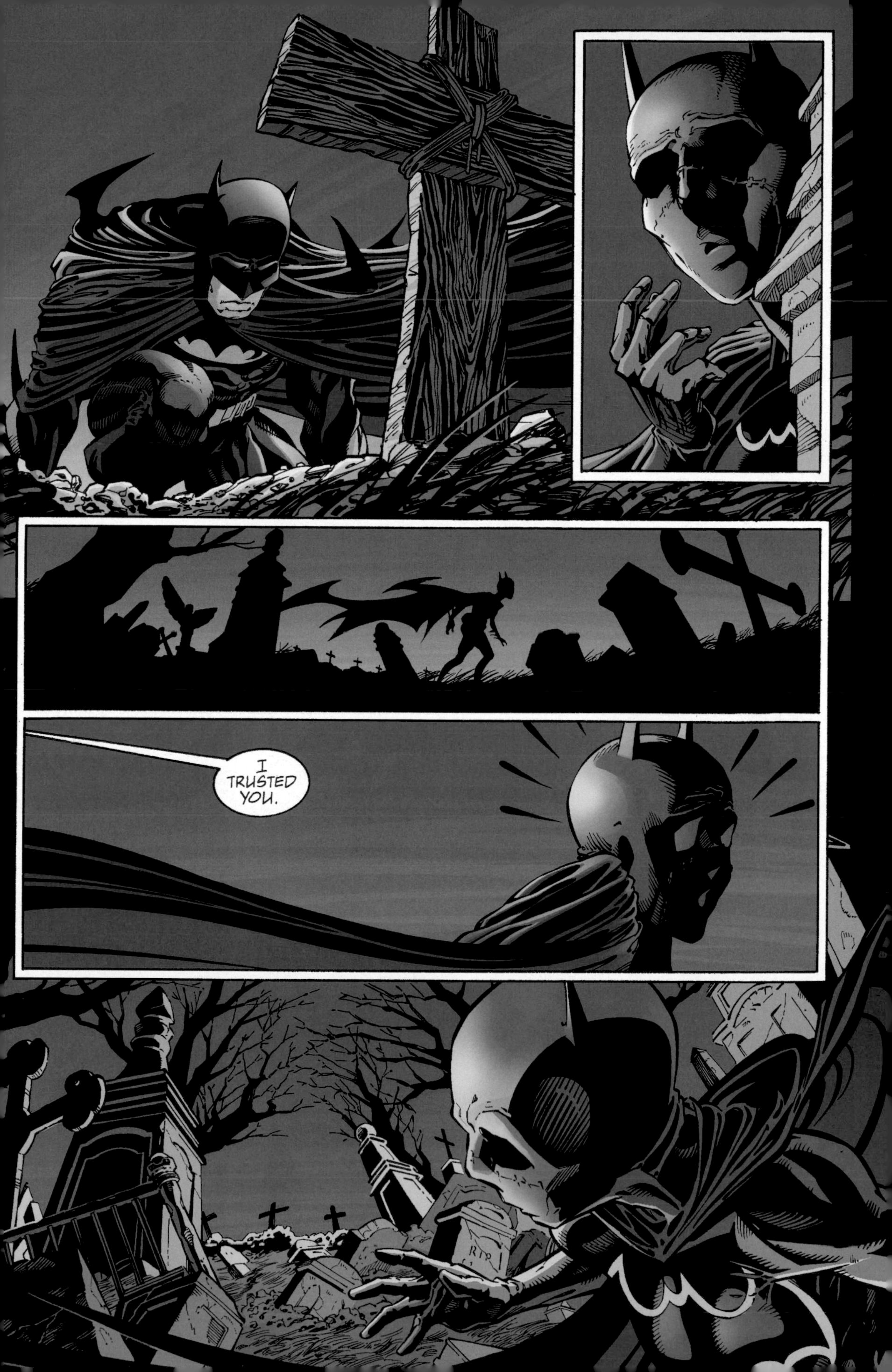

I TRUSTED YOU.

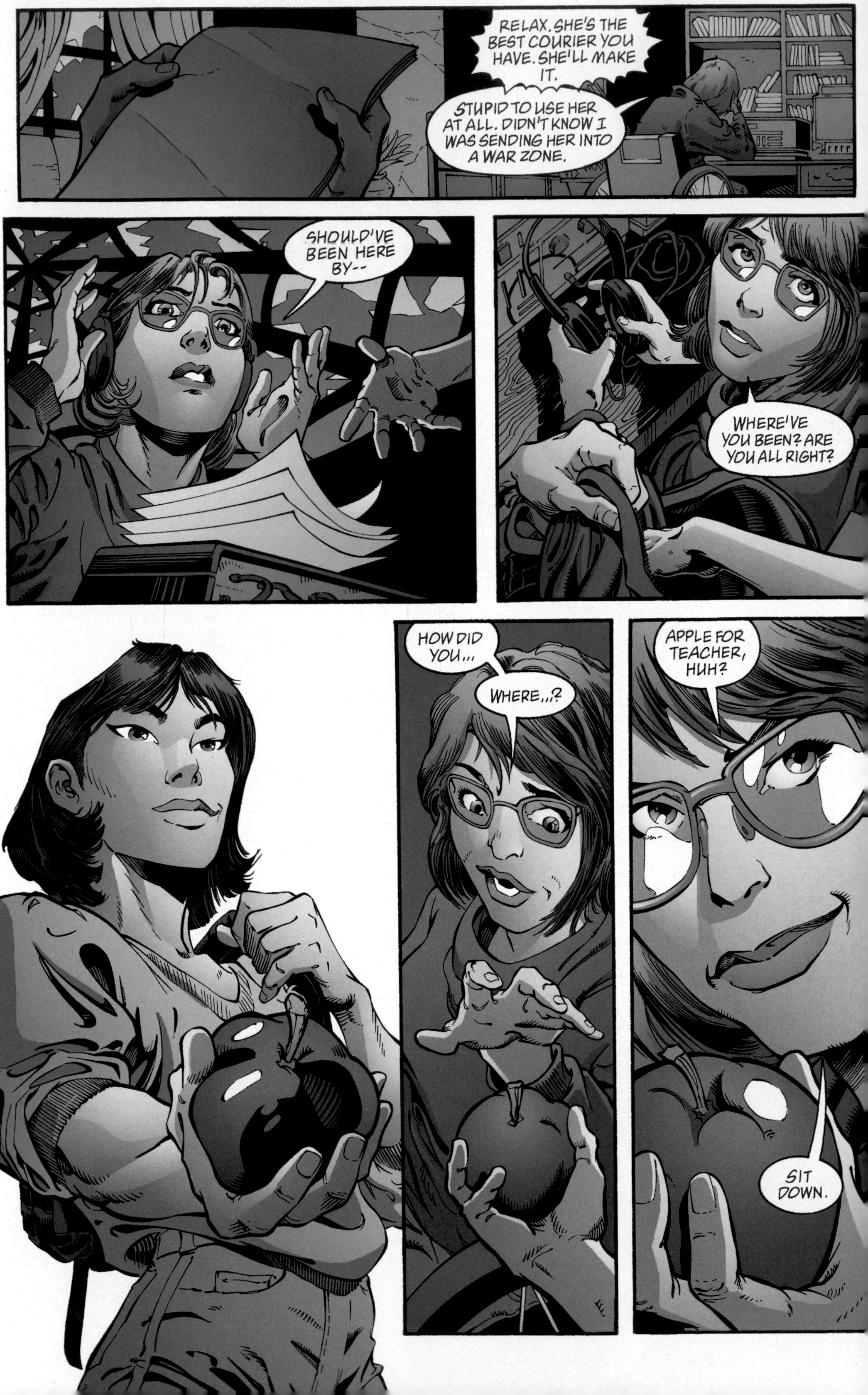
RELAX. SHE'S THE BEST COURIER YOU HAVE. SHE'LL MAKE IT.
STUPID TO USE HER AT ALL. DIDN'T KNOW I WAS SENDING HER INTO A WAR ZONE.
SHOULD'VE BEEN HERE BY--
WHERE'VE YOU BEEN? ARE YOU ALL RIGHT?
HOW DID YOU...
WHERE...?
APPLE FOR TEACHER, HUH?
SIT DOWN.

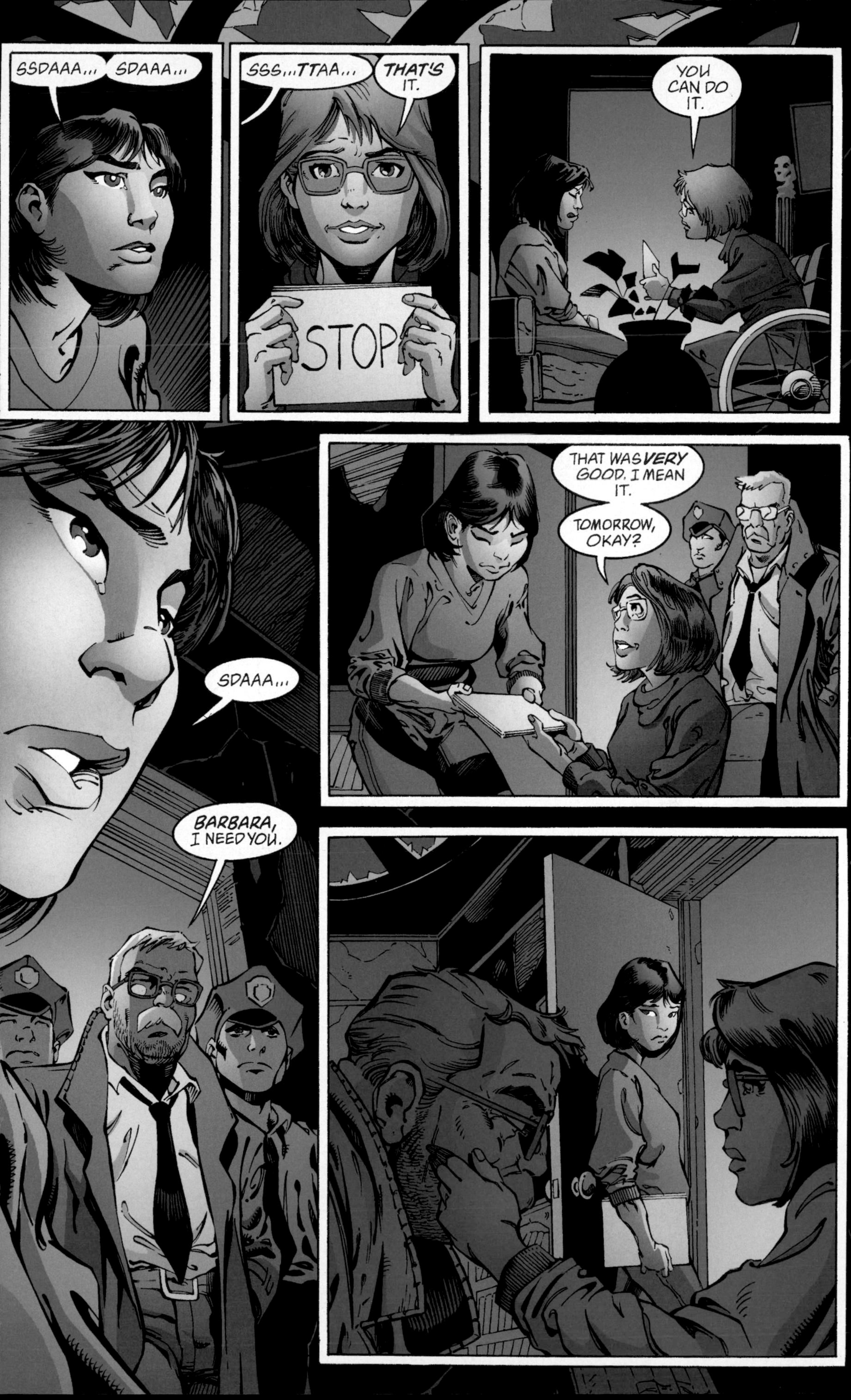
SSDAAA... SDAAA...
SSS...TTAA...
THAT'S IT.
STOP
YOU CAN DO IT.
SDAAA...
BARBARA, I NEED YOU.
THAT WAS VERY GOOD. I MEAN IT.
TOMORROW, OKAY?

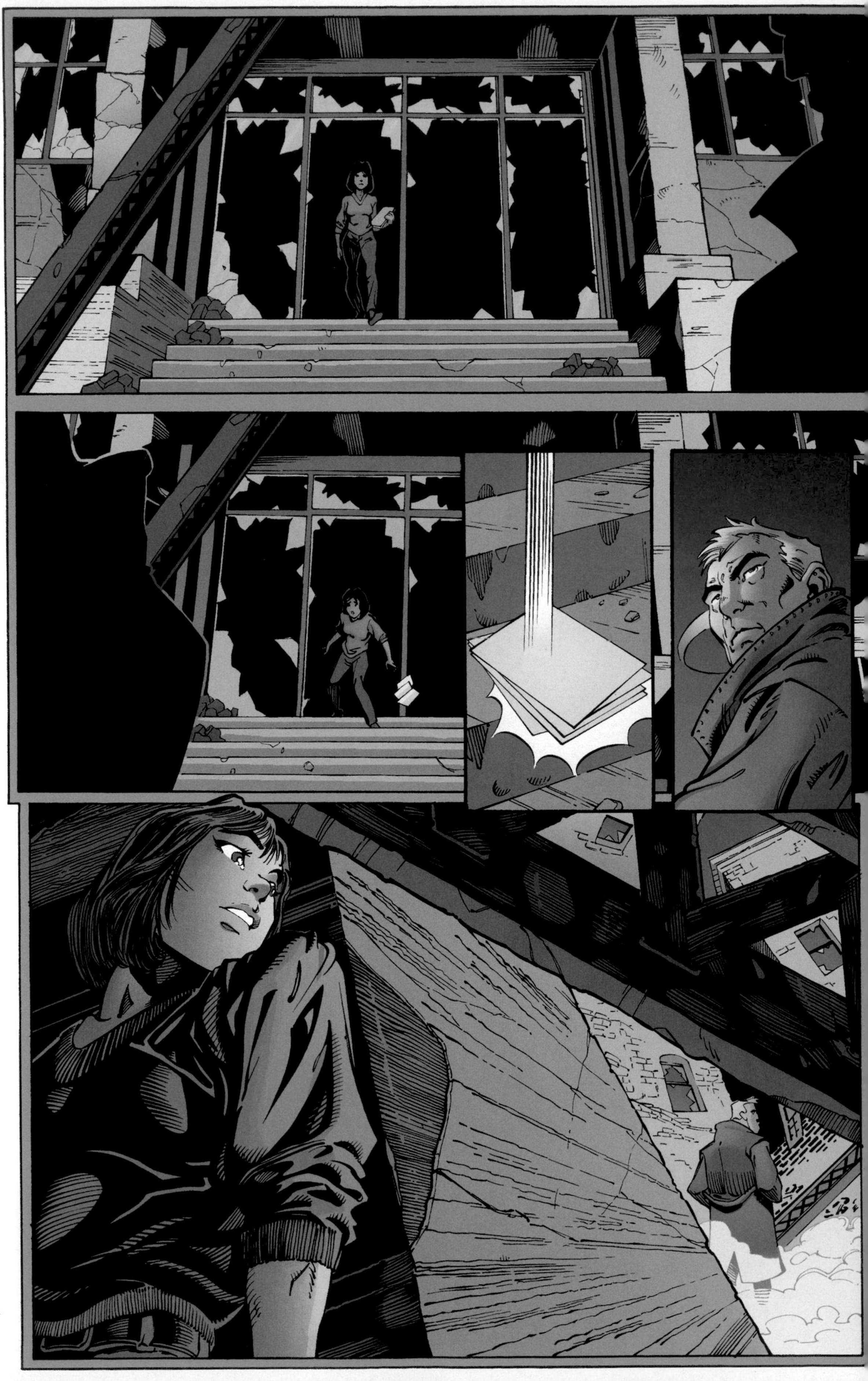

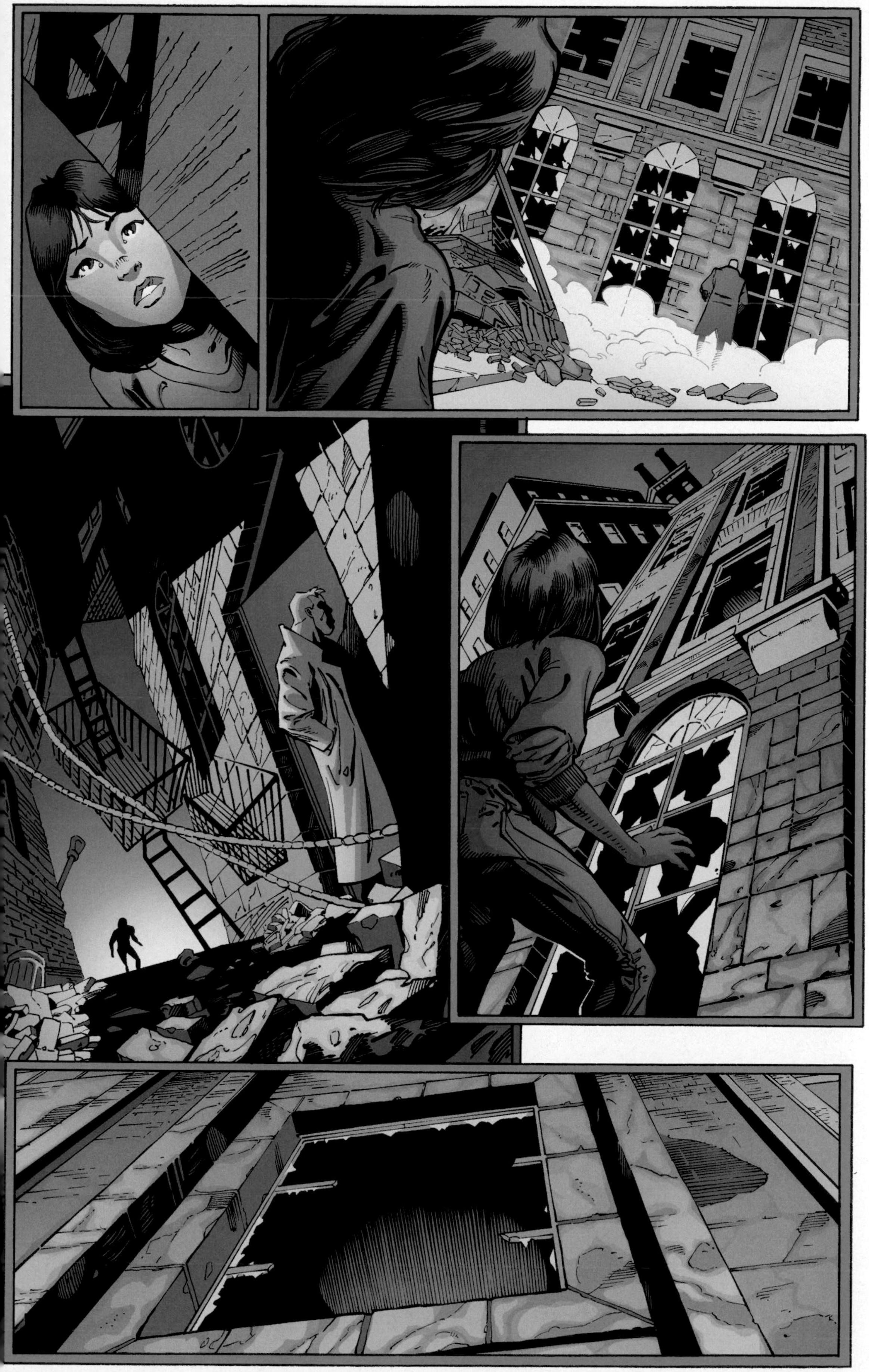

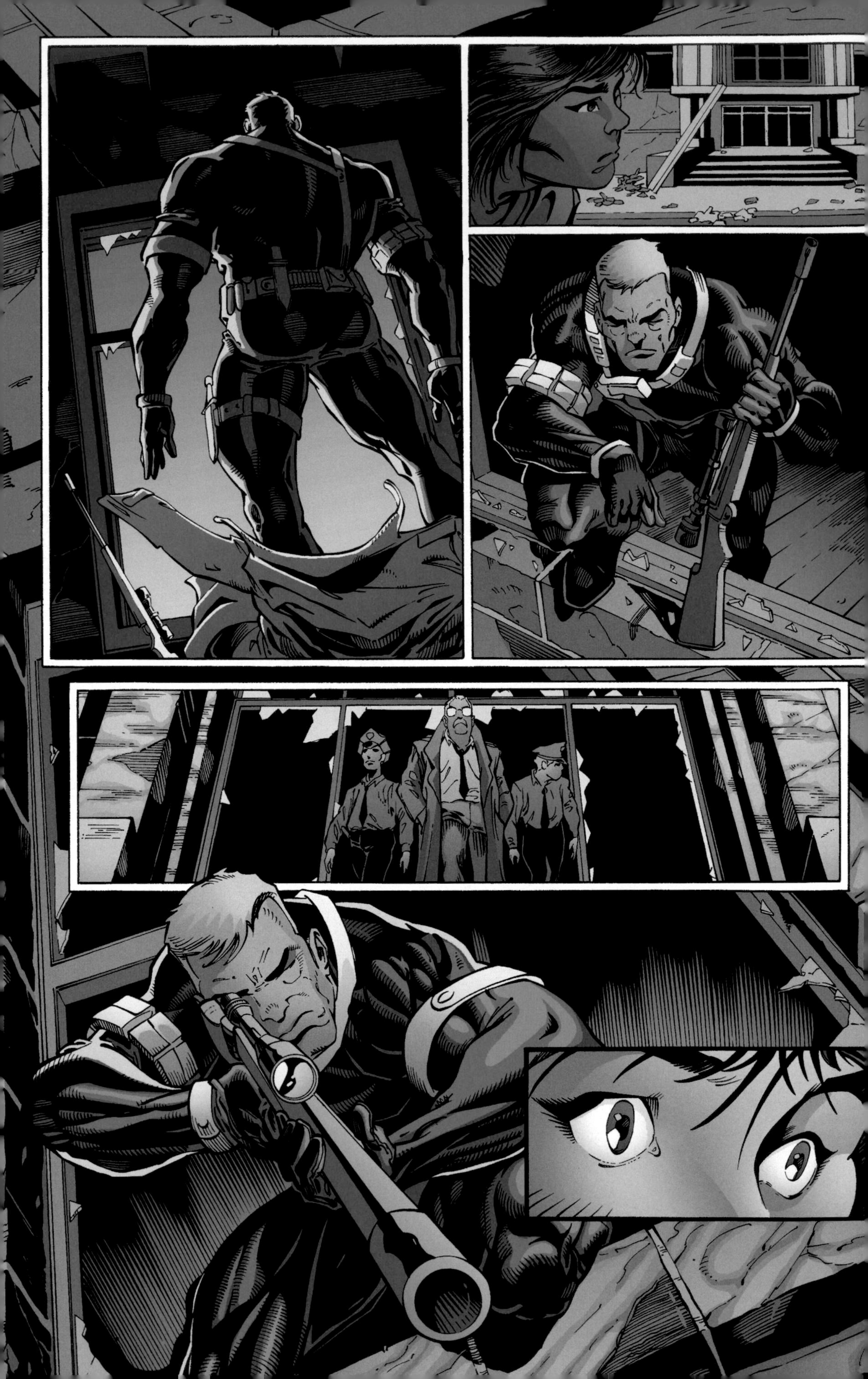

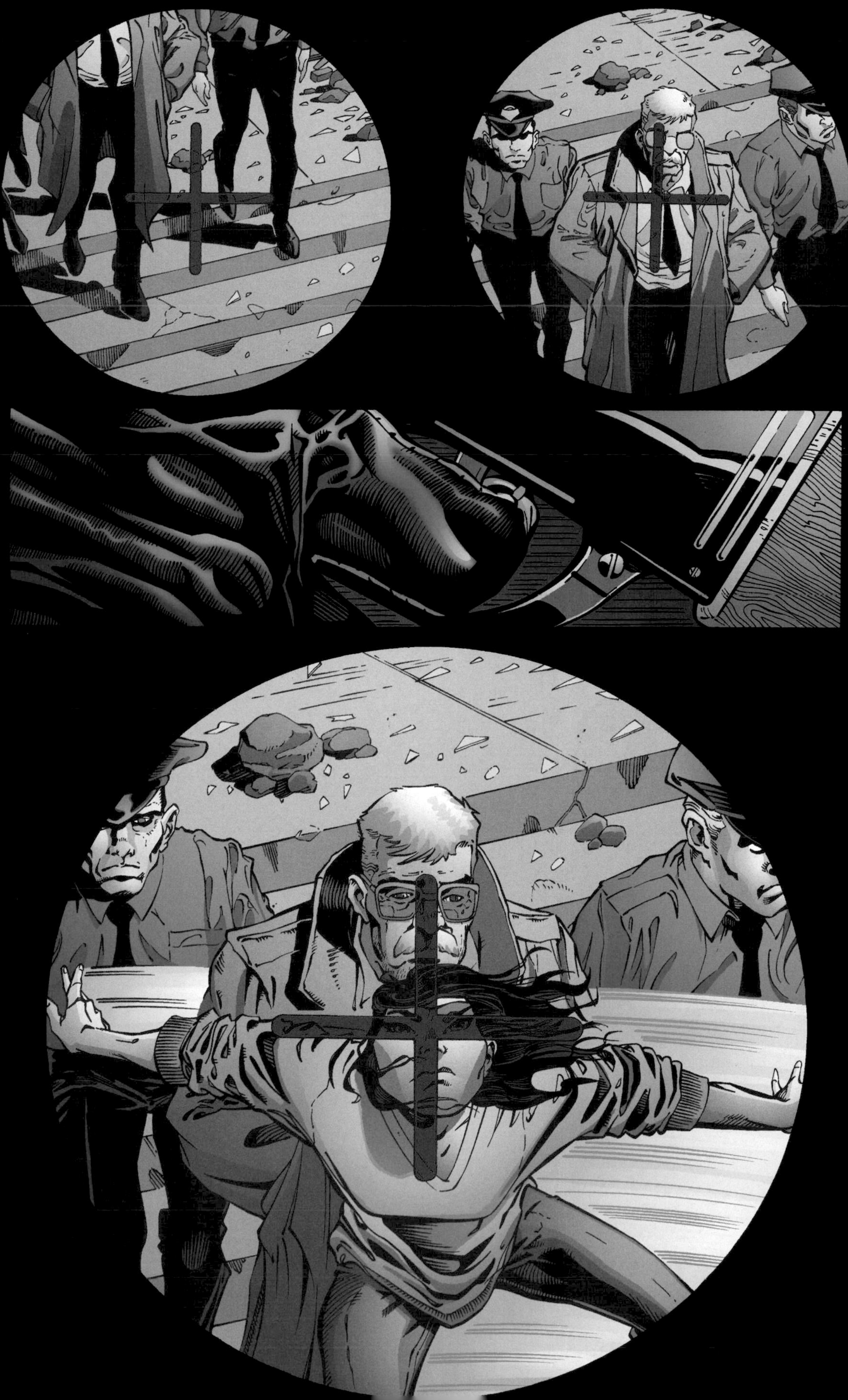

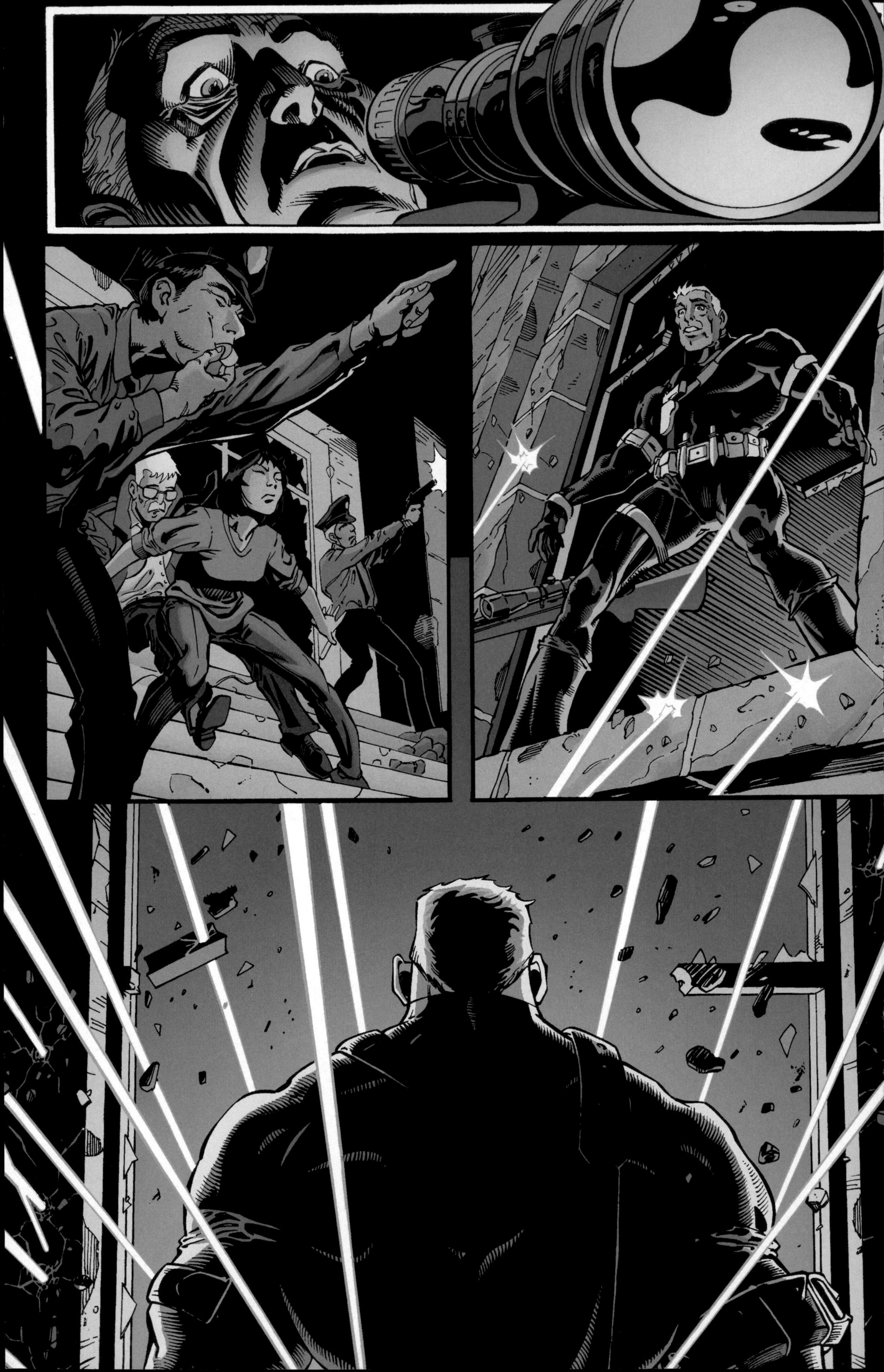

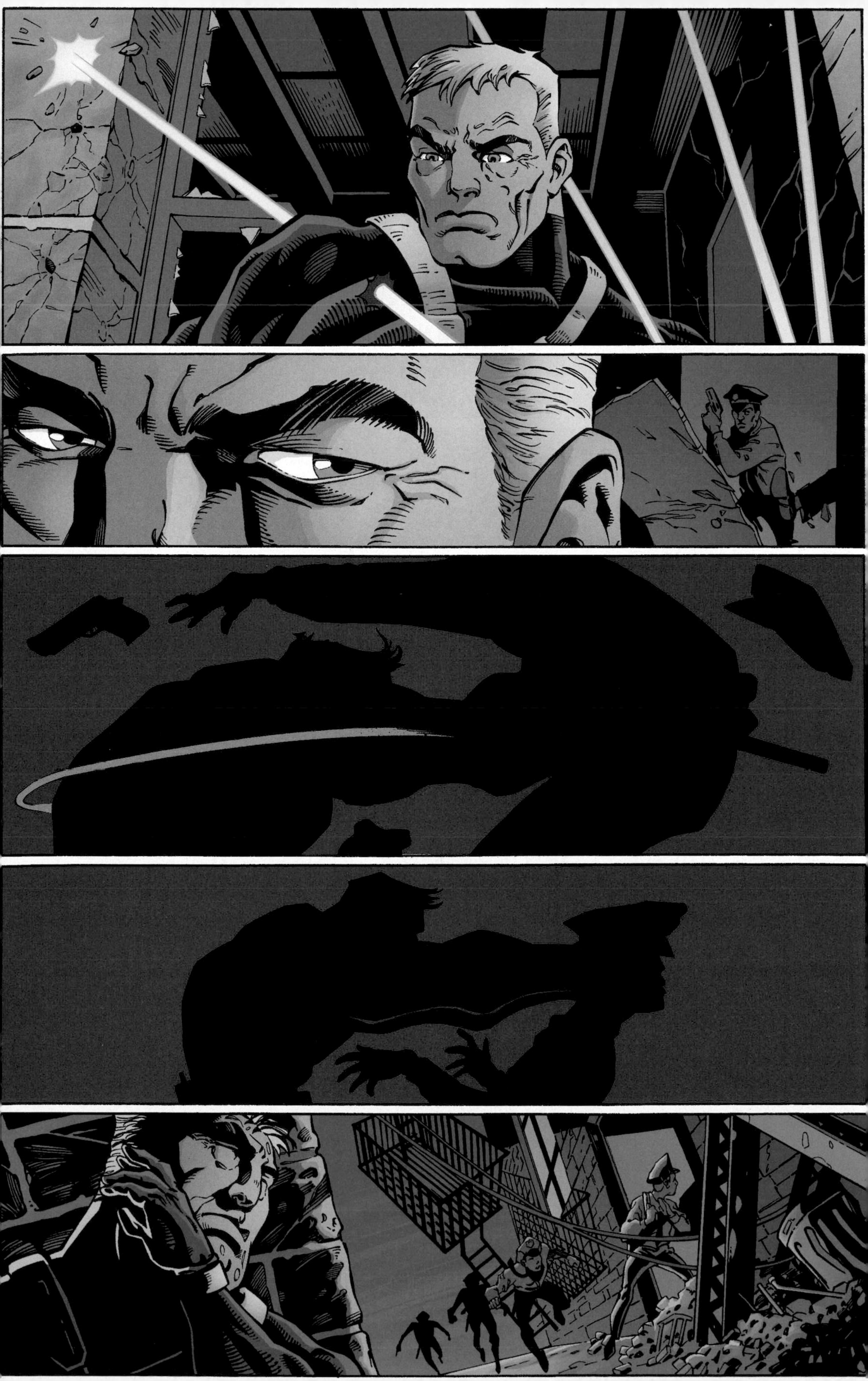

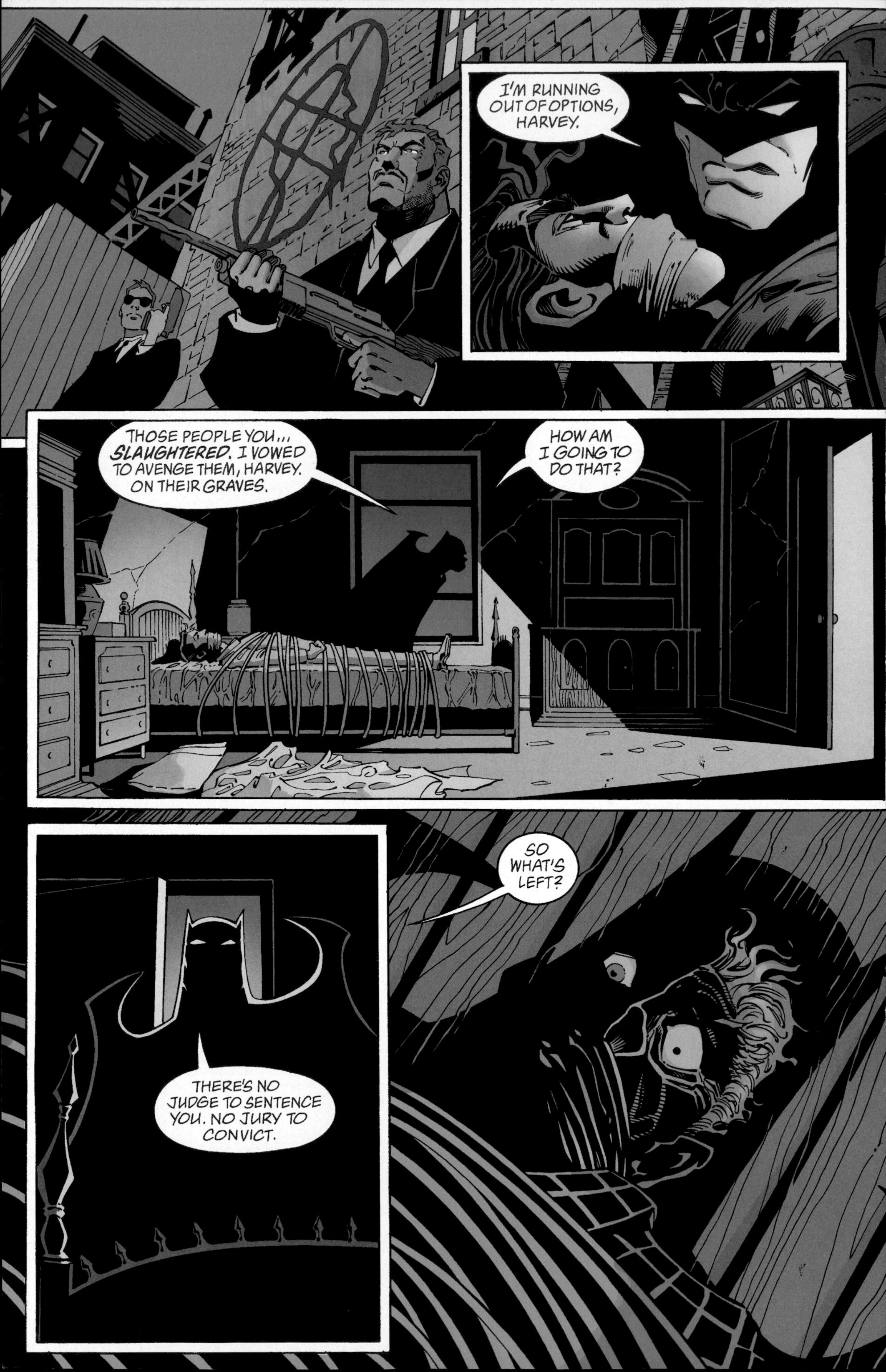
I'M RUNNING OUT OF OPTIONS, HARVEY.
THOSE PEOPLE YOU... SLAUGHTERED. I VOWED TO AVENGE THEM, HARVEY. ON THEIR GRAVES.
HOW AM I GOING TO DO THAT?
SO WHAT'S LEFT?
THERE'S NO JUDGE TO SENTENCE YOU. NO JURY TO CONVICT.

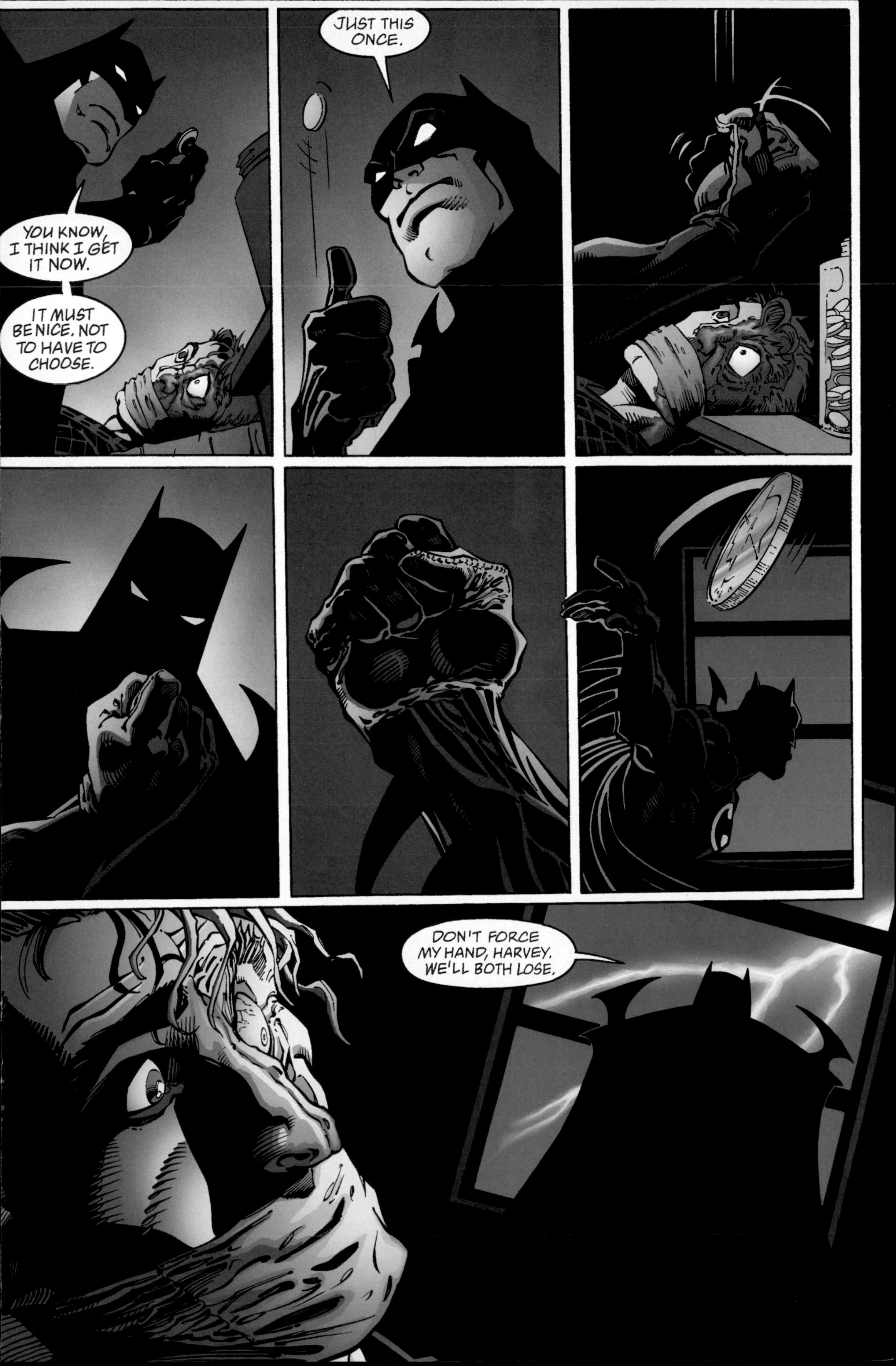
YOU KNOW, I THINK I GET IT NOW.
IT MUST BE NICE. NOT TO HAVE TO CHOOSE.
JUST THIS ONCE.
DON'T FORCE MY HAND, HARVEY. WE'LL BOTH LOSE.

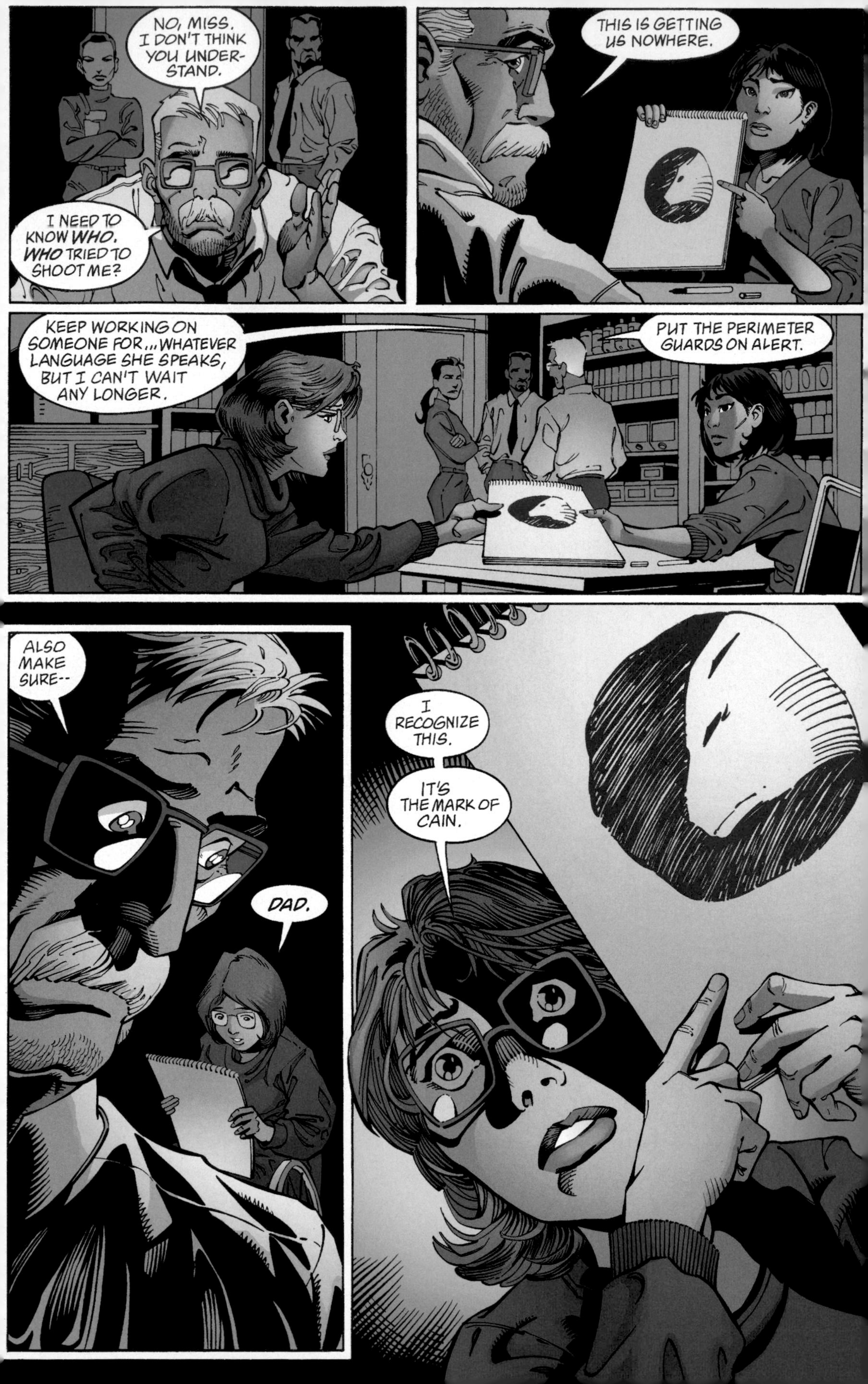
NO, MISS. I DON'T THINK YOU UNDERSTAND.
I NEED TO KNOW WHO. WHO TRIED TO SHOOT ME?
THIS IS GETTING US NOWHERE.
KEEP WORKING ON SOMEONE FOR... WHATEVER LANGUAGE SHE SPEAKS, BUT I CAN'T WAIT ANY LONGER.
PUT THE PERIMETER GUARDS ON ALERT.
ALSO MAKE SURE--
DAD.
I RECOGNIZE THIS.
IT'S THE MARK OF CAIN.

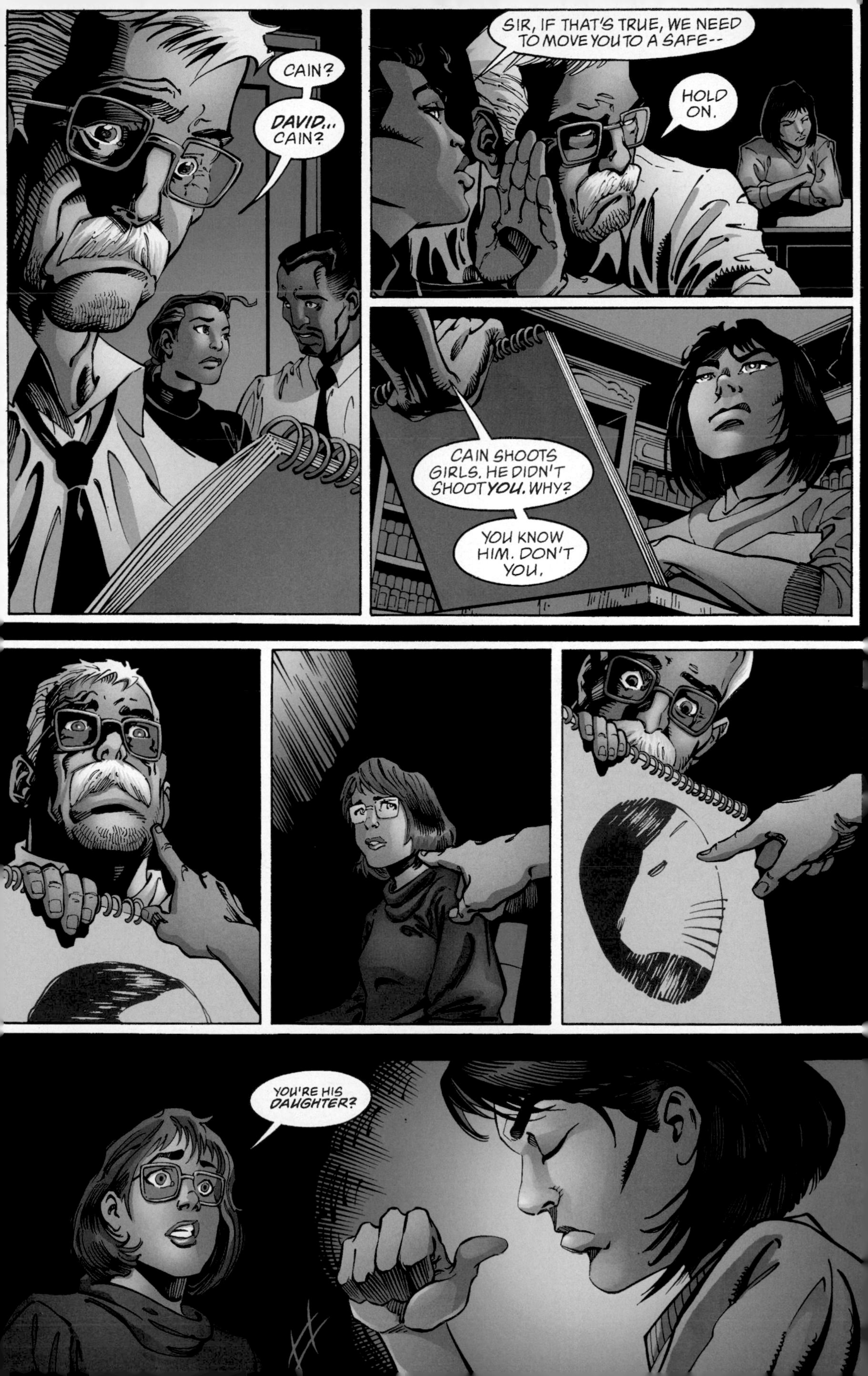
CAIN?
DAVID... CAIN?
SIR, IF THAT'S TRUE, WE NEED TO MOVE YOU TO A SAFE--
HOLD ON.
CAIN SHOOTS GIRLS. HE DIDN'T SHOOT YOU. WHY?
YOU KNOW HIM. DON'T YOU.
YOU'RE HIS DAUGHTER?

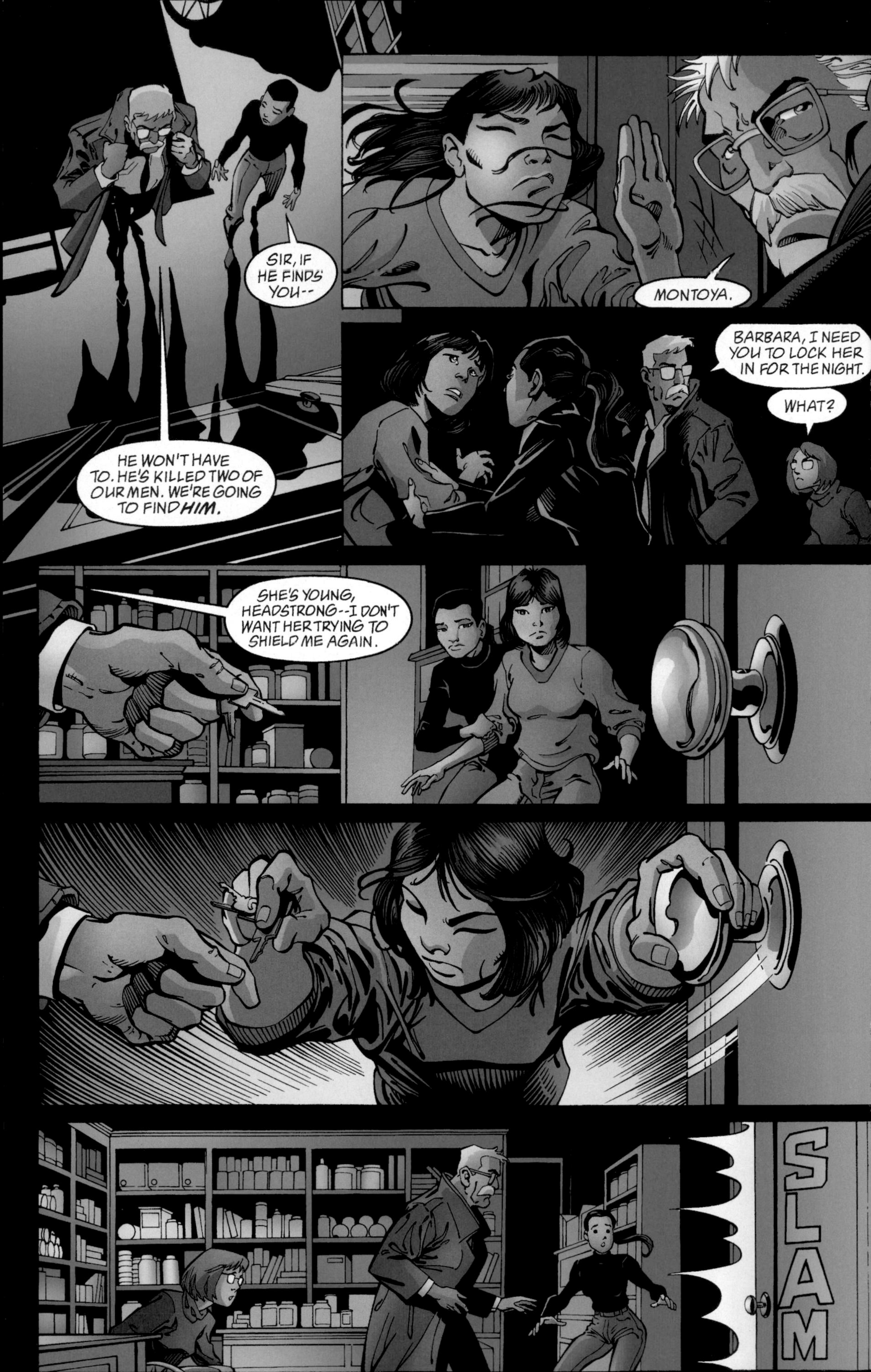
SIR, IF HE FINDS YOU--
HE WON'T HAVE TO. HE'S KILLED TWO OF OUR MEN. WE'RE GOING TO FIND HIM.
MONTOYA.
BARBARA, I NEED YOU TO LOCK HER IN FOR THE NIGHT.
WHAT?
SHE'S YOUNG, HEADSTRONG--I DON'T WANT HER TRYING TO SHIELD ME AGAIN.
SLAM

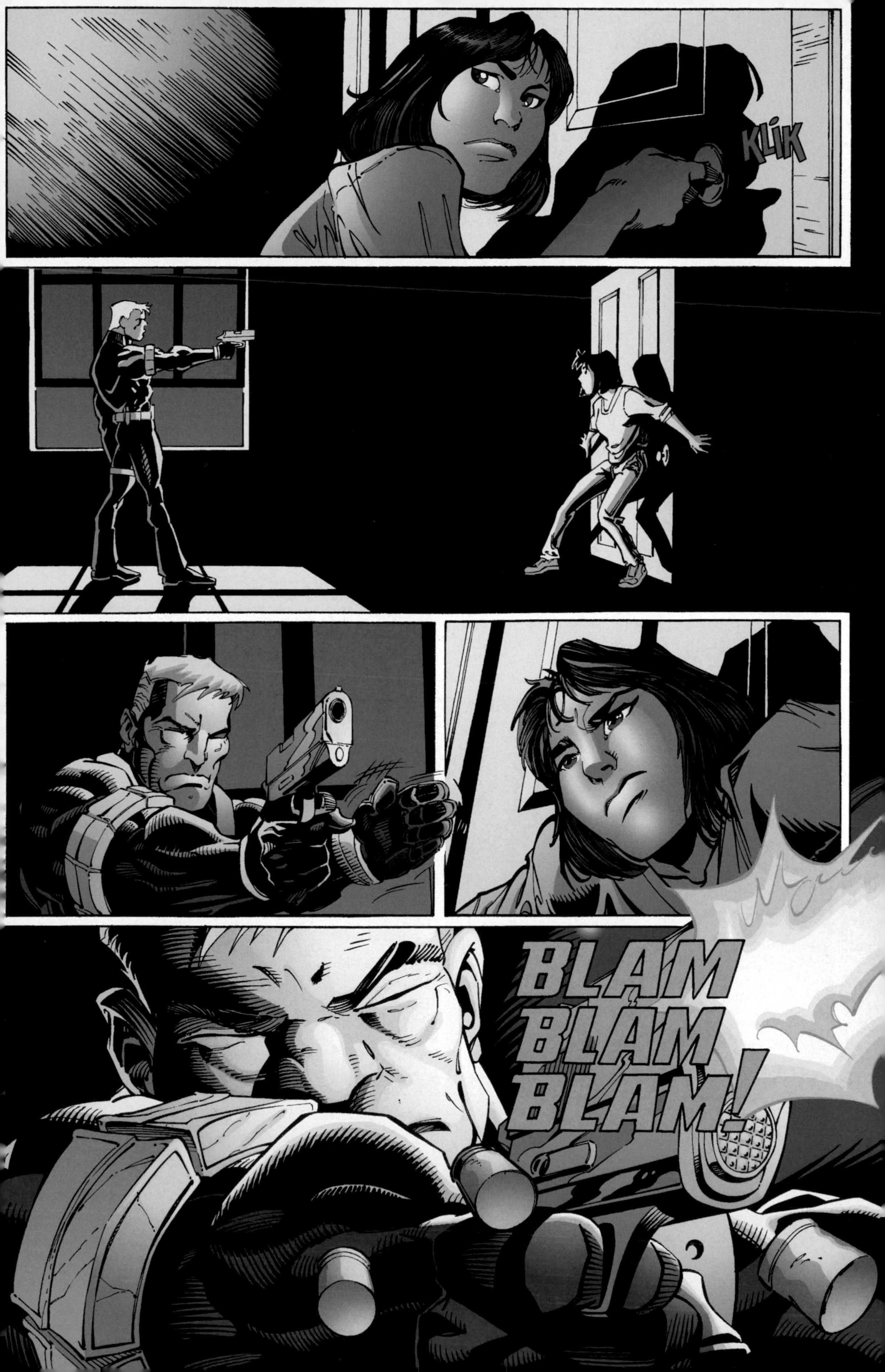
KLIK
BLAM
BLAM
BLAM!

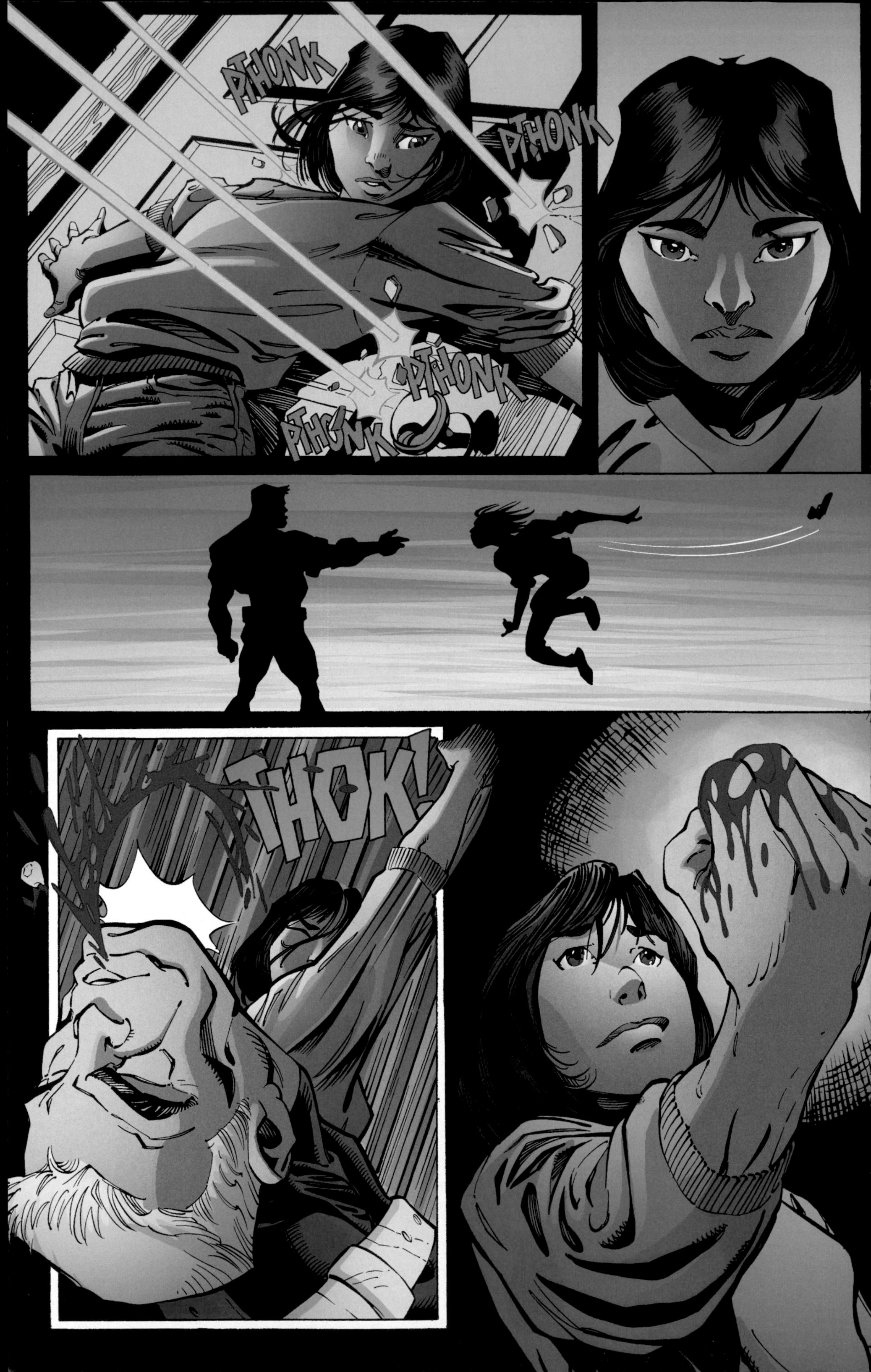
PTHONK
PTHONK
PTHONK
PTHONK
THOK!

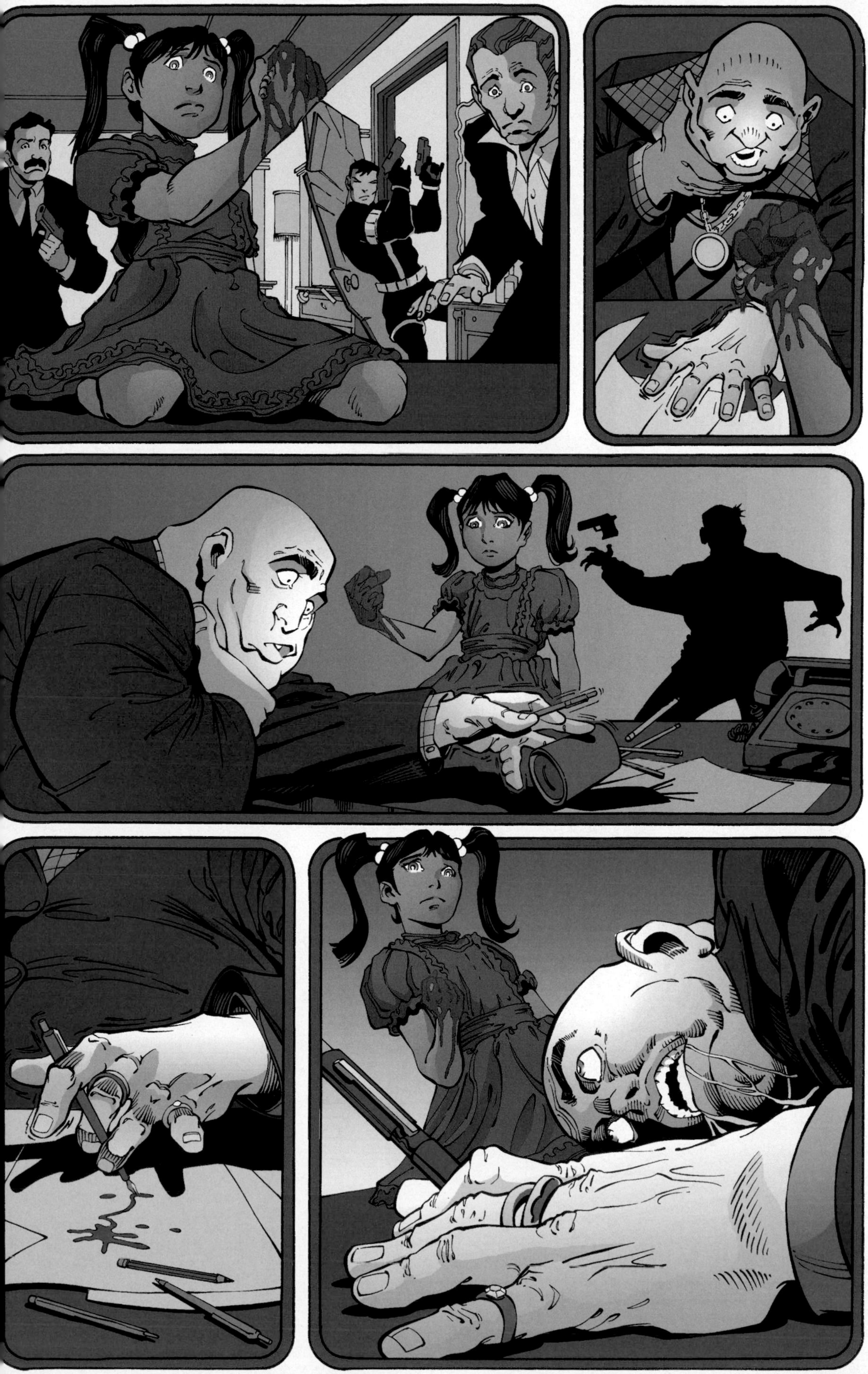

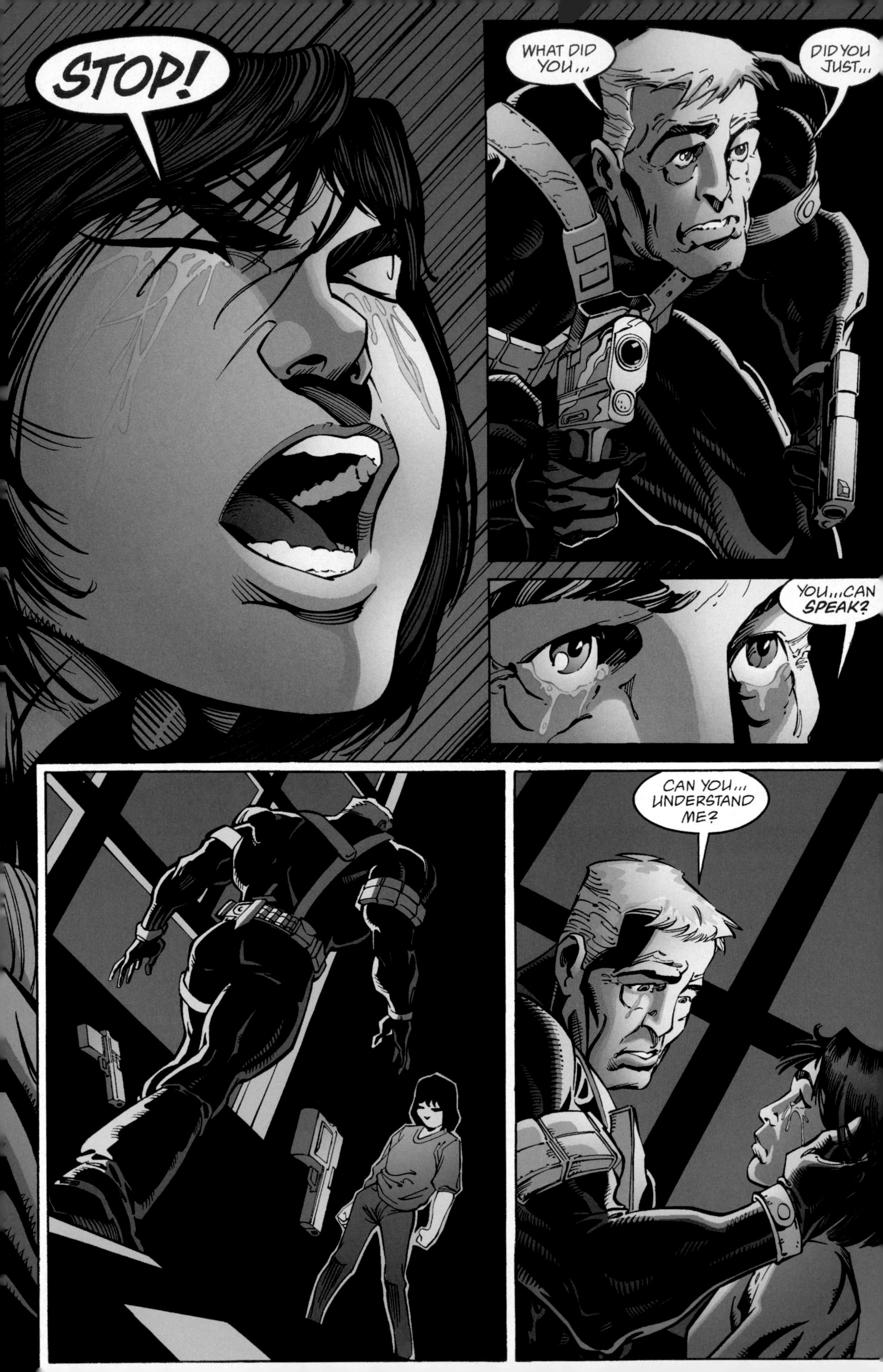
STOP!
WHAT DID YOU...
DID YOU JUST...
YOU...CAN SPEAK?
CAN YOU... UNDERSTAND ME?

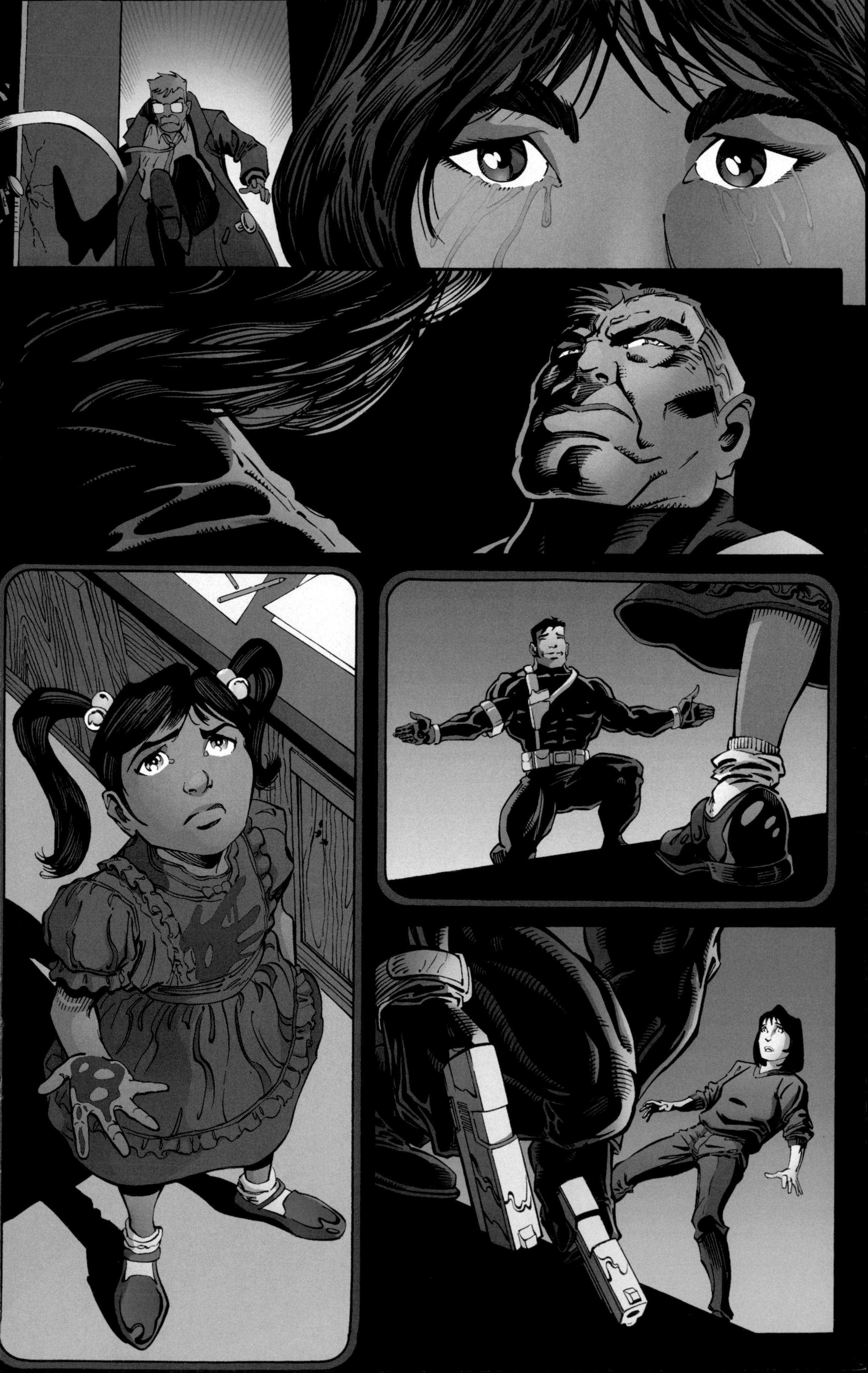

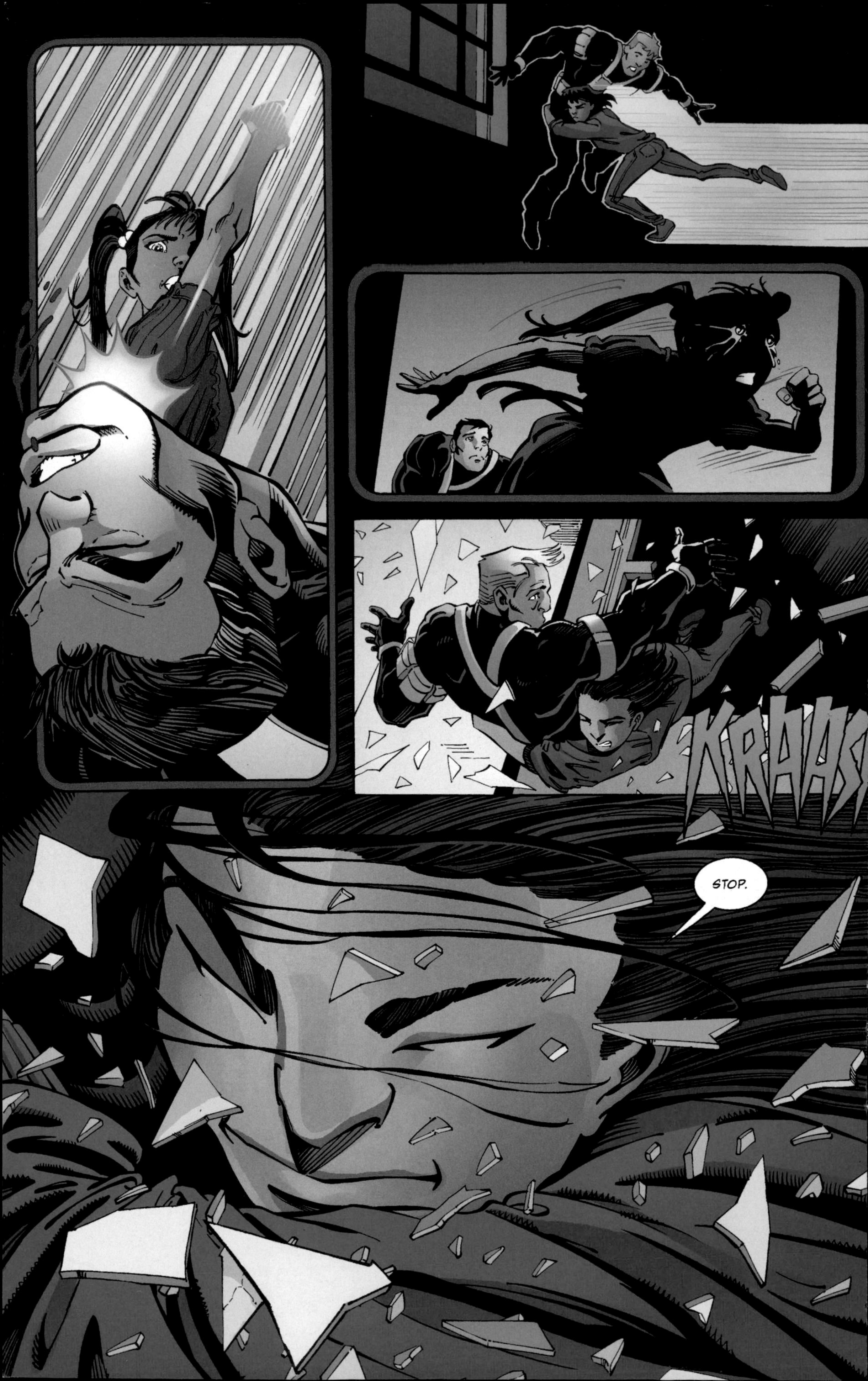
KRAASH
STOP.

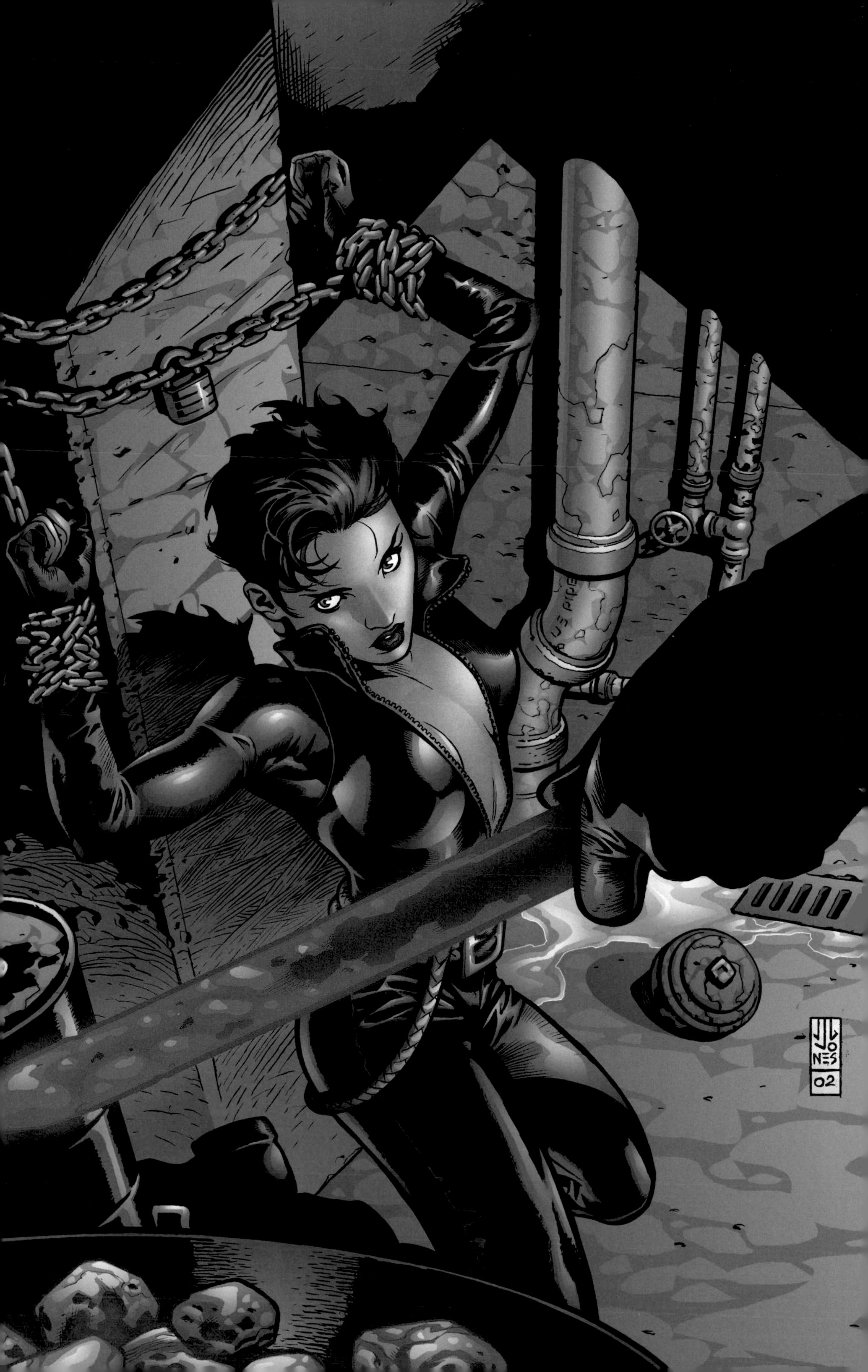
JG JONES 02

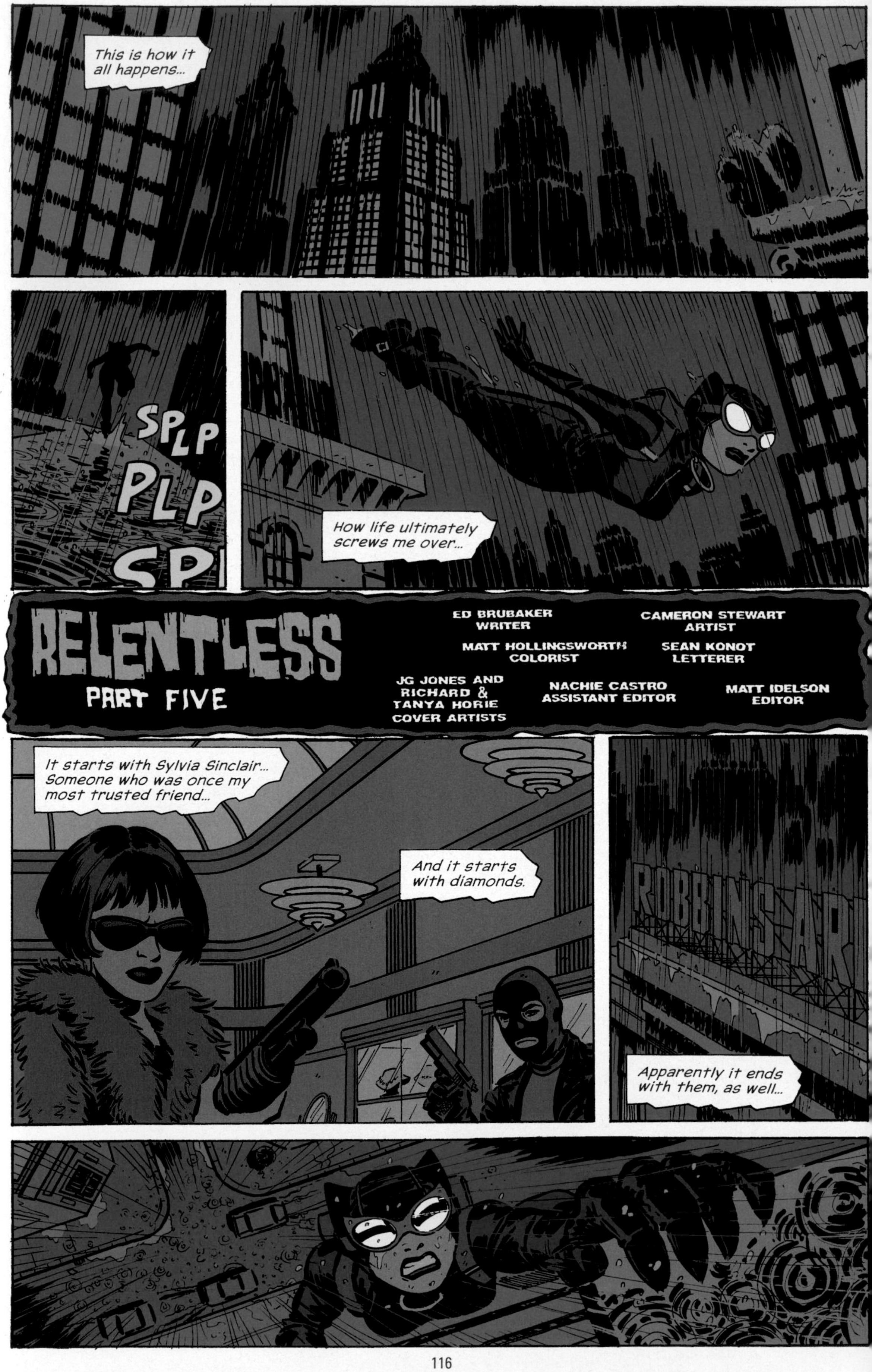
This is how it all happens...
SPLP
PLP
SP
How life ultimately screws me over...
RELENTLESS
PART FIVE
ED BRUBAKER WRITER
CAMERON STEWART ARTIST
MATT HOLLINGSWORTH COLORIST
SEAN KONOT LETTERER
JG JONES AND RICHARD & TANYA HORIE COVER ARTISTS
NACHIE CASTRO ASSISTANT EDITOR
MATT IDELSON EDITOR
It starts with Sylvia Sinclair... Someone who was once my most trusted friend...
And it starts with diamonds.
ROBBINS-AR
Apparently it ends with them, as well...

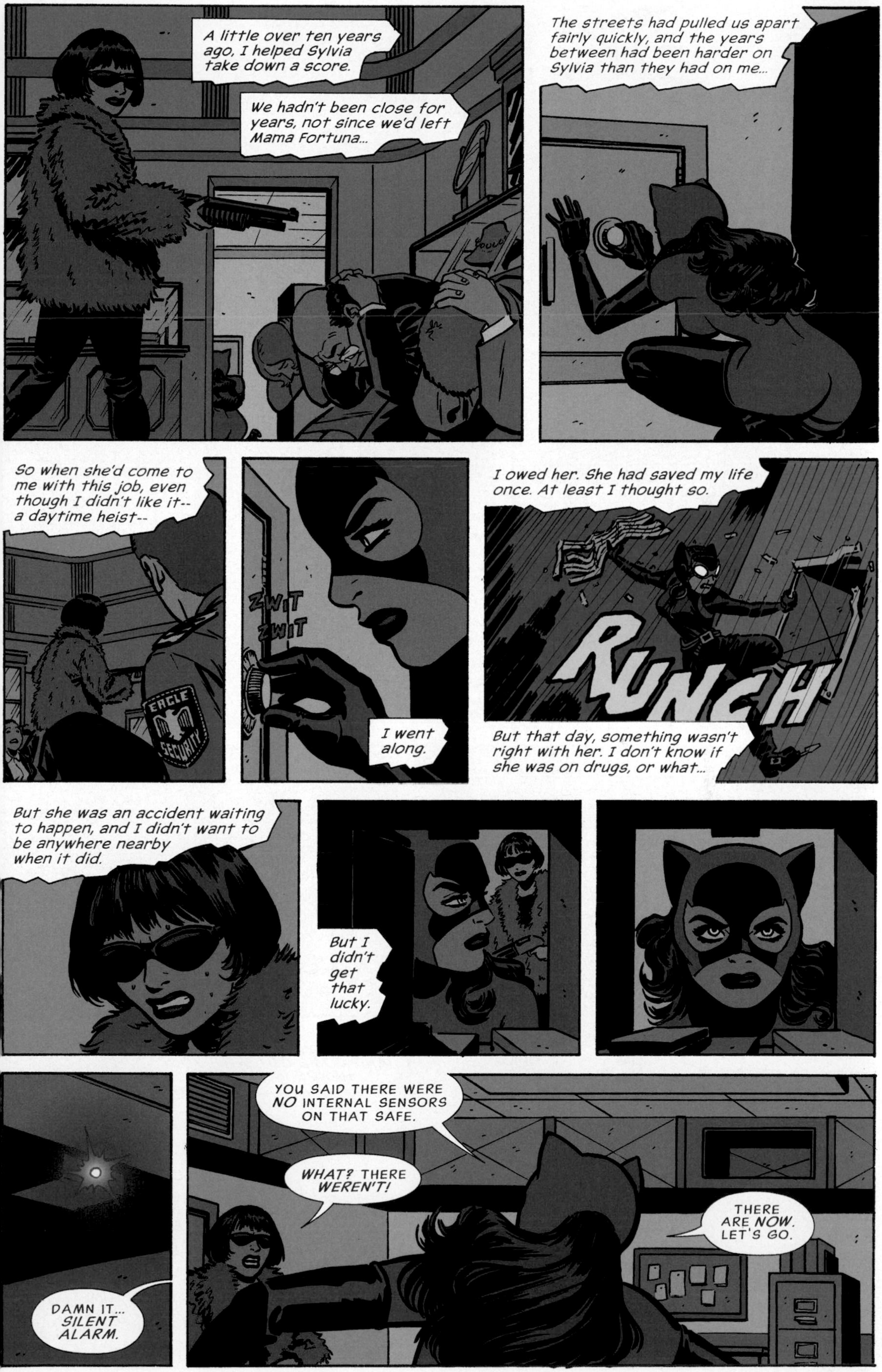
A little over ten years ago, I helped Sylvia take down a score.
We hadn't been close for years, not since we'd left Mama Fortuna...
The streets had pulled us apart fairly quickly, and the years between had been harder on Sylvia than they had on me...
So when she'd come to me with this job, even though I didn't like it-- a daytime heist--
EAGLE SECURITY
ZWIT ZWIT
I went along.
I owed her. She had saved my life once. At least I thought so.
RUNCH
But that day, something wasn't right with her. I don't know if she was on drugs, or what...
But she was an accident waiting to happen, and I didn't want to be anywhere nearby when it did.
But I didn't get that lucky.
DAMN IT... SILENT ALARM.
YOU SAID THERE WERE NO INTERNAL SENSORS ON THAT SAFE.
WHAT? THERE WEREN'T!
THERE ARE NOW. LET'S GO.

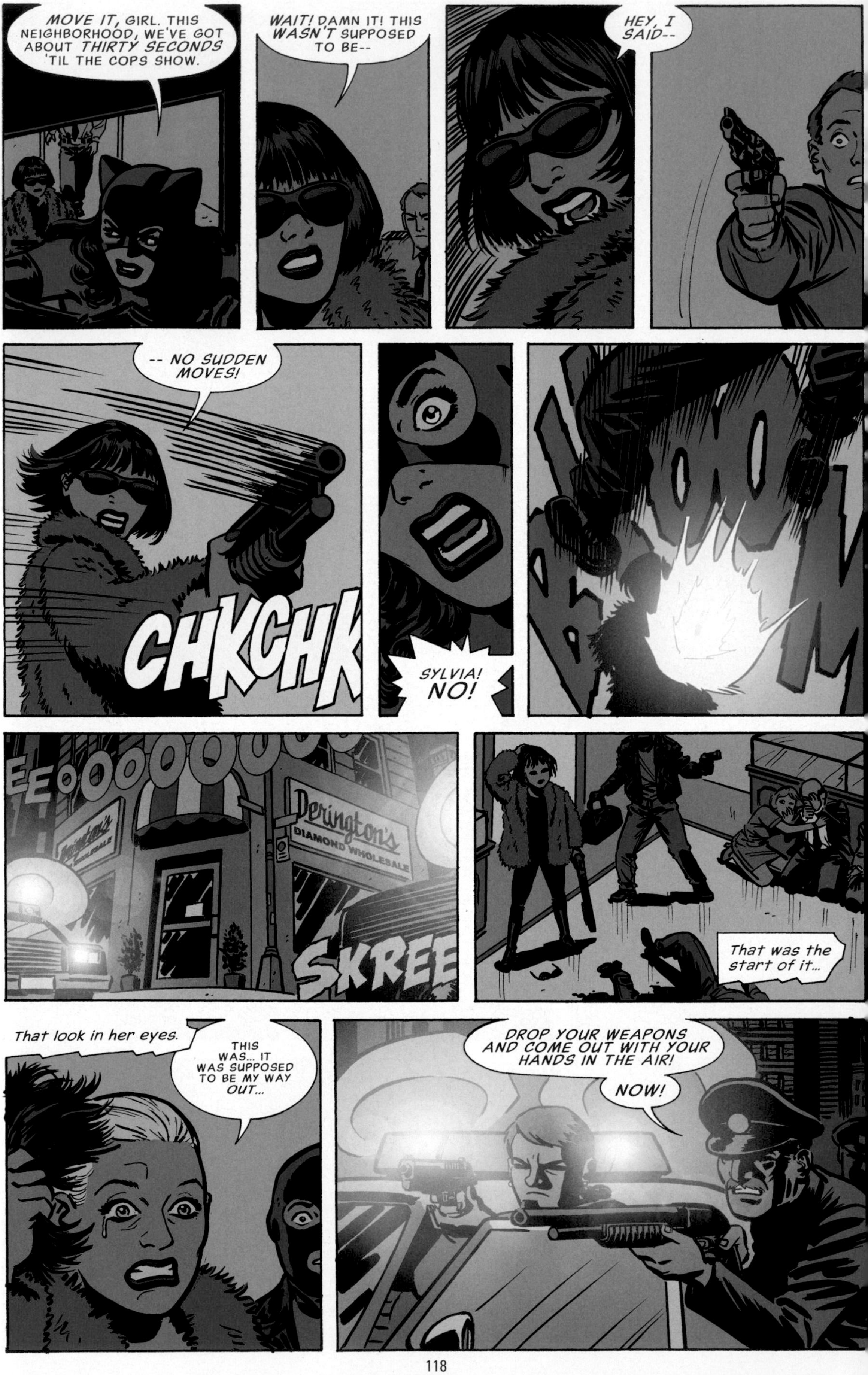
MOVE IT, GIRL. THIS NEIGHBORHOOD, WE'VE GOT ABOUT THIRTY SECONDS 'TIL THE COPS SHOW.
WAIT! DAMN IT! THIS WASN'T SUPPOSED TO BE--
HEY, I SAID--
-- NO SUDDEN MOVES!
CHKCHK
SYLVIA! NO!
EE-OOOOOOO
Derington's
Derington's DIAMOND WHOLESALE
SKREE
That was the start of it...
That look in her eyes.
THIS WAS... IT WAS SUPPOSED TO BE MY WAY OUT...
DROP YOUR WEAPONS AND COME OUT WITH YOUR HANDS IN THE AIR!
NOW!

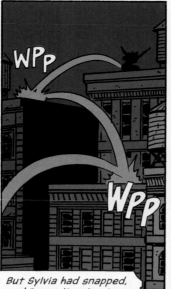

WPP

WPP

BLAM
BLAM
BLAM
BLAM

I suppose my survival instinct was my sin.

But Sylvia had snapped, and I wasn't going to go down the drain with her...

... Much as I loved her, I couldn't.

The strange part is, I didn't think she'd hold it against me... I guess you never know what prison will do to someone.

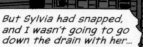

And the Black Mask...

But apparently he's remade himself into someone much more serious-- A drug kingpin trying to rule the East End in anonymity.

And like I said, life has been surprising me in ugly ways lately... My sister and her husband kidnapped. My friends attacked. My achievements destroyed.

Hard to believe it all comes down to diamonds and pride.

Until tonight I thought he was just a typical Gotham freak. Some fruitcake obsessed with masks.

ZZKSSHH

Well, I'm going to depose this would-be king...

SHK

x

119

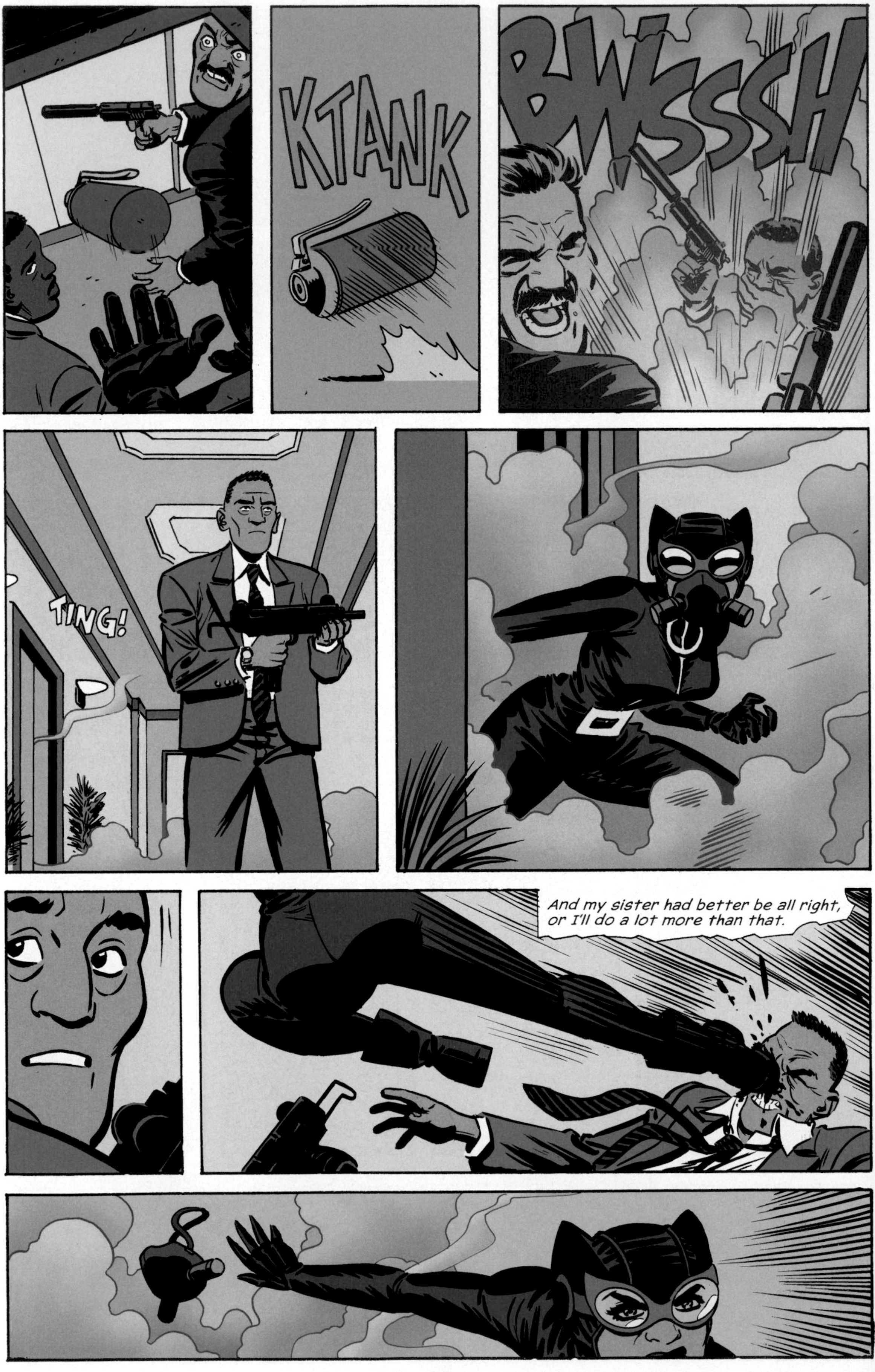

KTANK
BWSSSH
TING!
And my sister had better be all right, or I'll do a lot more than that.

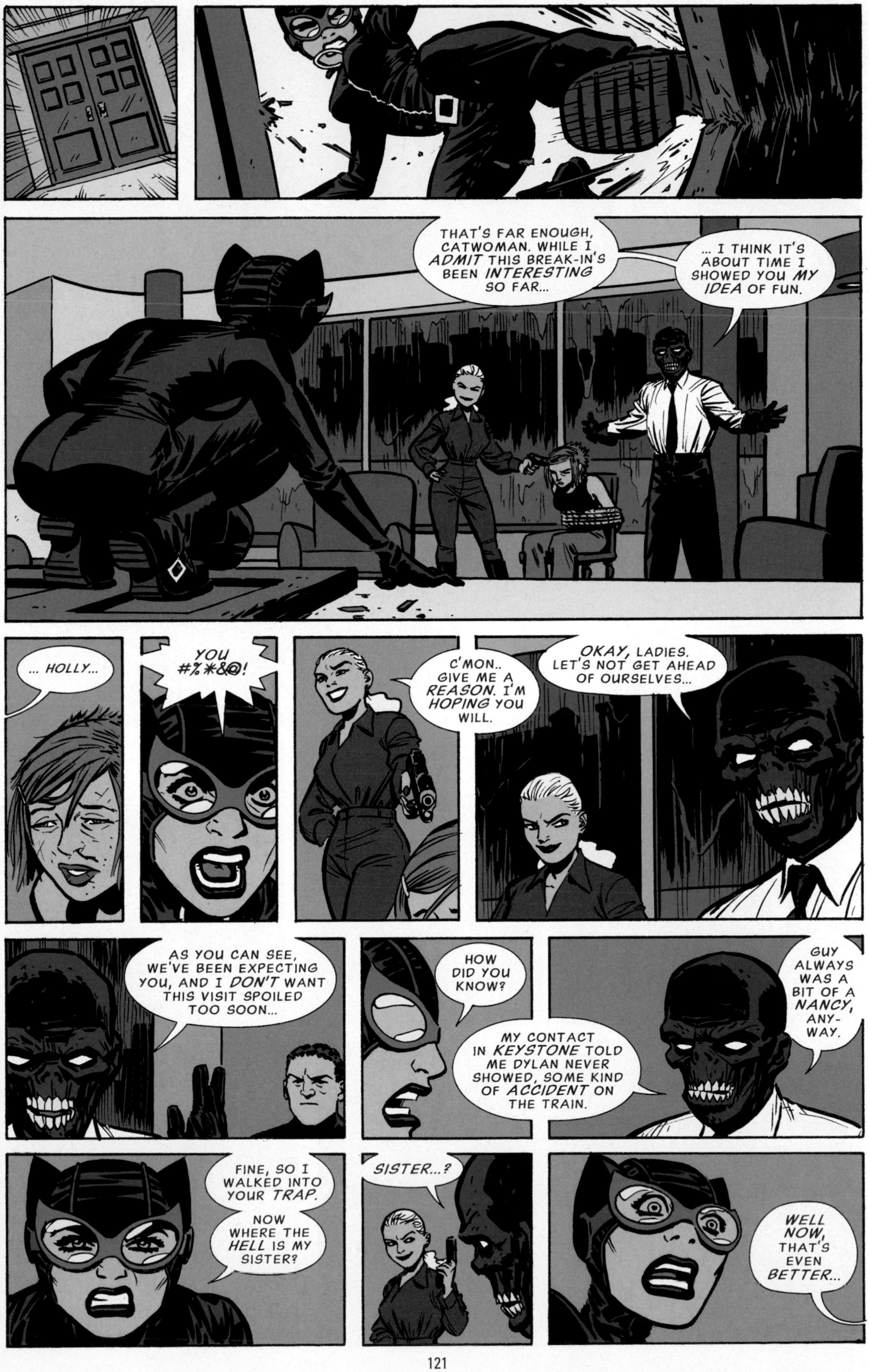

THAT'S FAR ENOUGH, CATWOMAN. WHILE I *ADMIT* THIS BREAK-IN'S BEEN *INTERESTING* SO FAR...
... I THINK IT'S ABOUT TIME I SHOWED YOU *MY IDEA* OF FUN.
... *HOLLY*...
YOU #%✱&@!
C'MON.. GIVE ME A *REASON*. I'M *HOPING* YOU WILL.
OKAY, LADIES. LET'S NOT GET AHEAD OF OURSELVES...
AS YOU CAN SEE, WE'VE BEEN EXPECTING YOU, AND I *DON'T* WANT THIS VISIT SPOILED TOO SOON...
HOW DID YOU KNOW?
MY CONTACT IN *KEYSTONE* TOLD ME DYLAN NEVER SHOWED, SOME KIND OF *ACCIDENT* ON THE TRAIN.
GUY ALWAYS WAS A BIT OF A *NANCY*, ANYWAY.
FINE, SO I WALKED INTO YOUR *TRAP*.
NOW WHERE THE *HELL* IS MY SISTER?
SISTER...?
WELL NOW, THAT'S EVEN *BETTER*...

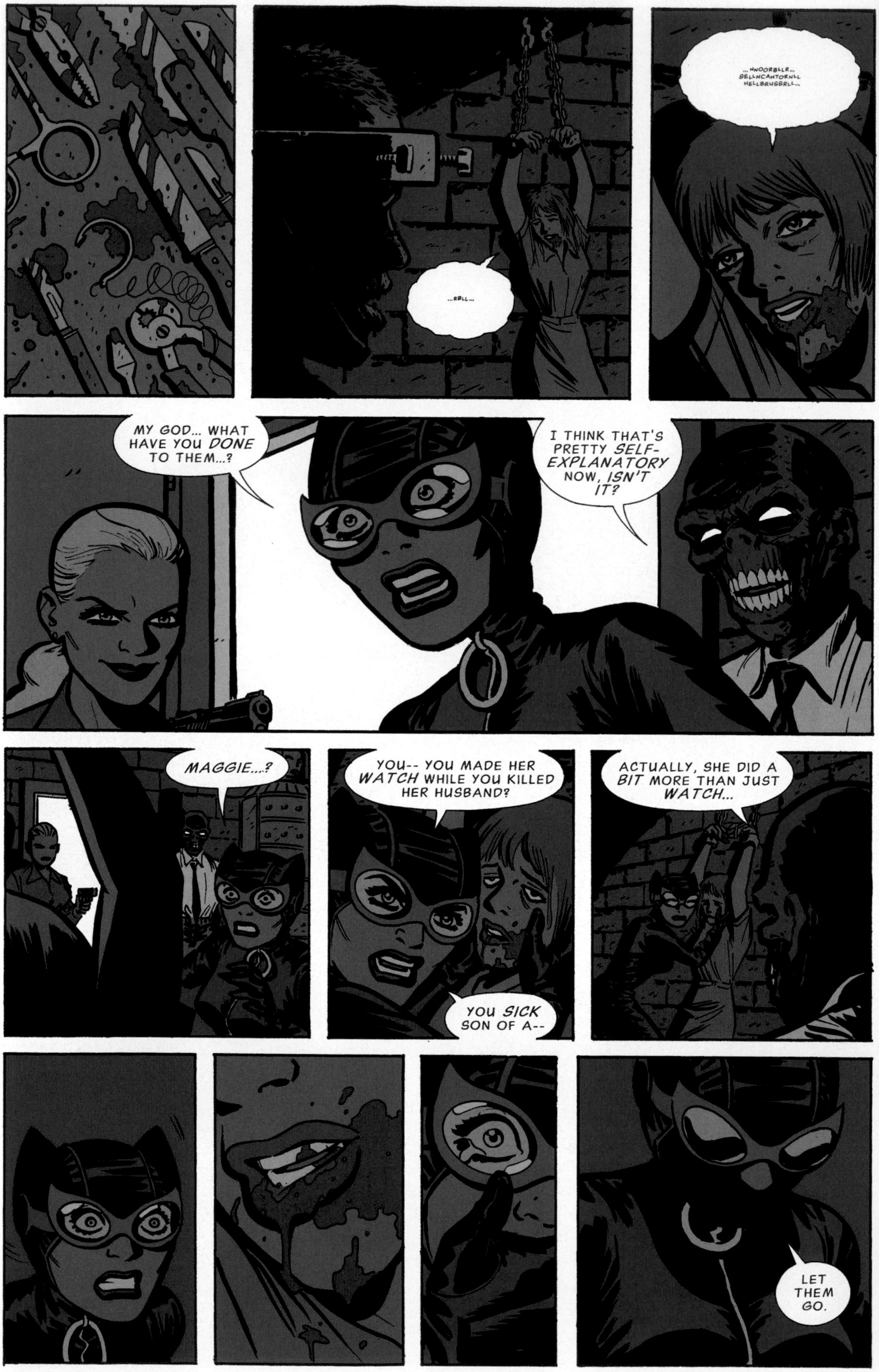
...RBLL...
...NNOORBLLR...
BELLNCANTORNLL
HELLBRUSSRLL...
MY GOD... WHAT HAVE YOU DONE TO THEM...?
I THINK THAT'S PRETTY SELF-EXPLANATORY NOW, ISN'T IT?
MAGGIE...?
YOU-- YOU MADE HER WATCH WHILE YOU KILLED HER HUSBAND?
YOU SICK SON OF A--
ACTUALLY, SHE DID A BIT MORE THAN JUST WATCH...
LET THEM GO.

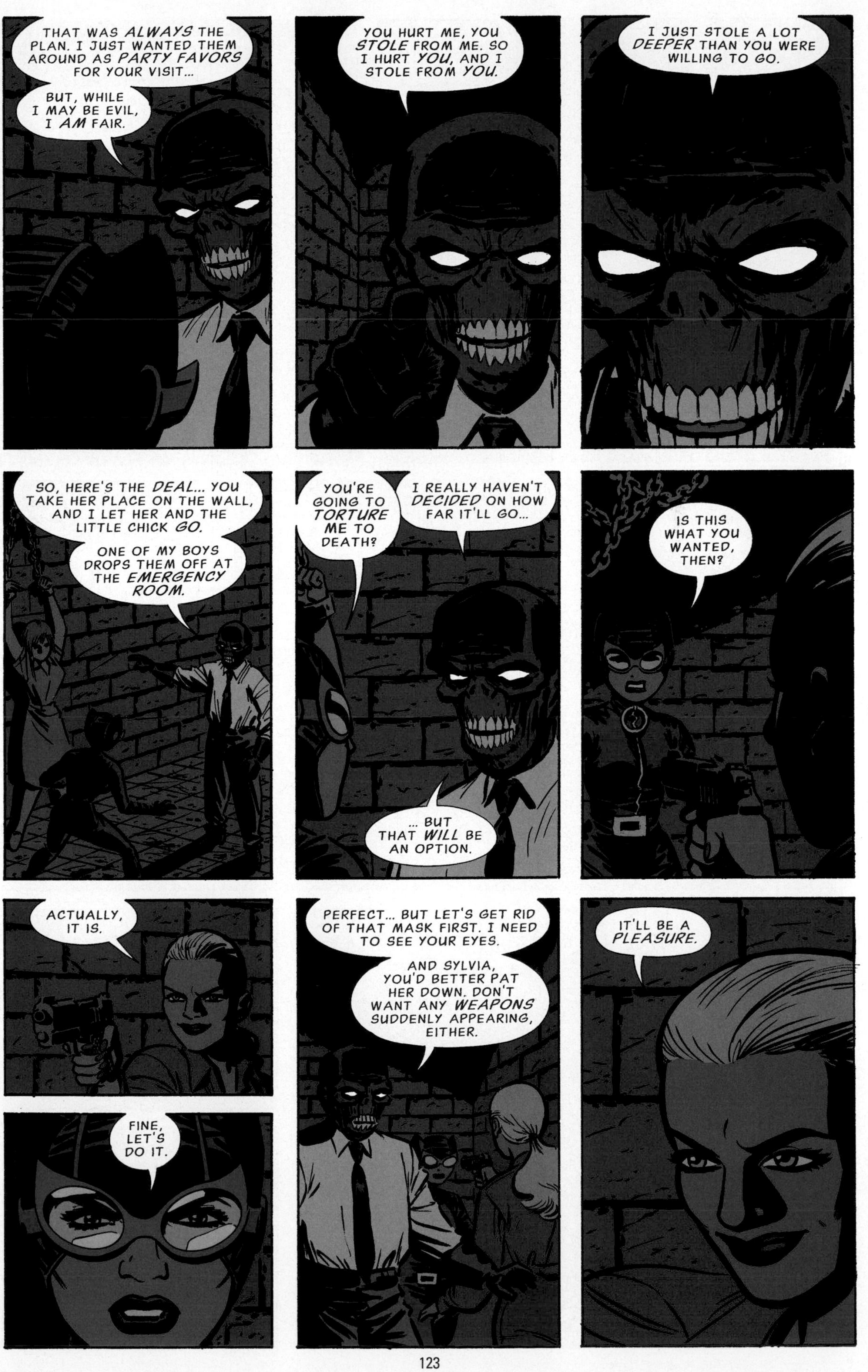
THAT WAS ALWAYS THE PLAN. I JUST WANTED THEM AROUND AS PARTY FAVORS FOR YOUR VISIT...
BUT, WHILE I MAY BE EVIL, I AM FAIR.
YOU HURT ME, YOU STOLE FROM ME. SO I HURT YOU, AND I STOLE FROM YOU.
I JUST STOLE A LOT DEEPER THAN YOU WERE WILLING TO GO.
SO, HERE'S THE DEAL... YOU TAKE HER PLACE ON THE WALL, AND I LET HER AND THE LITTLE CHICK GO.
ONE OF MY BOYS DROPS THEM OFF AT THE EMERGENCY ROOM.
YOU'RE GOING TO TORTURE ME TO DEATH?
I REALLY HAVEN'T DECIDED ON HOW FAR IT'LL GO...
... BUT THAT WILL BE AN OPTION.
IS THIS WHAT YOU WANTED, THEN?
ACTUALLY, IT IS.
FINE, LET'S DO IT.
PERFECT... BUT LET'S GET RID OF THAT MASK FIRST. I NEED TO SEE YOUR EYES.
AND SYLVIA, YOU'D BETTER PAT HER DOWN. DON'T WANT ANY WEAPONS SUDDENLY APPEARING, EITHER.
IT'LL BE A PLEASURE.

SHE ONLY HAD A FEW *LOCK-PICKS* ON HER...

... NOTHING *DANGEROUS*.

GOOD. YOU MADE SURE TO CHAIN HER *TIGHTLY*?

I'M *NOT* AN IDIOT.

NOW THAT I'VE GOT YOU LIKE THIS, I THINK I *WILL* KILL YOU, AFTER ALL.

JUST VERY SLOWLY.

WHAT ABOUT HER *SISTER*, AND THE *GIRL*?

WHAT DO YOU *THINK*?

KILL THEM.

OH, I DIDN'T LEAD YOU TO BELIEVE I WAS A MAN OF MY *WORD* NOW, DID I?

NOT AT *ALL*...

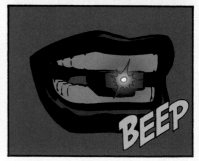

BEEP

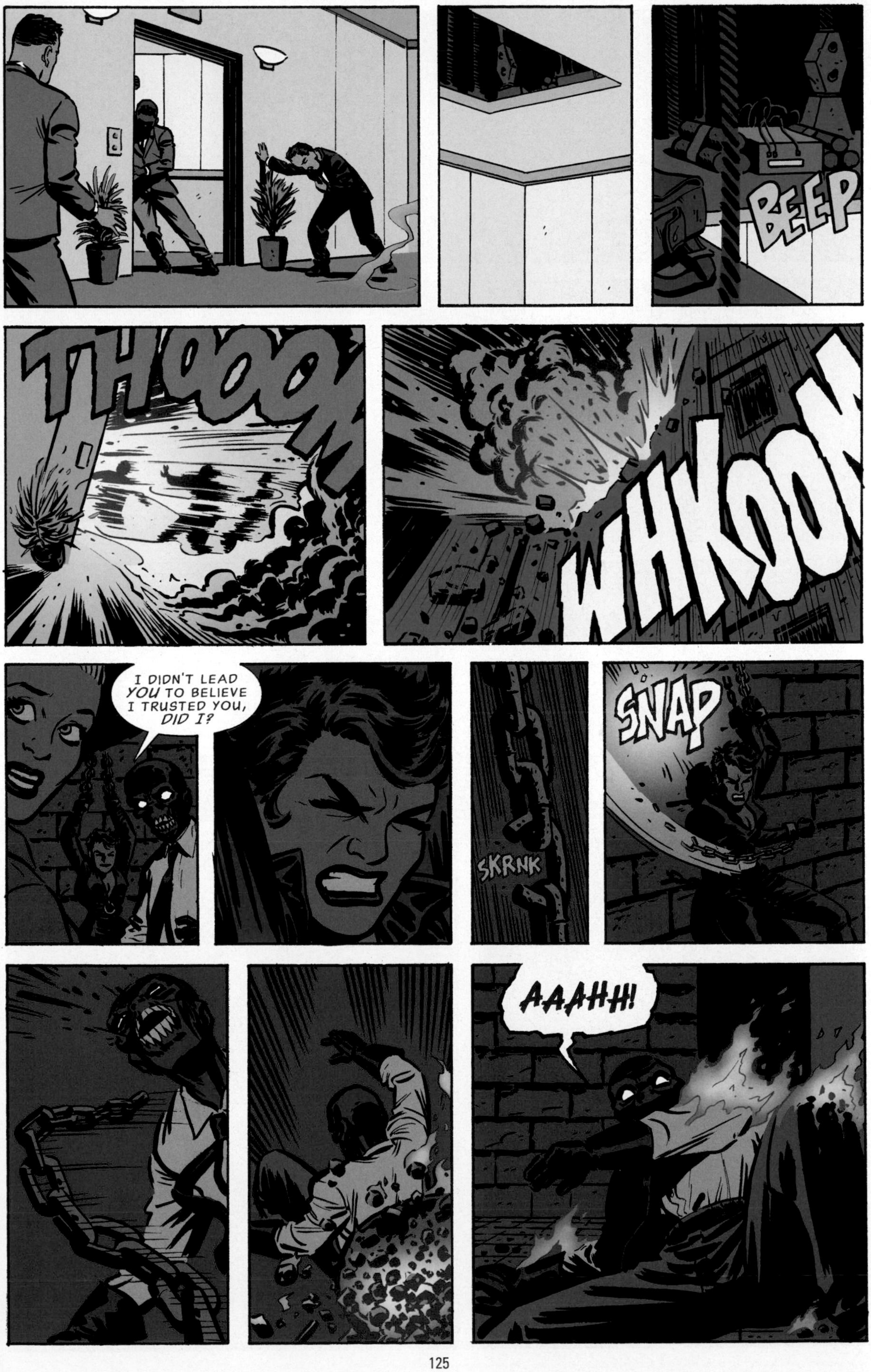
BEEP
THOOOM
WHKOOOM
I DIDN'T LEAD YOU TO BELIEVE I TRUSTED YOU, DID I?
SKRNK
SNAP
AAAHH!

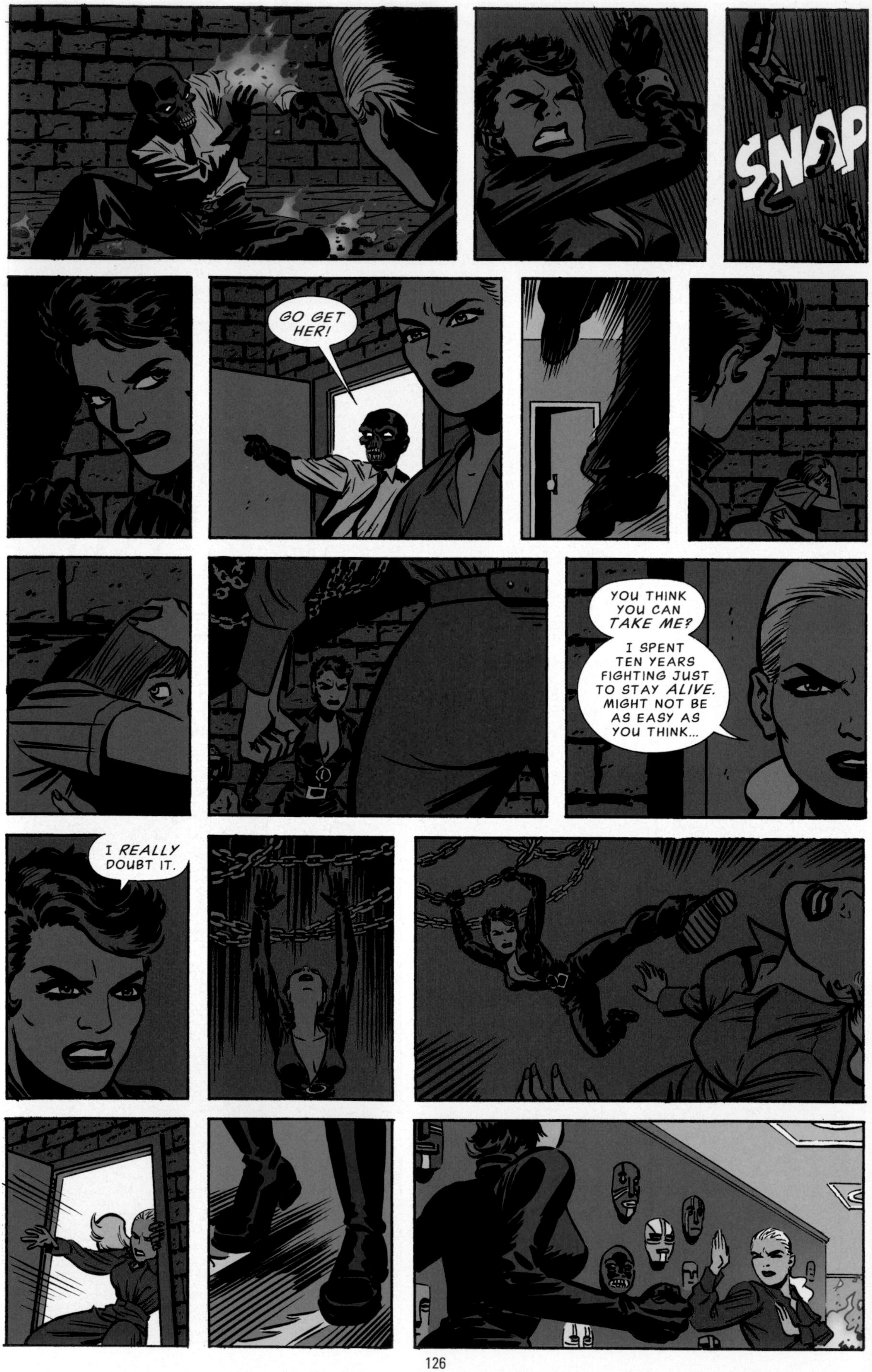
SNAP
GO GET HER!
YOU THINK YOU CAN TAKE ME?
I SPENT TEN YEARS FIGHTING JUST TO STAY ALIVE. MIGHT NOT BE AS EASY AS YOU THINK...
I REALLY DOUBT IT.

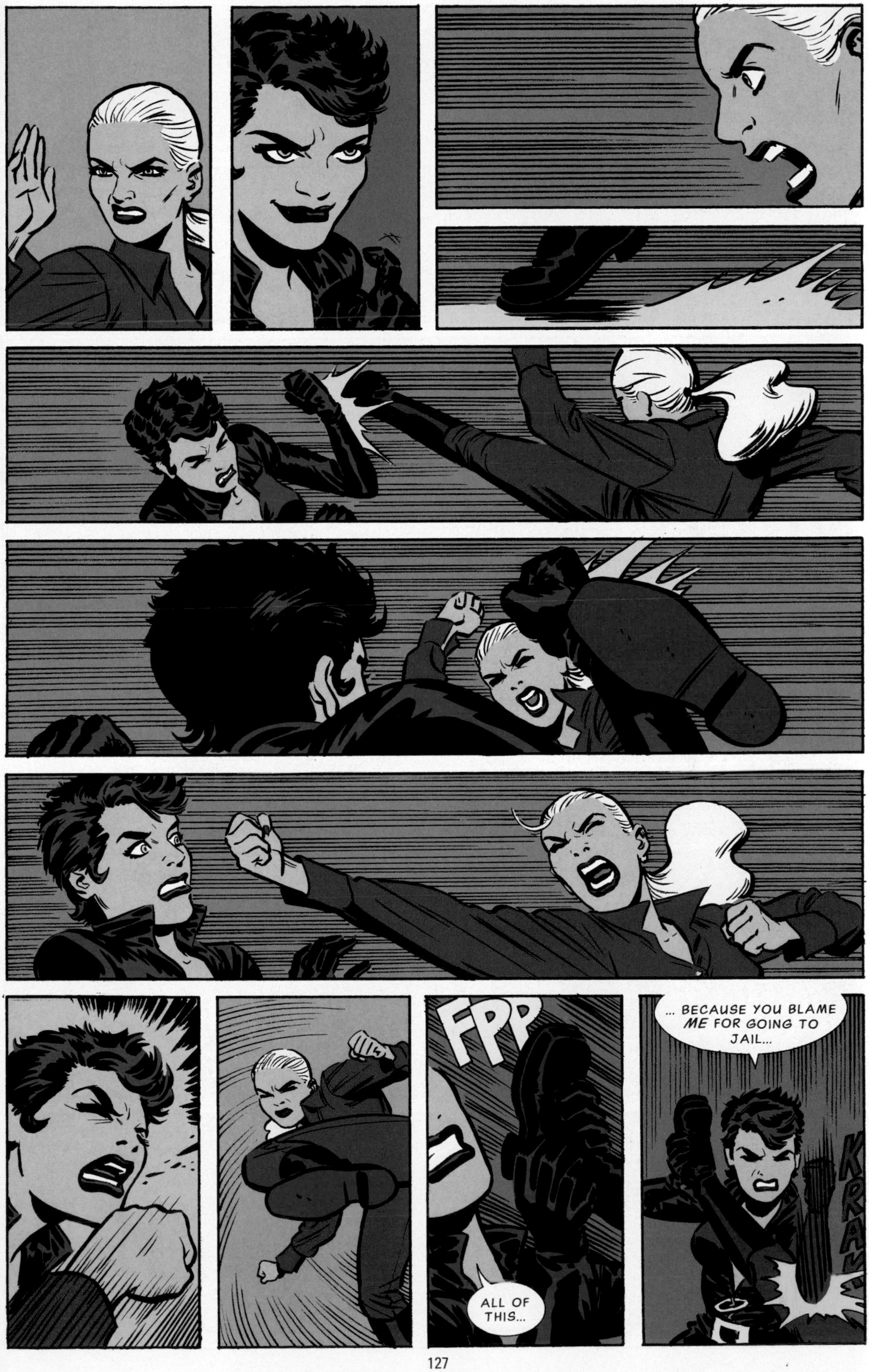
FPP
ALL OF THIS...
... BECAUSE YOU BLAME ME FOR GOING TO JAIL...
KRA

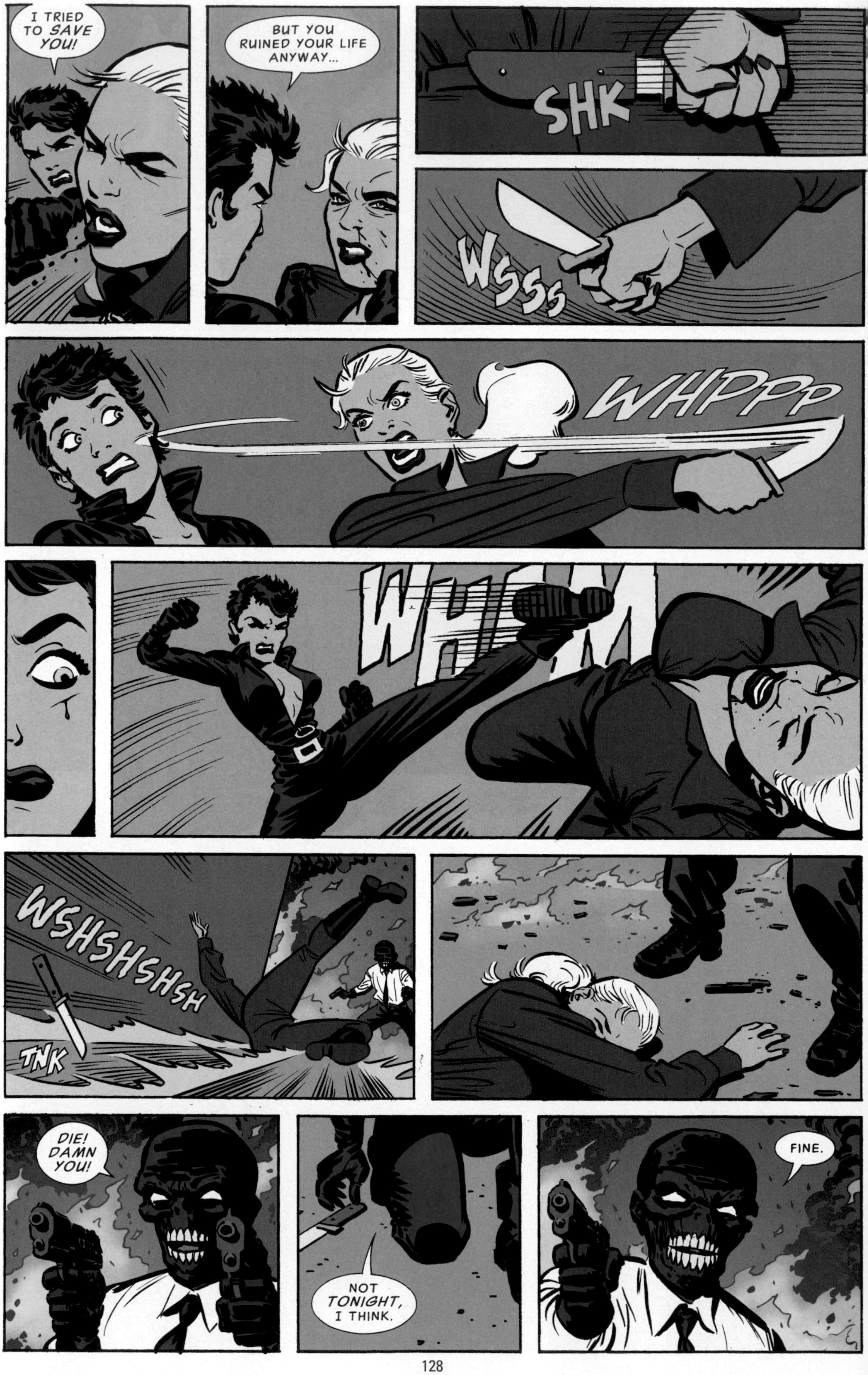
I TRIED TO *SAVE* YOU!
BUT YOU RUINED YOUR LIFE ANYWAY...
SHK
WSSSS
WHPPP
WSHSHSHSHSH
TNK
DIE! DAMN YOU!
NOT *TONIGHT*, I THINK.
FINE.

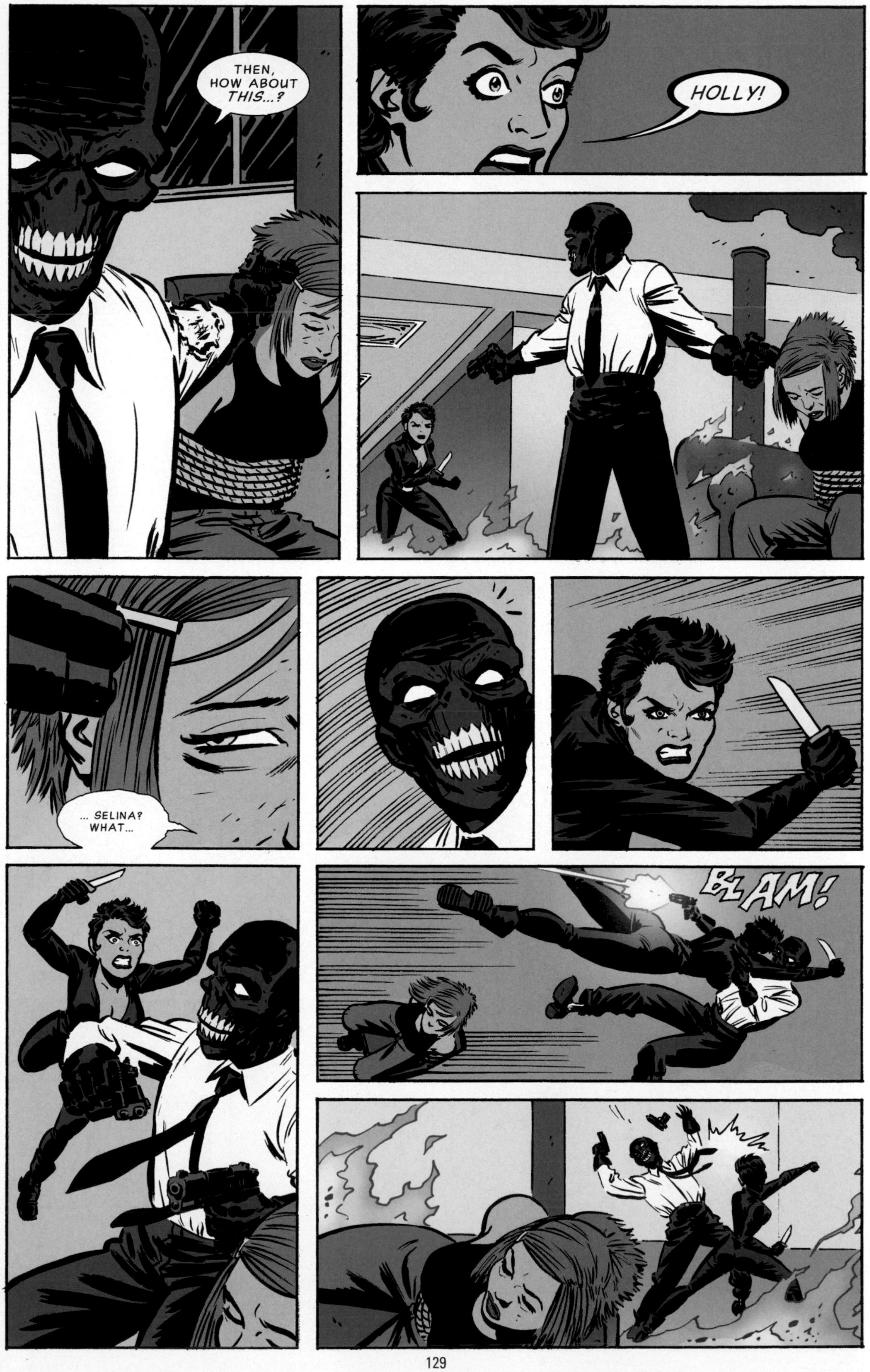
THEN, HOW ABOUT THIS...?
HOLLY!
... SELINA? WHAT...
BLAM!

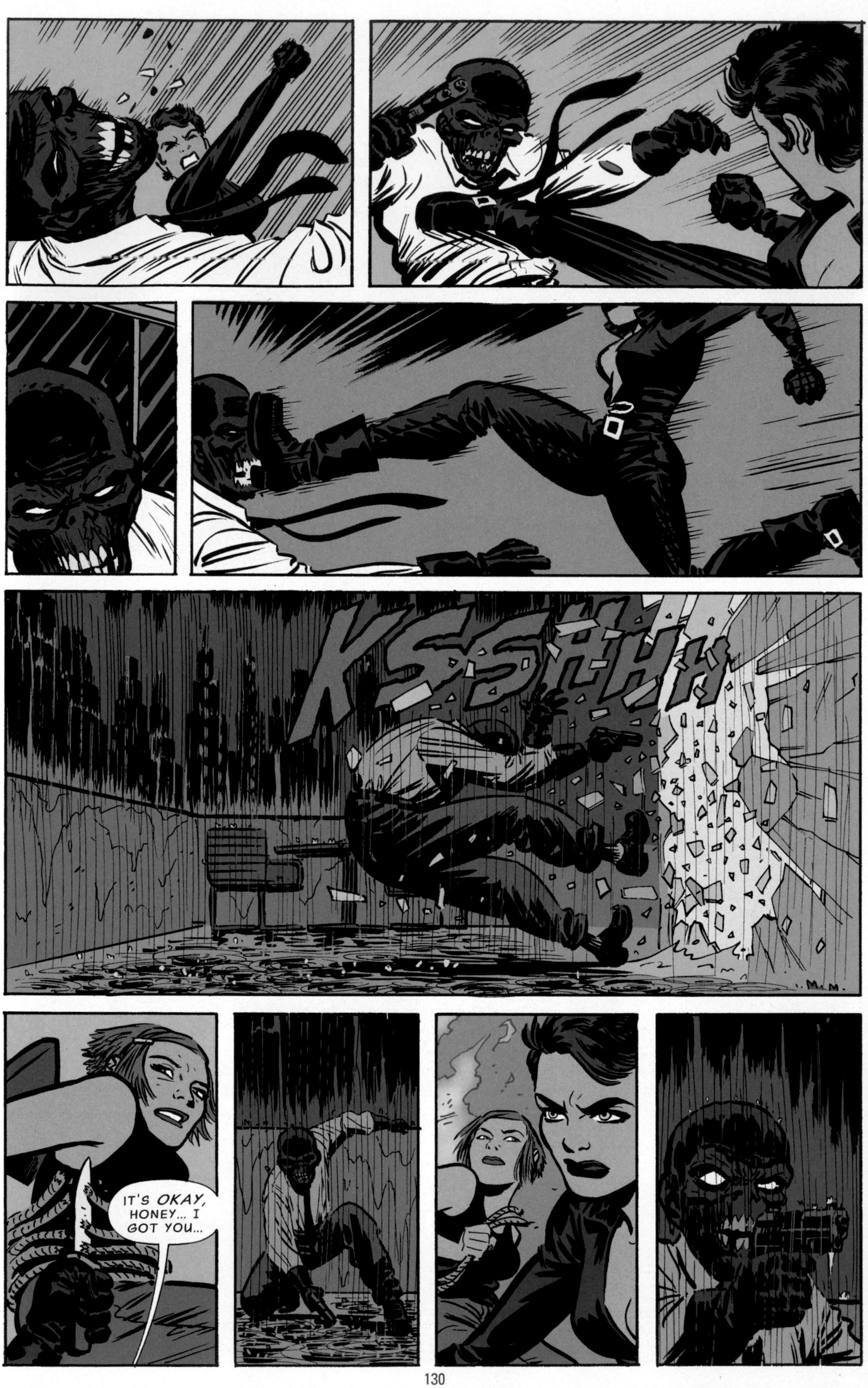
KSSHHH
IT'S OKAY, HONEY... I GOT YOU...

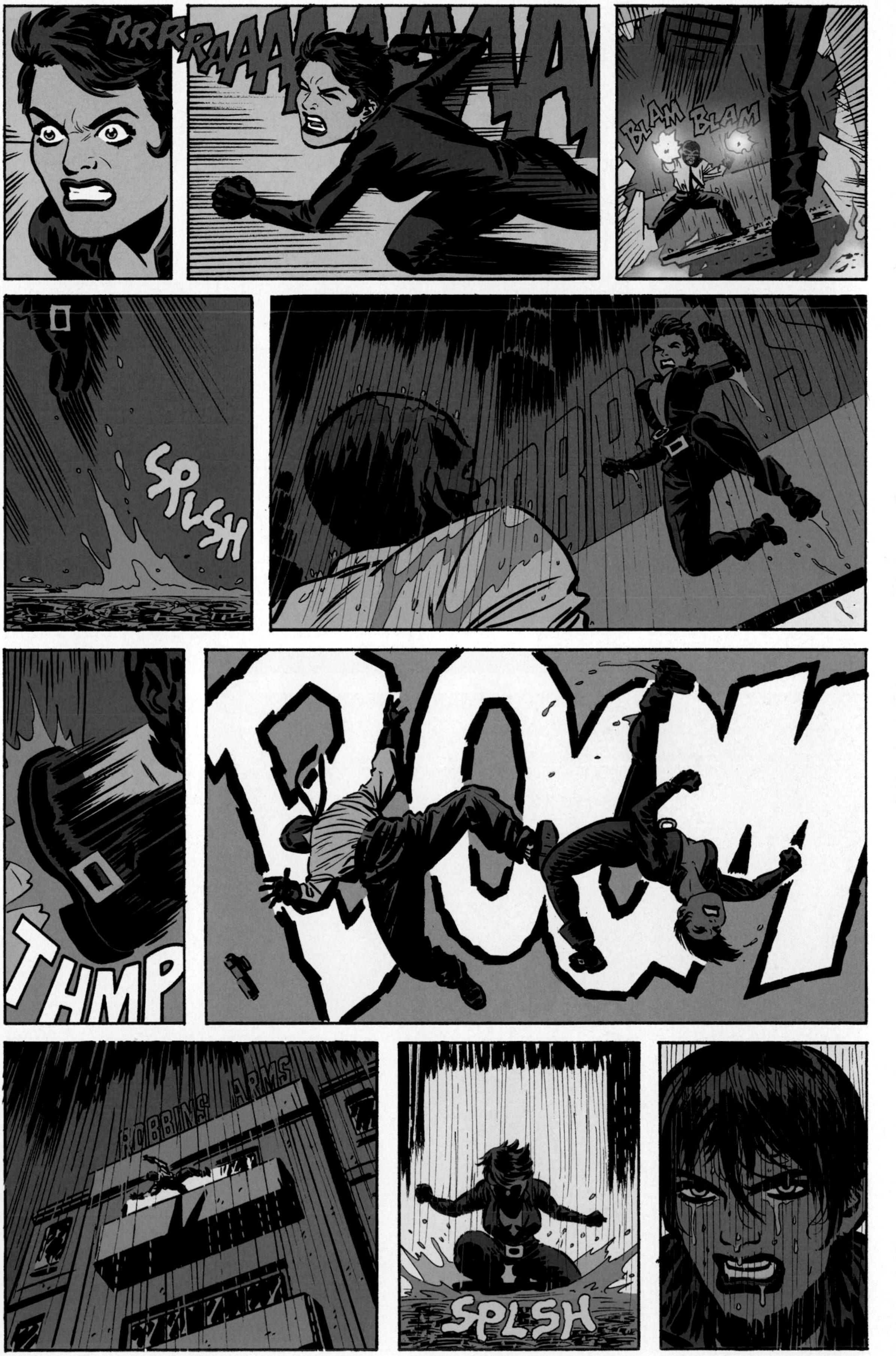
RRRRAAAAAAA
BLAM BLAM
SPLSH
THMP
ROBBINS ARMS
SPLSH

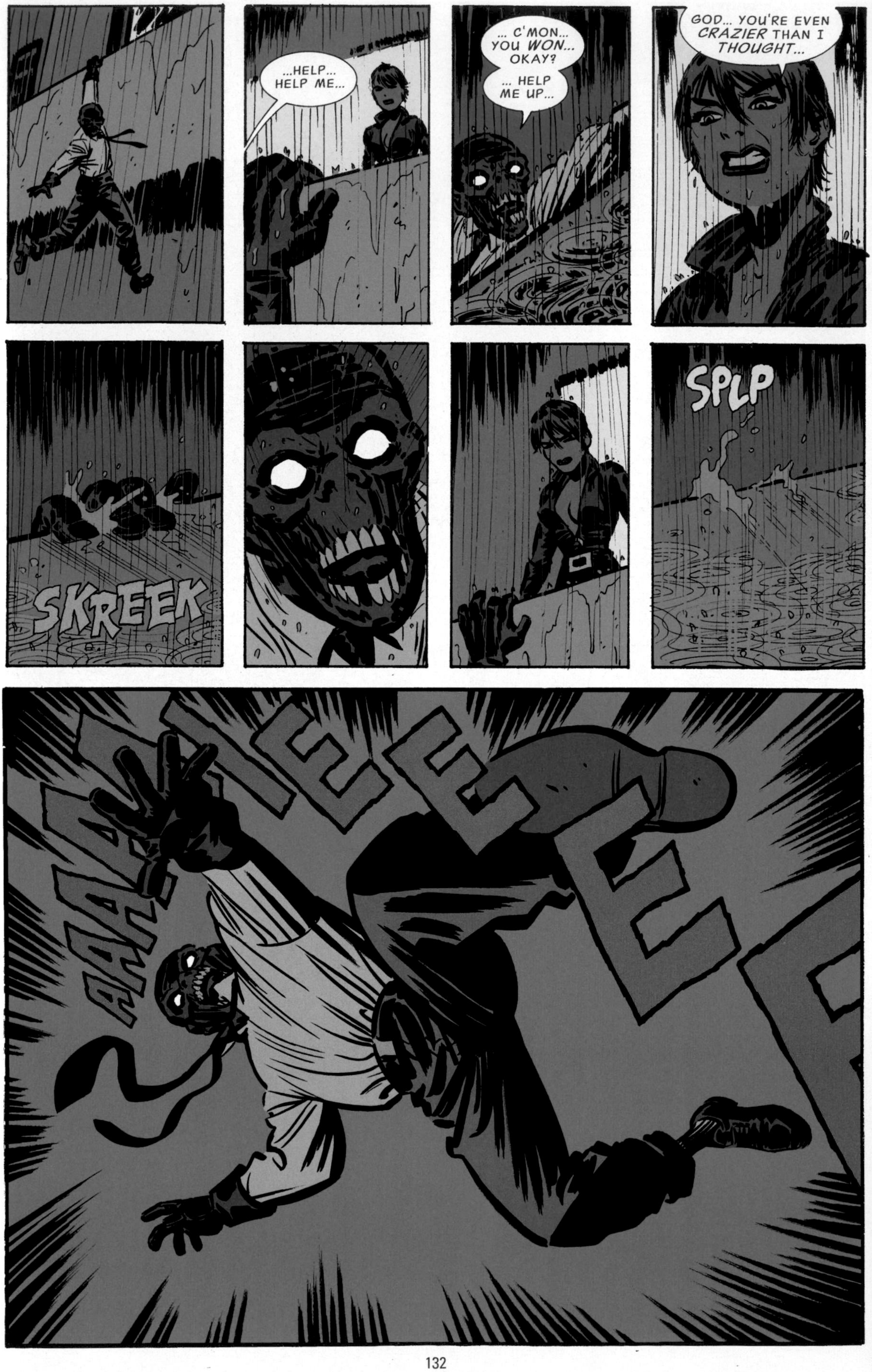
...HELP... HELP ME...
... C'MON... YOU WON... OKAY?
... HELP ME UP...
GOD... YOU'RE EVEN CRAZIER THAN I THOUGHT...
SKREEK
SPLP

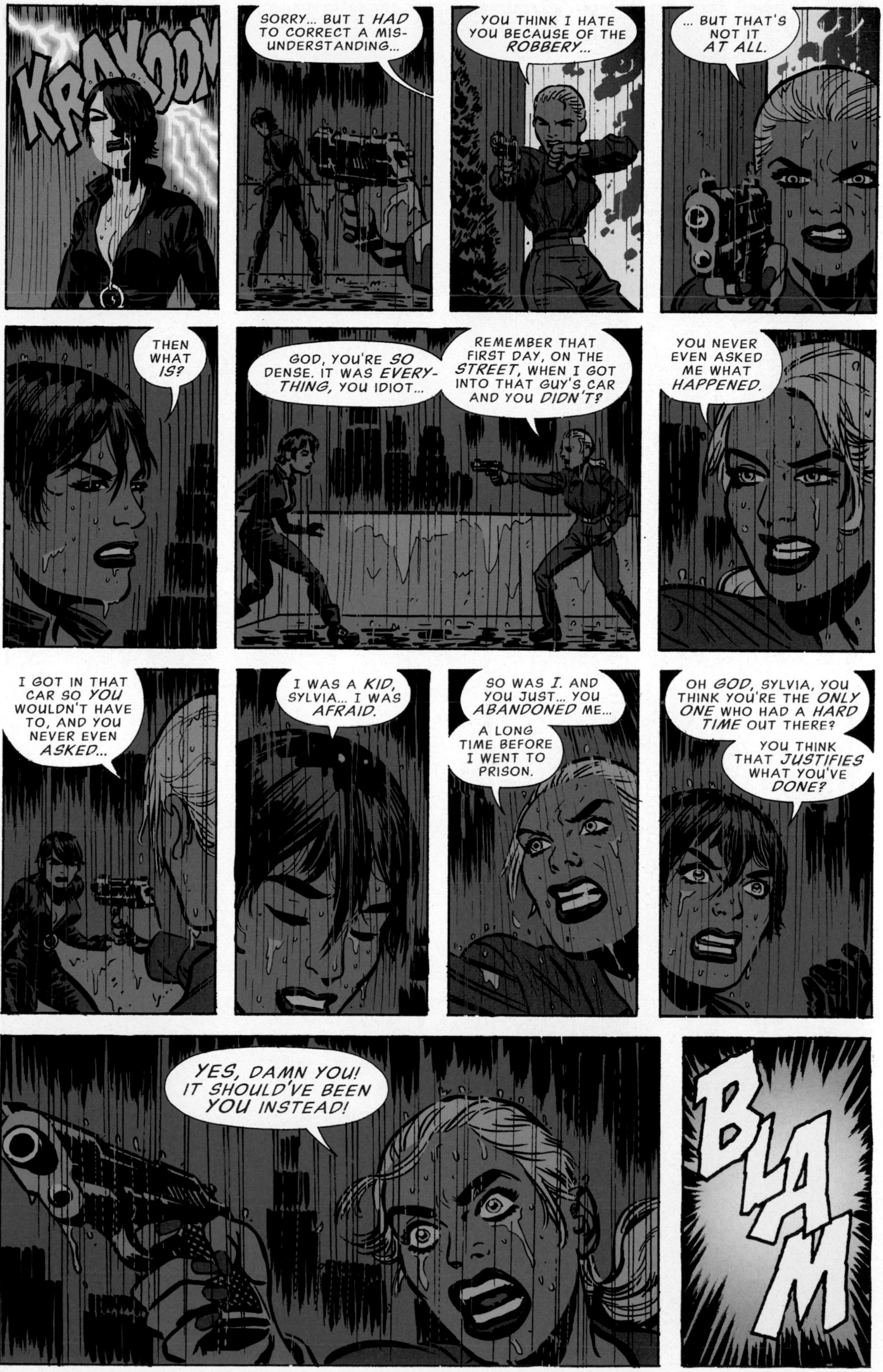
KRAKOOM
SORRY... BUT I HAD TO CORRECT A MIS-UNDERSTANDING...
YOU THINK I HATE YOU BECAUSE OF THE ROBBERY...
... BUT THAT'S NOT IT AT ALL.
THEN WHAT IS?
GOD, YOU'RE SO DENSE. IT WAS EVERYTHING, YOU IDIOT...
REMEMBER THAT FIRST DAY, ON THE STREET, WHEN I GOT INTO THAT GUY'S CAR AND YOU DIDN'T?
YOU NEVER EVEN ASKED ME WHAT HAPPENED.
I GOT IN THAT CAR SO YOU WOULDN'T HAVE TO, AND YOU NEVER EVEN ASKED...
I WAS A KID, SYLVIA... I WAS AFRAID.
SO WAS I. AND YOU JUST... YOU ABANDONED ME...
A LONG TIME BEFORE I WENT TO PRISON.
OH GOD, SYLVIA, YOU THINK YOU'RE THE ONLY ONE WHO HAD A HARD TIME OUT THERE?
YOU THINK THAT JUSTIFIES WHAT YOU'VE DONE?
YES, DAMN YOU! IT SHOULD'VE BEEN YOU INSTEAD!
BLAM

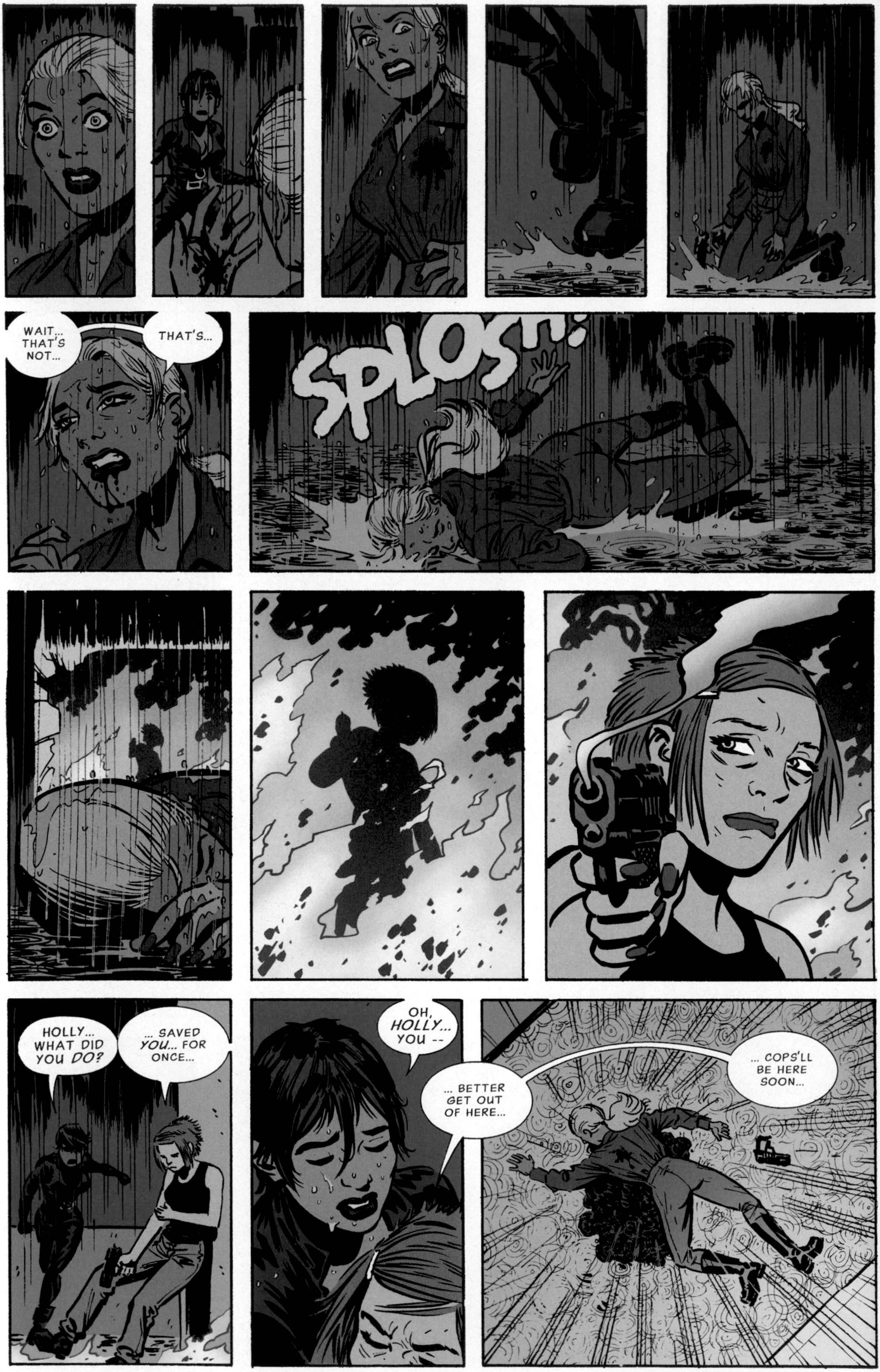
WAIT... THAT'S NOT...
THAT'S...
SPLOSH!
HOLLY... WHAT DID YOU DO?
... SAVED YOU... FOR ONCE...
OH, HOLLY... YOU --
... BETTER GET OUT OF HERE...
... COPS'LL BE HERE SOON...

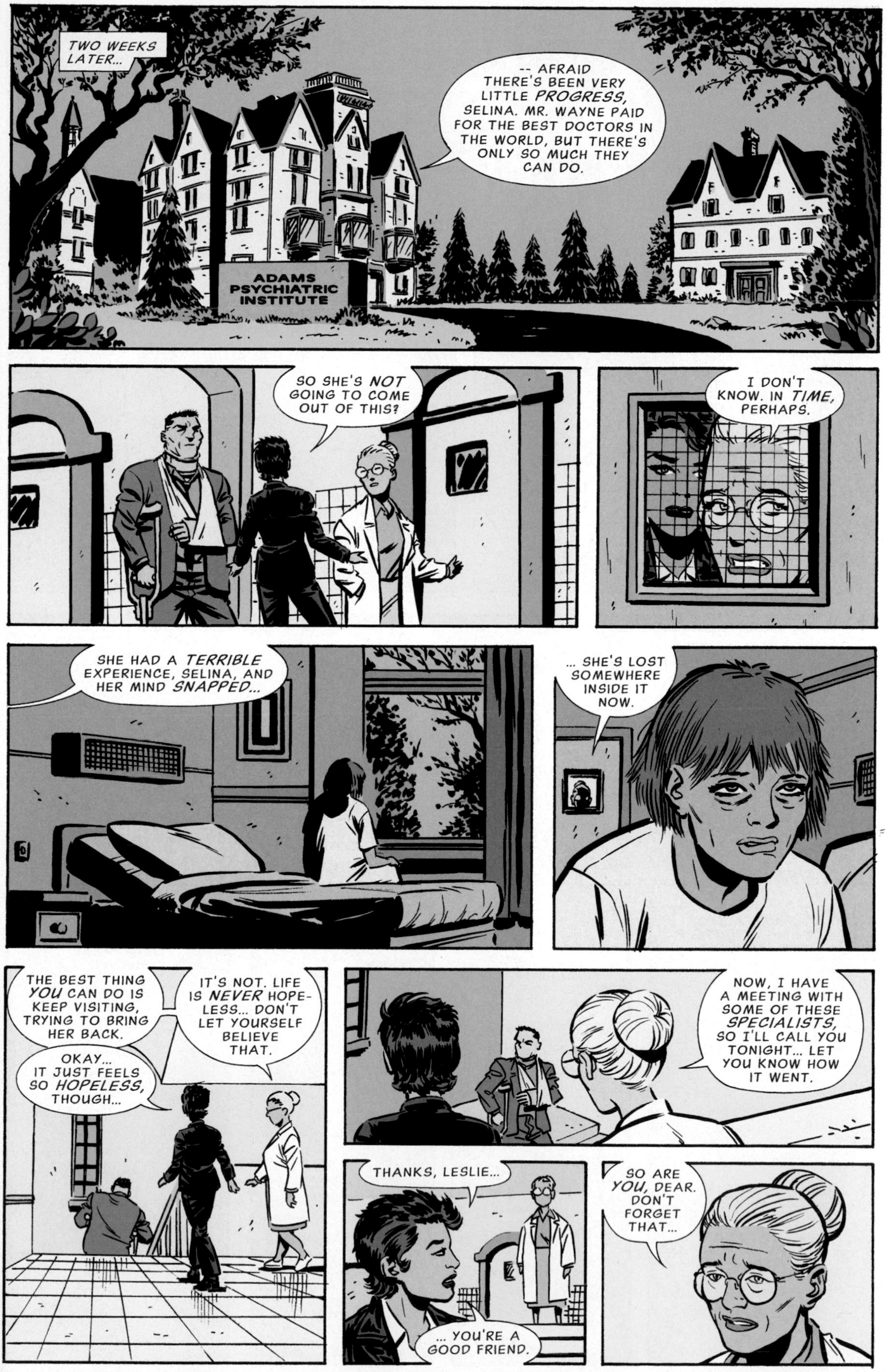
TWO WEEKS LATER...
ADAMS PSYCHIATRIC INSTITUTE
-- AFRAID THERE'S BEEN VERY LITTLE PROGRESS, SELINA. MR. WAYNE PAID FOR THE BEST DOCTORS IN THE WORLD, BUT THERE'S ONLY SO MUCH THEY CAN DO.
SO SHE'S NOT GOING TO COME OUT OF THIS?
I DON'T KNOW. IN TIME, PERHAPS.
SHE HAD A TERRIBLE EXPERIENCE, SELINA, AND HER MIND SNAPPED...
... SHE'S LOST SOMEWHERE INSIDE IT NOW.
THE BEST THING YOU CAN DO IS KEEP VISITING, TRYING TO BRING HER BACK.
OKAY... IT JUST FEELS SO HOPELESS, THOUGH...
IT'S NOT. LIFE IS NEVER HOPELESS... DON'T LET YOURSELF BELIEVE THAT.
NOW, I HAVE A MEETING WITH SOME OF THESE SPECIALISTS, SO I'LL CALL YOU TONIGHT... LET YOU KNOW HOW IT WENT.
THANKS, LESLIE...
... YOU'RE A GOOD FRIEND.
SO ARE YOU, DEAR. DON'T FORGET THAT...

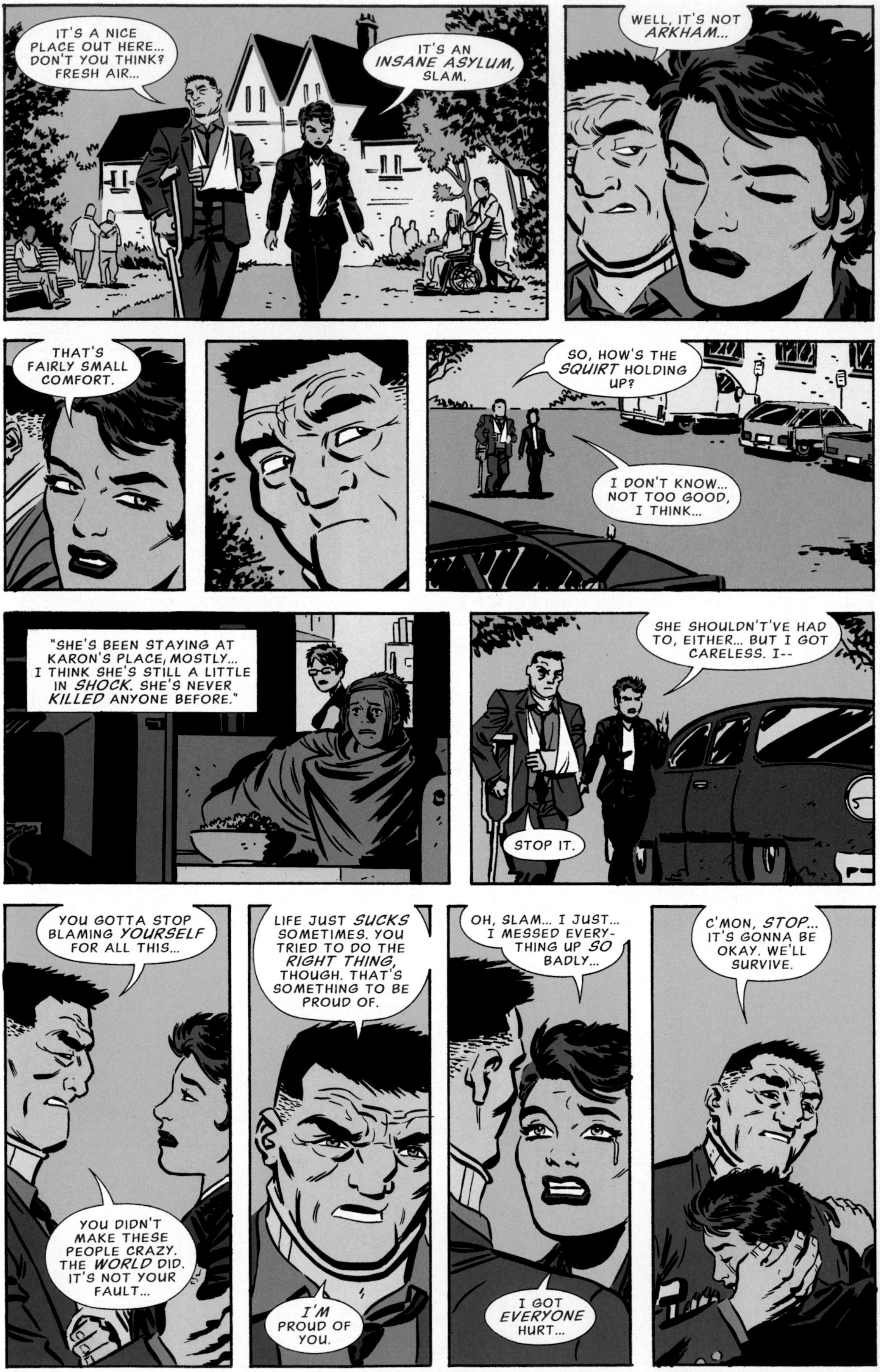
IT'S A NICE PLACE OUT HERE... DON'T YOU THINK? FRESH AIR...
IT'S AN INSANE ASYLUM, SLAM.
WELL, IT'S NOT ARKHAM...
THAT'S FAIRLY SMALL COMFORT.
SO, HOW'S THE SQUIRT HOLDING UP?
I DON'T KNOW... NOT TOO GOOD, I THINK...
"SHE'S BEEN STAYING AT KARON'S PLACE, MOSTLY... I THINK SHE'S STILL A LITTLE IN SHOCK. SHE'S NEVER KILLED ANYONE BEFORE."
SHE SHOULDN'T'VE HAD TO, EITHER... BUT I GOT CARELESS. I--
STOP IT.
YOU GOTTA STOP BLAMING YOURSELF FOR ALL THIS...
YOU DIDN'T MAKE THESE PEOPLE CRAZY. THE WORLD DID. IT'S NOT YOUR FAULT...
LIFE JUST SUCKS SOMETIMES. YOU TRIED TO DO THE RIGHT THING, THOUGH. THAT'S SOMETHING TO BE PROUD OF.
I'M PROUD OF YOU.
OH, SLAM... I JUST... I MESSED EVERY-THING UP SO BADLY...
I GOT EVERYONE HURT...
C'MON, STOP... IT'S GONNA BE OKAY. WE'LL SURVIVE.

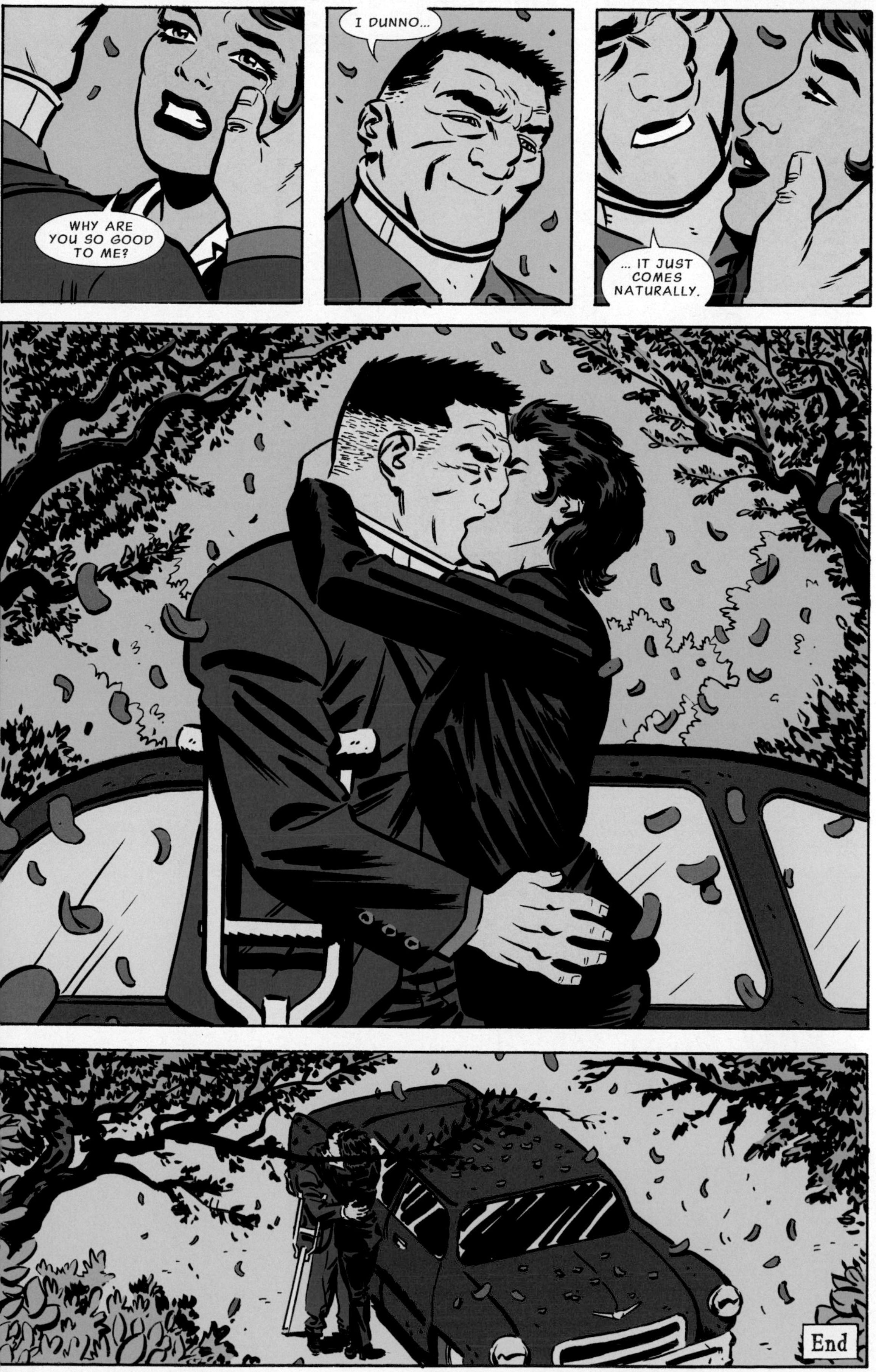
WHY ARE YOU SO GOOD TO ME?
I DUNNO...
... IT JUST COMES NATURALLY.
End

HARLEY QUINN

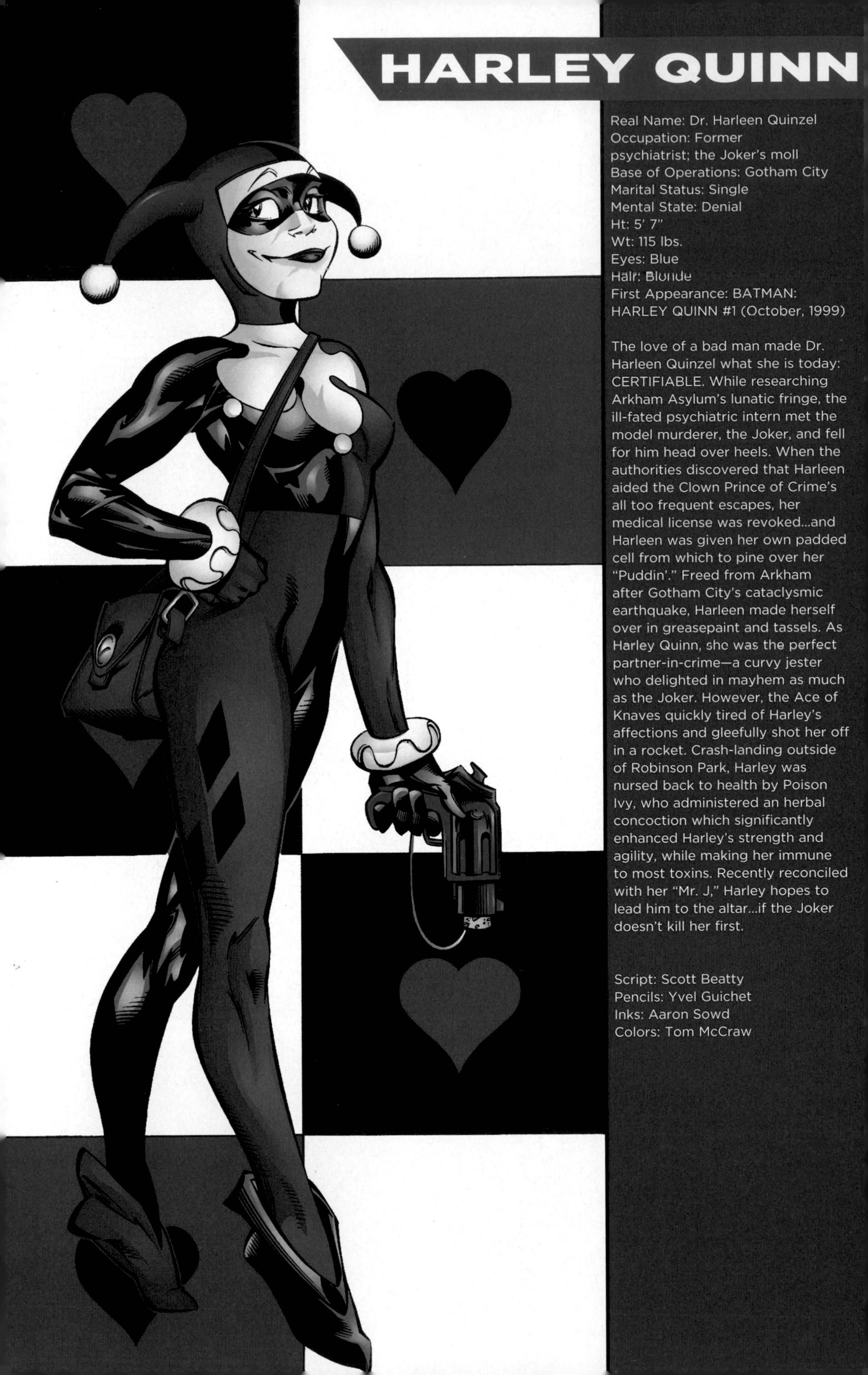

Real Name: Dr. Harleen Quinzel
Occupation: Former psychiatrist; the Joker's moll
Base of Operations: Gotham City
Marital Status: Single
Mental State: Denial
Ht: 5' 7"
Wt: 115 lbs.
Eyes: Blue
Hair: Blonde
First Appearance: BATMAN: HARLEY QUINN #1 (October, 1999)

The love of a bad man made Dr. Harleen Quinzel what she is today: CERTIFIABLE. While researching Arkham Asylum's lunatic fringe, the ill-fated psychiatric intern met the model murderer, the Joker, and fell for him head over heels. When the authorities discovered that Harleen aided the Clown Prince of Crime's all too frequent escapes, her medical license was revoked...and Harleen was given her own padded cell from which to pine over her "Puddin'." Freed from Arkham after Gotham City's cataclysmic earthquake, Harleen made herself over in greasepaint and tassels. As Harley Quinn, she was the perfect partner-in-crime—a curvy jester who delighted in mayhem as much as the Joker. However, the Ace of Knaves quickly tired of Harley's affections and gleefully shot her off in a rocket. Crash-landing outside of Robinson Park, Harley was nursed back to health by Poison Ivy, who administered an herbal concoction which significantly enhanced Harley's strength and agility, while making her immune to most toxins. Recently reconciled with her "Mr. J," Harley hopes to lead him to the altar...if the Joker doesn't kill her first.

Script: Scott Beatty
Pencils: Yvel Guichet
Inks: Aaron Sowd
Colors: Tom McCraw

BLACK CANARY

Real Name: Dinah Laurel Lance
Occupation: Crime Fighter
Base of Operations: Gotham City
Height: 5' 4"
Weight: 115 lbs.
Eyes: Blue-Grey
Hair: Bleached Blonde
First Appearance: JUSTICE LEAGUE OF AMERICA (first series) #75 (November, 1969)

The Black Canary wasn't the first so-called Bird of Prey employed by Oracle. That distinction is held by the adventuress known as Power Girl, who dissolved her partnership-in-crimefighting with Barbara Gordon after an unavoidably disastrous mission.

Choosing the Canary as Power Girl's successor was a logical choice for Oracle.

In her teens, Barbara thrilled to the exploits of Gotham City's newest homegrown heroine, who wore the familiar fishnets-and-leather costume of her mother, a member of the legendary Justice Society of America.

And Dinah Lance was her mother's namesake in more ways than one.

Like the original Black Canary, Dinah is an expert at judo as well as being schooled in other fighting skills by her heroic "uncles" in the JSA. The younger Dinah, however, was unique in possessing her own metagene-activated superpower: a hypersonic "Canary Cry" capable of staggering opponents and rending steel.

Dinah briefly lost this ability following injuries sustained in a horrible personal attack, but found her vocal cords miraculously healed after Oracle submerged her in one of eco-terrorist Ra's al Ghul's rejuvenating "Lazarus Pits" in order to save Dinah's life.

Today, Dinah is one of the hardest-working costumed heroines on the planet. As the modern Black Canary, she co-founded the Justice League of America, and currently serves as a member of the reconstituted Justice Society, though that role remains secondary to her position as Oracle's primary undercover field operative.

At first more strangers than partners, Dinah and Barbara Gordon are now fast friends, a relationship that continues to grow as these Birds of Prey work to make the world a better, safer place.

Script: Scott Young
Art: Phil Winslade
Colors: Hi-F

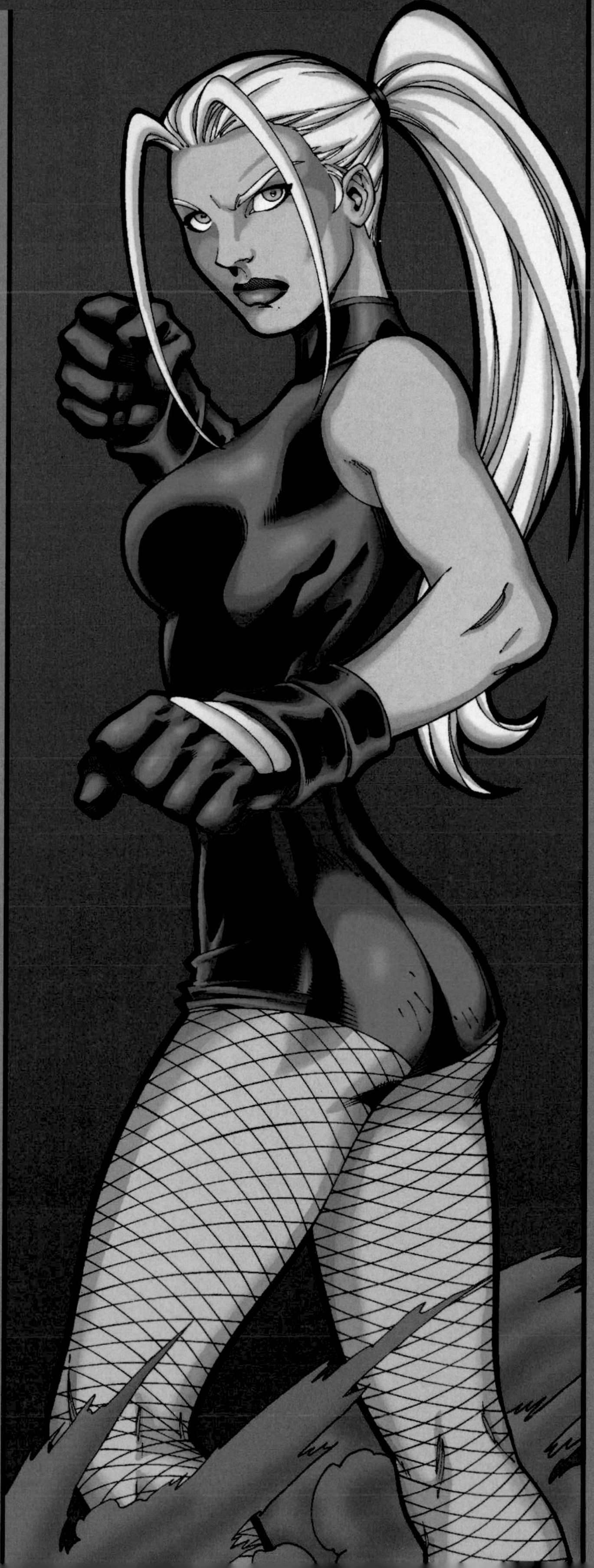

THE HUNTRESS

Real Name: Helena Rosa Bertinelli
Occupation: Special Education High School Teacher
Base of Operations: Gotham City
Marital Status: Single
Ht: 5' 11"
Wt: 148 lbs
Eyes: Brown
Hair: Black
First Appearance: HUNTRESS #1 (April, 1989)

The only surviving member of the Bertinelli family, the Huntress exists, in her mind, to do nothing but destroy the Mafia, the same organization she was born into, the same group ultimately responsible for the murders of all her relations. Isolated and manipulated by the Batman during the course of No Man's Land, Huntress took four bullets from the Joker's gun in an attempt to save innocent lives. Now nearly recovered from those injuries, she feels more alone in her fight against the Mafia than ever. Pursuing her vendetta with an ever more savage fury, the Batman once again keeps a wary eye on her actions, waiting for her to cross the line. Since the rebuilding of Gotham, another has watched her, as well—a man known as The Question.

Script: Greg Rucka
Art: Rick Burchett
Colors: Tom McCraw

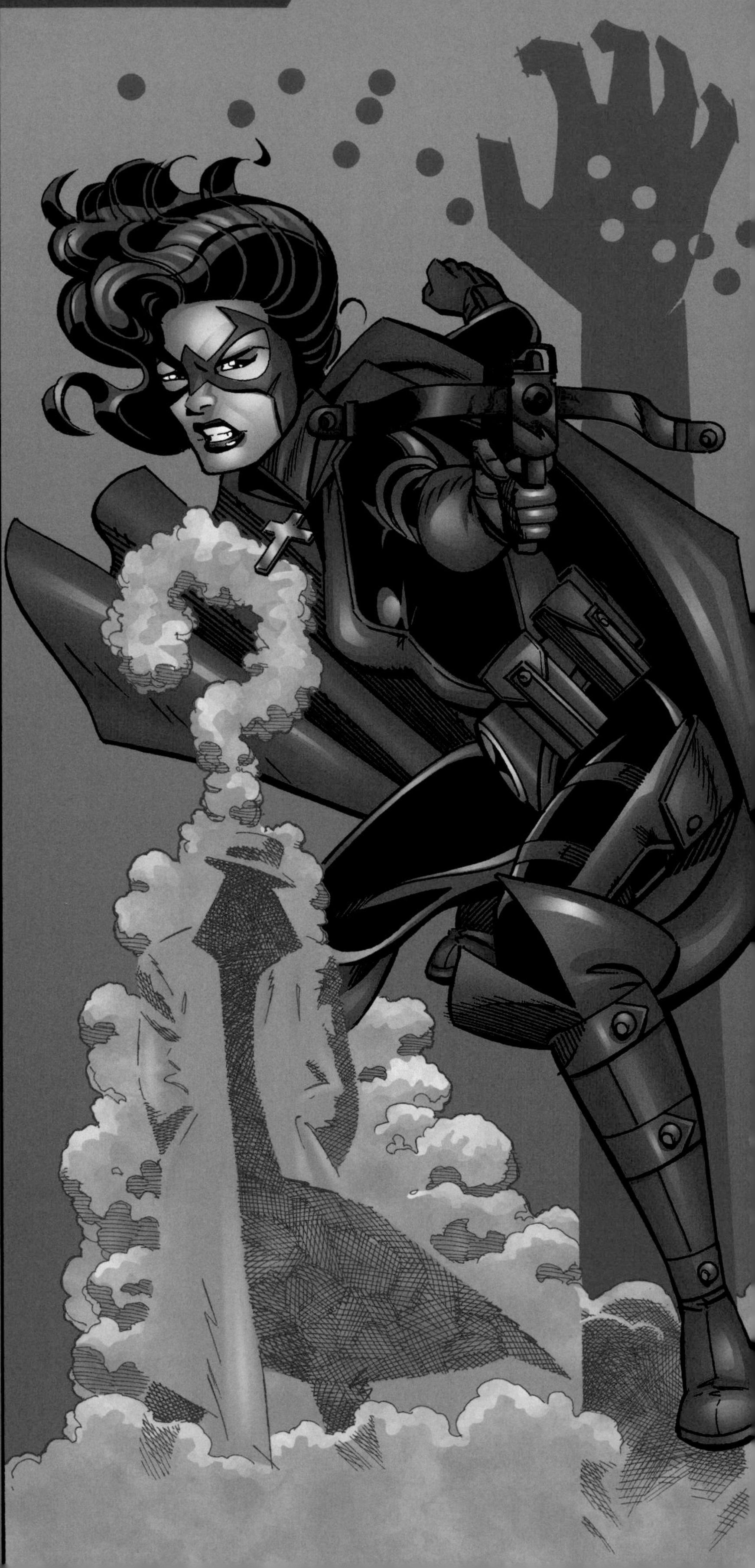

G.C.P.D.

FIRST APPEARANCES:
James Gordon DETECTIVE COMICS #27 (May, 1939)
Mackenzie Bock DETECTIVE COMICS #681 (January, 1996)
Harvey Bullock BATMAN #361 (July, 1983)
Reneé Montoya DETECTIVE COMICS #644 (May, 1992)
Crispus Allen DETECTIVE COMICS #742 (March, 2000)

As Gotham City continues to rebuild its splintered infrastructure, so do the Gotham police struggle to restore and maintain order. Police Commissioner JAMES GORDON leads Gotham's finest once more, promoting officers most loyal to him during "No Man's Land" to key positions within the re-chartered G.C.P.D. Gordon's second in command is Lt. HARVEY BULLOCK, who bristles under his new rank, a position most recently occupied by the late Lt. Sarah Essen-Gordon. Capt. MACKENZIE BOCK, nicknamed "Hardback" for his insatiable reading, now heads the organized crime division. RENEE MONTOYA owes her promotion to Lt. Essen-Gordon, who conferred upon Montoya the detective's shield shortly before her untimely death. Montoya is currently partnered with CRISPUS ALLEN, a former Metropolis homicide detective devoted equally to his job and deeply rooted sense of social responsibility. From the seasoned officers topping the G.C.P.D. hierarchy down to the rawest recruits on the street, Gordon and his cops are determined to make Gotham a decent and honest place to live.

Script: Scott Beatty
Pencils: Pablo Raimondi
Inks: Walden Wong
Colors: Tom McCraw

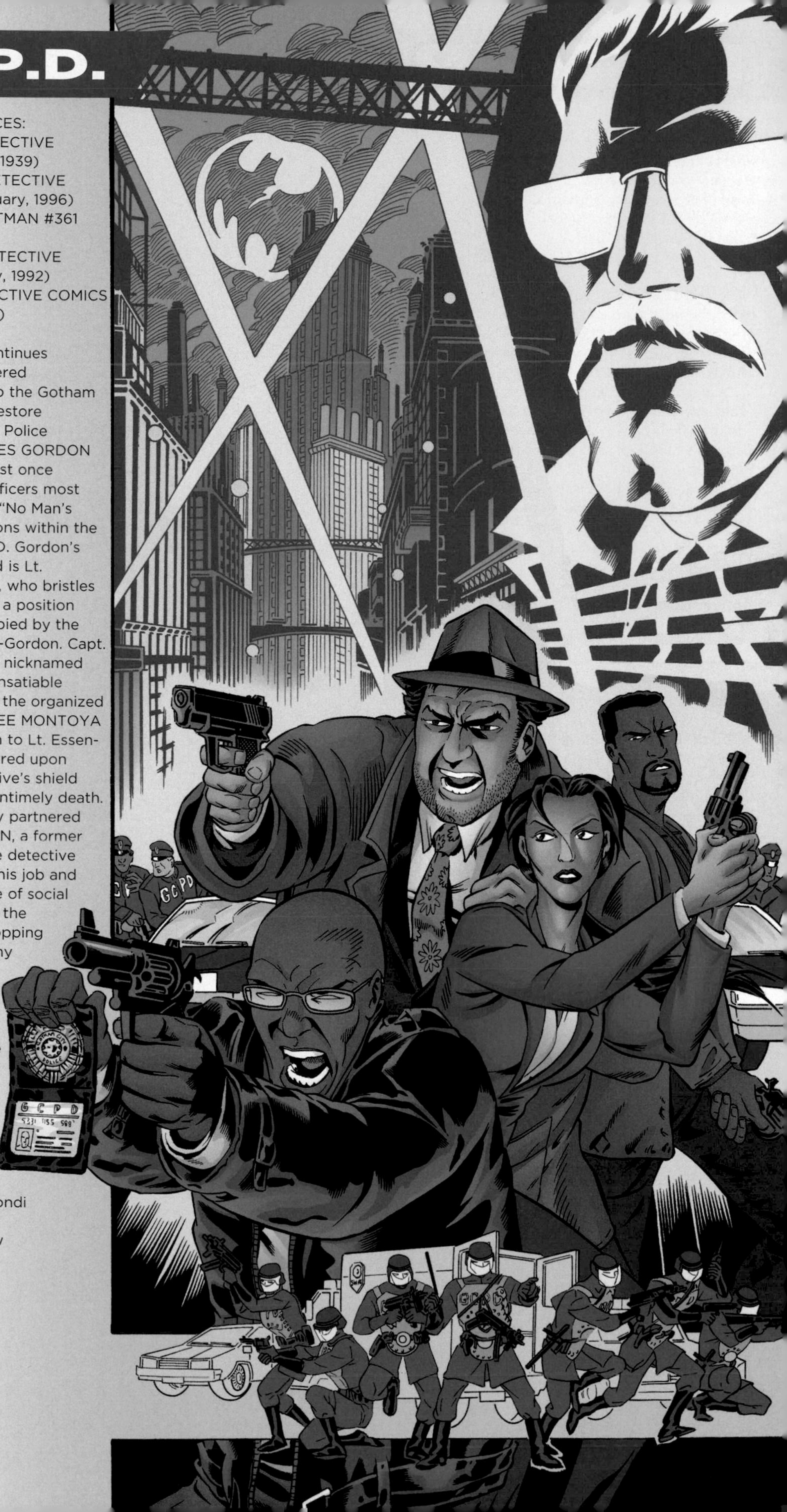
GCPD

BATGIRL

Real Name: Cassandra Cain
Occupation: Crime Fighter
Base of Operations: Gotham City
Height: 5' 5" Weight: 110 lbs.
Eyes: Brown Hair: Black
First Appearance: BATMAN #567 (July, 1999)

Before Cassandra Cain was offered the mantle of Batgirl, the then-mute teenager served as one of many "orphan operatives" acting as couriers for Oracle during Gotham City's year of post-earthquake misery as a lawless and feudal "No Man's Land."

Cass's considerable martial-arts prowess made her especially valuable when put to the task of helping Batman and his allies reclaim Gotham's streets. With Barbara's blessing, she became the new Batgirl as a reward.

The daughter of assassin David Cain, Cassandra spent years being molded into the perfect assassin. Denied vocal stimuli, she was trained to communicate with violence. But Cain was unsuccessful in supplanting her conscience, and she eventually escaped, seeking asylum in Gotham. Since then, she has rapidly acquired language skills and made a few very deadly enemies, including Lady Shiva Wu-San, perhaps the greatest martial artist alive.

Currently, Batgirl remains one of Batman's secret weapons in his war on crime, operating out of a scaled-down satellite Batcave modified to her needs. Otherwise, she reports to Oracle, who now knows the burden of training (and worrying over) her own costumed protégée.

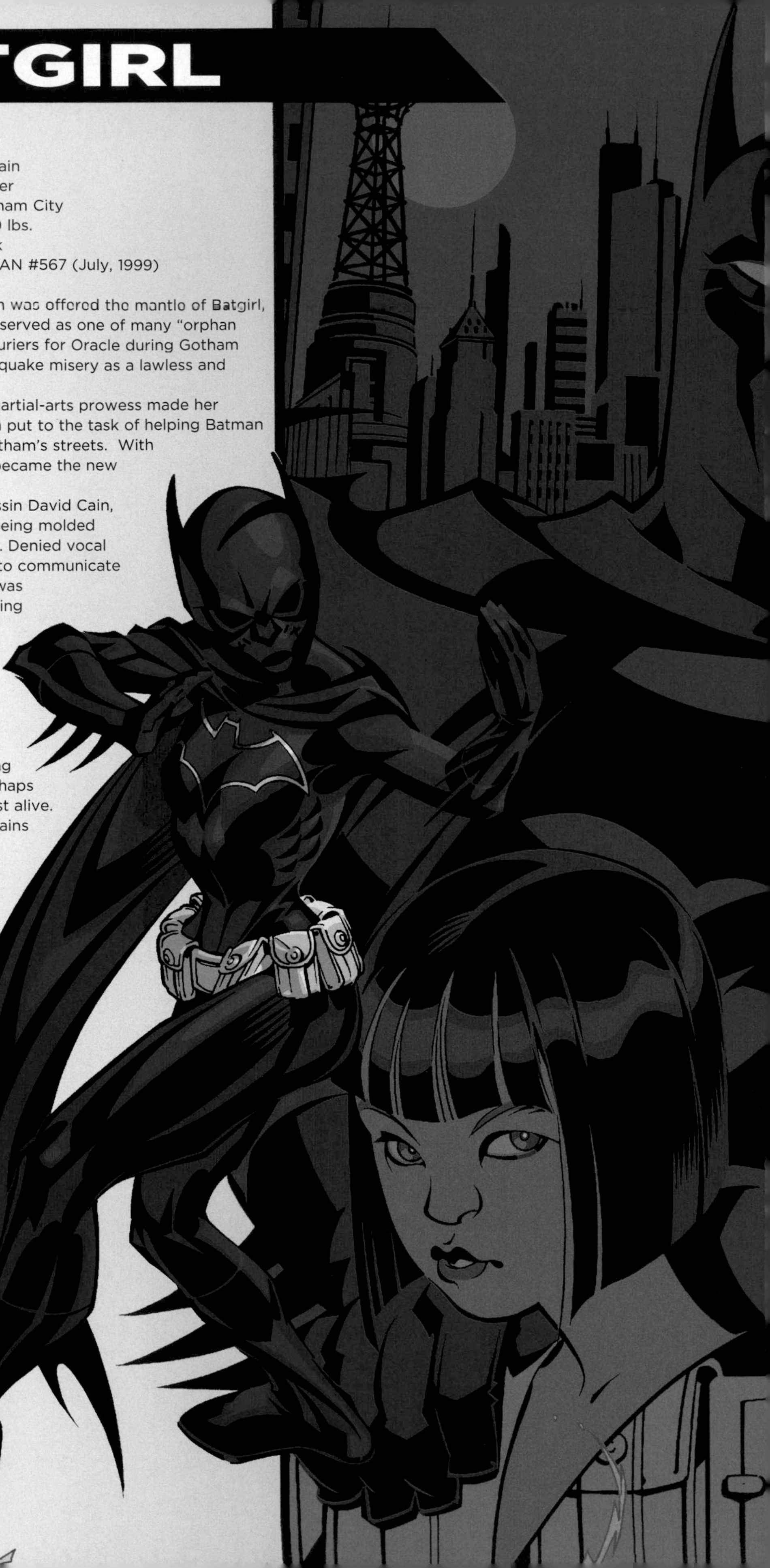

Script:
Scott Beatty
Art/Colors:
Brian Stelfreeze

BLACK MAS

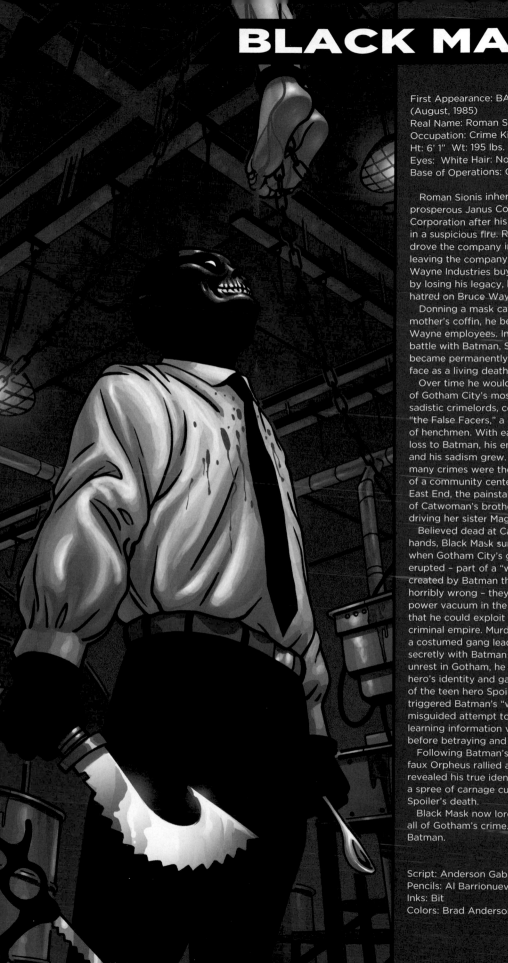

First Appearance: BATMAN
(August, 1985)
Real Name: Roman Sionis
Occupation: Crime King
Ht: 6' 1" Wt: 195 lbs.
Eyes: White Hair: None
Base of Operations: Gotham C

Roman Sionis inherited the
prosperous Janus Cosmetics
Corporation after his parents di
in a suspicious fire. Roman quick
drove the company into the red,
leaving the company open to a
Wayne Industries buyout. Driven r
by losing his legacy, he turned his
hatred on Bruce Wayne.
Donning a mask carved from his
mother's coffin, he began murdering
Wayne employees. In the ensuing
battle with Batman, Sionis's mask
became permanently burned into his
face as a living death mask.
Over time he would become one
of Gotham City's most ruthless and
sadistic crimelords, commanding
"the False Facers," a masked army
of henchmen. With each subsequent
loss to Batman, his empire shrank
and his sadism grew. Among his
many crimes were the destruction
of a community center on Gotham's
East End, the painstaking murder
of Catwoman's brother-in-law, and
driving her sister Maggie insane.
Believed dead at Catwoman's
hands, Black Mask survived, and
when Gotham City's gang wars
erupted – part of a "war game"
created by Batman that went
horribly wrong – they created a
power vacuum in the underworld
that he could exploit to build a
criminal empire. Murdering Orpheus,
a costumed gang leader working
secretly with Batman to end the
unrest in Gotham, he took the tragic
hero's identity and gained the trust
of the teen hero Spoiler (who had
triggered Batman's "war games" in a
misguided attempt to prove herself),
learning information vital to his cause
before betraying and torturing her.
Following Batman's plans, the
faux Orpheus rallied all the factions,
revealed his true identity and initiated
a spree of carnage culminating with
Spoiler's death.
Black Mask now lords over nearly
all of Gotham's crime...thanks to the
Batman.

Script: Anderson Gabrych
Pencils: Al Barrionuevo
Inks: Bit
Colors: Brad Anderson

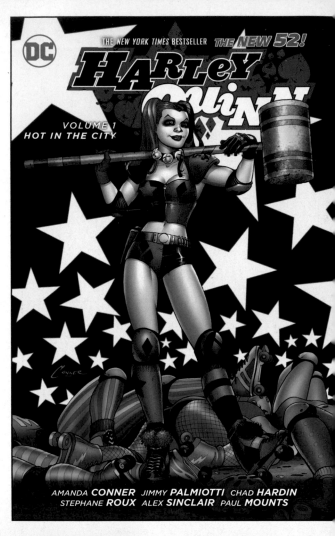